A Research Agenda for Manufacturing Industries in the Global Economy

Elgar Research Agendas outline the future of research in a given area. Leading scholars are given the space to explore their subject in provocative ways, and map out the potential directions of travel. They are relevant but also visionary.

Forward-looking and innovative, Elgar Research Agendas are an essential resource for PhD students, scholars and anybody who wants to be at the forefront of research.

Titles in the series include:

A Research Agenda for Manufacturing Industries in the Global Economy

Edited by

JOHN R. BRYSON

Birmingham Business School, University of Birmingham, UK

CHLOE BILLING

City-Region Economic Development Institute, University of Birmingham, UK

WILLIAM GRAVES

Department of Geography and Earth Sciences, University of North Carolina at Charlotte, USA

GODFREY YEUNG

Department of Geography, National University of Singapore, Singapore

Elgar Research Agendas

 Edward Elgar
PUBLISHING

Cheltenham, UK • Northampton, MA, USA

Published by
Edward Elgar Publishing Limited
The Lypiatts
15 Lansdown Road
Cheltenham
Glos GL50 2JA
UK

Edward Elgar Publishing, Inc.
William Pratt House
9 Dewey Court
Northampton
Massachusetts 01060
USA

A catalogue record for this book
is available from the British Library

Library of Congress Control Number: 2021949010

This book is available electronically in the **Elgar**online
Geography, Planning and Tourism subject collection
http://dx.doi.org/10.4337/9781789908510

ISBN 978 1 78990 850 3 (cased)
ISBN 978 1 78990 851 0 (eBook)

Printed and bound by CPI Group (UK) Ltd, Croydon, CR0 4YY

Contents

Figures

Tables

Contributors

Chloe Billing is a Research Fellow at the City-Region Economic Development Institute (City-REDI), Birmingham Business School, UK. Her role at City-REDI involves carrying out policy-oriented research to better understand city-regions and to provide academic outputs that inform and influence regional and national economic growth policies. She is an economic geographer, focusing on firm-level competitiveness, commercialization, innovation, skills and regional productivity, with particular expertise and interest in the space sector.

John R. Bryson has held research and teaching posts at the Universities of St Andrews, Cambridge and Aberystwyth in the UK, and most recently at the University of Birmingham, UK where he is Professor of Enterprise and Economic Geography. His research focuses on understanding people and organizations in place and space and the ways in which place-based adaptation occurs, including understanding barriers and enablers to adaptation. Much of his research has focused on developing an integrated approach to understanding city-regions. His books include *Service Management: Theory and Practice* (Palgrave, 2020), *Ordinary Cities, Extraordinary Geographies: People, Place and Space* (Edward Elgar Publishing, 2021) and *Living with Pandemics: Places, People and Policy* (Edward Elgar Publishing, 2021).

Harrison S. Campbell, Jr is a Professor of Geography at the University of North Carolina at Charlotte, USA, where he specializes in economic geography, urban and regional development, policy analysis, spatial income distribution, and the geography of economic well-being.

David Yuen Tung Chan is a senior research assistant in the Department of Geography at Hong Kong Baptist University. He is a PhD graduate in Geography from Hong Kong Baptist University. His research interests cover regional economic development in China and Southeast Asia, globalization, industrial transformation, urbanization, global production networks, global value chains by using both qualitative and quantitative methods. He has published papers in *Tijdschrift voor economische en sociale geografie*.

Jan Godsell is a Professor of Operations and Supply Chain Strategy at Warwick Manufacturing Group (WMG), University of Warwick, UK. Jan's work focuses on the design of end-to-end supply chains to enable responsibility, sustainability, flexibility and productivity. She leads the Supply Chain Research Group and the Supply Chains in Practice (SCIP) industrial collaborator forum. As a chartered engineer, Jan has more than two decades of combined industry experience in product development, innovation, supply chain strategy, and process improvement working for ICI, AstraZeneca and Dyson. She has advised government and industry on supply chain strategy and its relationship to industrial and business strategy.

William Graves is an Associate Professor of Geography at the University of North Carolina at Charlotte, USA where he specializes in economic geography, urban change, and the role of culture on economic change in the Southern United States. Recent research projects have examined how the venture capital industry, the automotive industry and the retail location process are unique in the US South.

Anne Green is Professor of Regional Economic Development at City-REDI (Region Economic Development Institute), University of Birmingham, UK. Her research interests span employment, non-employment, regional and local labour market issues, skills strategies, sector studies, urban and regional development, migration and commuting, associated policy issues and evaluation. She has published in high-profile journals and has written numerous reports for UK Government departments and agencies. She was a member of the Lead Expert Group for the UK Government Office for Science foresight project on the Future of Manufacturing. Current projects focus on productivity, universities and skills, megatrends and future cities.

Douglas R. Gress is Professor of Economic Geography in the Department of Geography Education at Seoul National University, South Korea. With nearly 30 years of experience living and working in South Korea, his research interests primarily include Korean firms, firm networks, and theories and practices associated with the geography of innovation. He has published extensively on diverse topics including foreign direct investment (FDI), trade, (regional) innovation networks, global production networks, and gender at Korean firms, and on the machine tool, solar photovoltaics (PV), and additive manufacturing industries. Most recently, he served as a consultant on Korea's International Science and Business Belt project.

Chantal Hales completed a PhD at the University of Birmingham, UK that explored female entrepreneurship in Senegal. She was involved in a number of academic research projects and currently works in industry.

Jennifer Johns is a Reader in International Business at the University of Bristol, UK, working at the interface of economic geography, work and organization studies and international business. Broadly concerned with the unevenness of economic activity across space, her recent work focuses on digital technologies and their impacts on the geographies of production and global value chains. Recent empirical projects include the corporate strategies of multinational enterprises around remote working, and work on the development of distributive manufacturing solutions. Jennifer acts as Academic Advisor to the GTMA trade association and Reshoring UK and regularly speaks at industry events on additive manufacturing.

Ronald V. Kalafsky is a Professor of Geography at the University of Tennessee in Knoxville, Tennessee, USA. His research interests include the location-based challenges of exporters, urban-level trade performance, and the export-related strategies of small and medium-sized enterprises, including the geographies of their export markets. Recent research has explored these topics in Canada, South Korea and the Southern United States.

Donato Masi is Senior Lecturer in Operations and Supply Chain Management at Aston Business School in Birmingham, UK. He holds a PhD degree in Management Engineering and an MSc in Mechanical Engineering from Politecnico di Milano, Italy. He is a specialist in sustainable operations and supply chain management and has published several scientific papers in the top-ranked international journals for this area. He actively collaborates with industry through private- and public-funded research projects. He is currently focusing on how digitalization and the emerging Industry 4.0 approach can enhance the sustainability of operations and supply chains.

Rachel Mulhall completed a PhD at the University of Birmingham, UK on energy-intensive manufacturing companies. Between 2013 and 2016 she was a research fellow based at the Business School, University of Birmingham, working on projects on city-regions. From December 2016, Rachel has been working for the Energy Systems Catapult on energy market innovations.

Megan Ronayne completed a PhD at the University of Birmingham, UK on technical textiles. She is currently Programme Manager of the Productivity through Innovation project, University of Nottingham, UK.

Abigail Taylor is a Research Fellow at City-REDI, University of Birmingham, UK. Abigail completed her PhD at the University of Sheffield, UK. Particular interests include skills, regional and local labour markets, governance structures, and employment support policy. Her research often involves a cross-national focus. In 2019–20, Abigail undertook a part-time secondment to the Industrial Strategy Council during which she examined skills challenges facing the UK, how these challenges could be addressed, and how the UK system compares to international skills systems. Abigail has also conducted research into employer perspectives of the UK skills system, the process of developing Local Industrial Strategies, and international evidence on effective place-based interventions.

Chun Yang is Professor in the Department of Geography, Hong Kong Baptist University. Her research areas are in urban and regional development, global production networks and global value chains, transnational corporations and foreign investment, geography of innovation, industrial clusters, cross-border regions, and China, particularly the Pearl River Delta and Greater Bay Area, as well as Southeast Asian countries, particularly Vietnam. She has published extensively in internationally peer-reviewed journals including *Economic Geography*, *Political Geography*, *Urban Studies*, *Regional Studies*, *Geoforum* and *Environment and Planning A*.

Godfrey Yeung is Associate Professor of Economic Geography at the National University of Singapore. His research interests include foreign direct investment, international trade and production networks, financial geographies and regional development in China. As a Standing Committee member of the GPN@NUS, he is researching automotive production networks and their impacts on local economic development.

Dedication: Michael J. Taylor

John R. Bryson

Pioneer in the study of industrial geography, business processes, local economic development, and the theory of the firm

This edited collection is dedicated to Michael (Mike) J. Taylor in recognition of his academic leadership in the field of economic geography. Mike was one of the world's foremost economic geographers and is best known for his important contributions to the study of business enterprise and local development in the context of understanding the constraints on local growth imposed by processes of global change. He retired from the Chair of Human Geography at the School of Geography, Earth and Environmental Sciences, University of Birmingham, UK, in September 2011 and died at Bunbury, Western Australia on 22 May 2021, leaving a highly influential legacy of research and publications.

Following his undergraduate studies in geography and a PhD that explored spatial linkage and the West Midlands iron foundry industry at University College London (UCL), Mike developed an academic career that included posts at Auckland, Australian National University (ANU), UWA, Portsmouth and Birmingham (UK). He also held adjunct positions at the University of Western Australia (UWA) and the University of the Sunshine Coast (USC), Australia. His early publications focused on industrial geography with a focus on behavioural dimensions of economic activities. This includes his 1982 book co-authored with Philip McDermot on *Industrial Organisation and Location*. This book was an important contribution, as it set out to establish a geography of organizations, to develop an adequate conceptualization of the organization in industrial geography and to make a major contribution to micro-scale studies. Mike was one of the first geographers to recognize the growing importance of exploring micro-scale processes and developing a geography of firms and of firm behaviour. He pioneered research on business organization, segmentation and location by developing a process-oriented account (Taylor and Thrift, 1982a, 1982b, 1983) and published one of the first edited collections on the geography of multinationals (Taylor and Thrift, 1982c). He published over 150 papers and book chapters, and 15 books. Without question, Mike's work helped shape the study of manufacturing industries, local economic development, and geographical approaches to theorizing firms in place and across space.

Many of the world's most prominent economic geographers worked with Mike during his research career. His research both shaped academic debates, but informed policy development in the United Kingdom, New Zealand and Australia (Taylor, 2000). One of his cross-cutting research interests revolved around the theory of the firm and the concept of the firm in economic geography (Taylor and Asheim, 2001; Taylor and Oinas, 2006). This included research on temporary coalitions (Taylor, 1999), clusters (Taylor, 2010), and corporate location and performance (Tonts and Taylor, 2010). Much of his research included an Australian or West Midlands (UK) focus. The West Midlands work produced a set of papers on manufacturing that commenced with his early work on local linkage and iron foundries (Taylor, 1973, 1978), and concluded with papers on the manufacture of locks (Bryson et al., 2008) and group contracting and the organization of production in Birmingham in the nineteenth century (Bryson and Taylor, 2010). Throughout his publications there is a very clear emphasis placed on theory development and testing. This includes contributions to the theory of the firm (McDermot and Taylor, 1982; Taylor and Asheim, 2001; Taylor and Oinas, 2006), theories of local economic growth (Plummer and Taylor, 2001a, 2001b, 2003) and enterprise power (Taylor, 1996).

Mike had many talents. Despite undertaking a formidable amount of cutting-edge research, Mike was also an excellent PhD supervisor and teacher. He was always making something, and engaged in building and construction activities on his home. Making also included making stained glass windows, decorating cakes, and he was also a remarkably accomplished seamster. The latter talent included making ball gowns, bridesmaids' dresses and even wedding dresses.

It is appropriate that this book should be dedicated to Mike, given the contributions he made to unravelling the changing geography of manufacturing organizations and in understanding the spatial and organizational dimensions of firms. Mike liked to question existing approaches to understanding firms in place and space, and to identify new research agendas.

References

Bryson, J.R. and Taylor, M. (2010), 'Mutual dependency, diversity and alterity in production: cooperatives, group contracting and factories', in Fuller, D., Jonas, A.E.G. and Lee, R. (eds), *Interrogating Alterity*, Farnham: Ashgate, 75-94.

Bryson, J.R., Taylor, M. and Cooper, R. (2008), 'Competing by design, specialization and customization: manufacturing locks in the West Midlands (UK)', *Geografiska Annaler: Series B, Human Geography*, 90 (2), 173-186.

McDermot, P. and Taylor, M. (1982), *Industrial Organisation and Location*, Cambridge: Cambridge University Press.

Plummer P. and Taylor M. (2001a), 'Theories of local economic growth (part 1): concepts, models, and measurement', *Environment and Planning A: Economy and Space*, 33 (2), 219-236.

Plummer P. and Taylor M. (2001b), 'Theories of local economic growth (part 2): model specification and empirical validation', *Environment and Planning A: Economy and Space*, 33 (3), 385-398.

Plummer P. and Taylor, M. (2003), 'Theory and praxis in economic geography: "enterprising" and local growth in a global economy', *Environment and Planning C: Politics and Space*, 21 (5), 633-649.

Taylor, M.J. (1973), 'Local linkage, external economies and the iron foundry industry of the West Midlands and East Lancashire conurbations', *Regional Studies*, 7, 387-400.

Taylor, M.J. (1978), 'Linkage change and organisational growth: the case of the West Midlands iron foundry industry', *Economic Geography*, 54, 314-336.

Taylor, M.J. (1996), 'Industrialisation, enterprise power, and environmental change: an exploration of concepts', *Environment and Planning A*, 28, 1035-1051.

Taylor M.J. (1999), 'The small firm as a temporary coalition', *Entrepreneurship and Regional Development*, 11 (1), 1-19.

Taylor, M. (2000), 'The dynamics of Australian regional policy: lessons for Europe?', *Regional and Federal Studies*, 10 (2), 107-125.

Taylor, M. (2010), 'Clusters: a mesmerising mantra', *Tijdschrift voor economische en sociale geografie*, 101, 276-286.

Taylor, M. and Asheim, B. (2001), 'The concept of the firm in economic geography', *Economic Geography*, 77, 315-328.

Taylor, M. and Oinas, P. (2006), *Understanding the Firm: Spatial and Organizational Dimensions*, Oxford: Oxford University Press.

Taylor, M.J. and Thrift, N.J. (1982a), 'Industrial linkage and the segmented economy: 1. Some theoretical proposals', *Environment and Planning A*, 14, 1601-1613.

Taylor, M.J. and Thrift, N.J. (1982b), 'Industrial linkage and the segmented economy: 2. An empirical reinterpretation', *Environment and. Planning A*, 14, 1615-1632.

Taylor, M.J. and Thrift, N.J. (eds) (1982c), *The Geography of Multinationals*, London: Croom Helm.

Taylor, M. and Thrift, N. (1983), 'Business organization, segmentation and location', *Regional Studies*, 17 (6), 445-465.

Tonts, M. and Taylor, M. (2010), 'Corporate location, concentration and performance: large company headquarters in the Australian urban system', *Urban Studies*, 47 (12), 2641-2664.

Preface

As we completed this book in March 2021, we were living through the COVID-19 pandemic. This pandemic can be conceptualized as a cultural inflection point that rippled across all socio-economies, challenging established practices, expectations and routines. Overcoming COVID-19 required immediate solutions to the sudden increase in demand for personal protection equipment (PPE), hand sanitizer and medical equipment, combined with developments in new therapies, and the race to develop effective vaccines. It also included adjustments to homeworking for those employed to undertake tasks that could be delivered from home. Homeworking required developments in software and new working, teaching and learning routines. During the pandemic, businesses failed, jobs were created and destroyed, and new businesses were established. For some people and firms, the pandemic has represented a moment of creative destruction as existing business routines were displaced by online alternatives.

The pandemic should also be conceptualized as a discontinuity, in which policy and practice shifted towards tackling the pandemic and away from trying to develop solutions, or mitigation and adaptation strategies, to ongoing global societal challenges; including the 17 Sustainable Development Goals (SDGs) identified by the United Nations in 2015, climate change and the race to decarbonize socio-economies. Once the pandemic is under control, then the policy agenda must return to decarbonization, in the context of the SDGs, combined with post-pandemic recovery. This requires the decarbonization of manufacturing in the context of a production ecosystem approach that includes logistics.

The next decade will be one of revolutionary and extremely disruptive innovations across production ecosystems that will transform the existing manufacturing research agenda. There are three important disruptions to consider.

The first must be the decarbonization of production ecosystems. This is a complex process involving technological innovation, redesigning products and their production processes, new approaches to reconfiguring global production networks (GPNs) that minimize carbon and environmental pollutants, and alterations in consumer behaviour. There must be a focus on maximizing recyclability, and this requires ensuring that all consumers participate in minimizing non-recyclable waste. This shift in emphasis towards decarbonization will alter the current geographical configuration of production ecosystems, but also transform product design and fabrication with an emphasis on recyclability. This includes the selection of raw materials to reduce pollutants and enhance recycling and/or alterations in the location of manufacturing plants to reduce the overall environmental impacts of production processes.

Second, technological sovereignty has recently become a major concern as one response to resisting economic coercion imposed by one nation-state on another. In 1997, the United States (US) published the Entity List of foreign organizations that were engaged in activities that were counter to US national security and/or foreign policy interests. This initially focused on military-related activities but has expanded into other areas. In her November 2019 inauguration speech, Ursula von der Leyen, the President of the European Commission, stated that the EU's top priorities for the next five years were technology and climate change. She noted that Europe 'must have *mastery and ownership of key technologies in Europe*. These include quantum computing, artificial intelligence, blockchain, and critical chip technologies' (von der Leyen, 2019). This strategy includes identifying areas where the European Union is dependent on other countries. The focus is on limiting the reach of US and Chinese technology across Europe, with a focus on ensuring security of access to key technologies. Similar strategies have been developed by other countries, including the US and China. The COVID-19 pandemic highlighted both the fragility and the agility of GPNs. Concerns over technological sovereignty will intensify as products become more data-intensive, combined with technological convergence. Technological convergence is linked to digital transformation. One consequence is that more production processes and infrastructure systems are increasingly exposed to cyberattacks. One consequence of technological convergence could be technological divergence, as major economies adopt their own standards to enhance economic and national security. Technological sovereignty will reconfigure GPNs, altering the balance between localized versus globalized production. Technological sovereignty is a complex issue involving strategic autonomy of critical technologies, regulatory sovereignty and digital sovereignty. All this suggests that there will be an intensification of the role governments play in economic activity.

Third, the ongoing digitalization of manufacturing will continue to transform production ecosystems. This includes additive, rapid manufacturing, and rapid prototyping. It also includes innovations in artificial intelligence (AI) and robotics, and the emergence of 'hyper factories' that would be able to create many different types of products. Developments in AI will transform the interface between workers and machines. This includes continued innovation in collaborative robots, or 'cobots', that are designed to share a workspace with humans. Developments in robots are making the adoption of automation by businesses of all sizes much simpler and more cost-effective. The introduction of universal robots has transformed the time required to set up a cobot from weeks to hours. Universal cobots can be redeployed to undertake multiple applications without altering production layouts. Development in cobotics, combined with other types of digital manufacturing, will continue to contribute to rebalancing the relationship between local and global production networks. GPNs may become more orientated towards producing 3D printers and their powders required to facilitate close-to-market production systems that will be increasingly designed around a circular economy.

All these changes mean that existing approaches to understanding manufacturing, production ecosystems and GPNs will need to be replaced by new approaches to understanding the changing nature of capitalist production systems. This book sets out an agenda for manufacturing research at the start of what will be a decade of rapid and extremely disruptive and destructive change that will transform consumption and production.

John R. Bryson, Malvern, UK
Chloe Billing, Birmingham, UK
William Graves, Charlotte, NC, USA
Godfrey Yeung, Singapore

March 2021

Reference

Von der Leyen, U. (2019), Speech by President-elect von der Leyen in the European Parliament Plenary on the occasion of the presentation of her College of Commissioners and their programme, accessed 1 March 2021, available at https://ec.europa.eu/commission/presscorner/detail/es/speech_19_6408.

Acknowledgements

Books are the outcome of a co-creation process, and this is especially the case for edited collections. The editors and the chapter authors have drawn upon the erudition of many scholars, practitioners and policymakers to shape the ideas developed in these chapters.

The origins of this book can be traced back to a multidisciplinary research project funded by the Institute of Advanced Studies (IAS), University of Birmingham, UK. This project explored regeneration economies and led to two edited books: *Handbook of Manufacturing Industries in the World Economy* (Bryson, Clark and Vanchan, Edward Elgar Publishing, 2015) and *A Research Agenda for Regeneration Economies: Reading City-Regions* (Bryson, Andres and Mulhall, Edward Elgar Publishing, 2018). The regeneration economies project led to the Urban Living Birmingham project that was funded by the Research Councils UK (RCUK) and Innovate UK, led by the Engineering and Physical Sciences Research Council (EPSRC), as part of the Urban Living Partnership (grant number EP/P002021/1). It also led to the Institute for Global Innovation, University of Birmingham, funded Challenge Theme that is focusing on exploring Resilient Cities. Completing the *Research Agenda for Regeneration Economies* book led to a discussion regarding the possibilities of extending the *Handbook of Manufacturing Industries in the World Economy* by developing this research agenda collection.

Producing an edited collection is a partnership between many different individuals: the editors, chapter authors and their families, but also firms, employees and policymakers who have given their time to discuss manufacturing and production processes. There were meant to be a series of face-to-face meetings over the last year or so in which the editors would come together to discuss the book. There would also have been opportunities to meet with chapter authors to discuss their chapters and the overall collection. COVID-19 prevented these meetings from occurring, and this collection is the outcome of discussions that occurred online. We are very aware that some chapter authors had to balance childcare, including home-schooling, with writing their chapters for this collection, whilst becoming accustomed to teaching online. We thank the contributors who willingly and constructively responded to feedback on their draft chapters and dealt quickly with various queries along the way. We also thank our colleagues, current and former PhD students and research assistants, for the many fascinating discussions we have had regarding ongoing alterations in the world of manufacturing. Finally, we appreciate the work of our editor at Edward Elgar Publishing, Matthew Pitman, for encouraging us to develop this collection and in seeing the project through to completion. We must also thank Natasha Rozenberg, Production Editor and Digital Specialist, and Stephanie Hartley, Senior Assistant Editor.

1 Reframing manufacturing research: place, production, risk and theory

John R. Bryson, Chloe Billing, William Graves and Godfrey Yeung

Manufacturing matters and will always matter. The COVID-19 pandemic is associated with the rapid acceleration of innovation and with enhanced digitalization of production systems and consumer behaviour (Bryson et al., 2020). The shift towards online shopping and online living that was associated with the COVID-19 pandemic produced alterations in consumer behaviour and some of these may be permanent. Companies had to cope with supply chain disruptions, alterations in working practices with the imposition of social distancing in the workplace, combined with alterations and disruptions in consumer demand. Some of these alterations in working practices will become permanent as companies alter the balance between working from home and working in company offices. Thus, in March 2021, BP announced that it would be introducing a new hybrid work model for office-based employees who would be expected to work 40 per cent of the time at home (BBC, 2021). The pandemic has highlighted the complex interrelationships that exist between the worlds of production and consumption and the ways in which these are mediated by supply chain management and logistics. This highlights that any attempt to theorize manufacturing, or production, must be placed within a wider framework that includes consumption and logistics.

Manufacturing is about transforming raw materials to create both use and exchange values that are released at the moment of consumption. This requires raw materials, components and packaging to be delivered to manufacturing plants, and for completed products to be provided to consumers at a specified place. This involves the design of operational systems within and between manufacturing plants that are supported by logistics. Data and data analytics play a critical role in both the management of operational systems and logistics. There are multiple moments of value creation. These include values related to the effective management of a company's operations and engagement with logistics. This is about efficiency combined with location. It is also about the ability of any one company to negotiate better outcomes compared to competitors. These better outcomes include configuring a supply chain that provides access to higher-quality and/or cheaper inputs as well as configurating more agile and cost-effective logistics. This includes companies configuring supply chains designed to balance cost control and price with the production of eco-friendly products (Peattie and Crane, 2005). It also includes non-price-based values that may play an important role in consumer decisions. Products may be sold on price based on production systems that focus on stripping out costs to maintain margins. For these products, there is a direct interrelationship between the sales price and production costs. Alternatively, products are differentiated in the marketplace based on non-price-based values including corporate social responsibility, environmentally friendly products, and companies which pay living wages and which try to ensure that their supply chains include no examples of modern-day slavery and labour exploitation. Products may also be embedded in value chains that are focused on the production and sale of additional value by the provision of product-related services. This includes finance packages for purchase and insurance, training, servicing and recycling.

There are many reasons why it is important to research manufacturing. First, everyday living across the world is dependent on a vast array of manufactured products. Many of these products are hidden from everyday citizens, for example, sewage and water pumps, electricity generators, and the optical fibre trunklines and satellites that are the internet's backbone.

Second, every consumption decision directly or indirectly engages with manufacturing. Every service is supported by manufacturing products and every manufactured product is enmeshed in services (Bryson et al., 2020). These consumption decisions link the consumer with different forms of labour practice, and this includes slave labour and labour exploitation. Every consumer decision creates and sustains employment but also contributes to environmental pollution. Identifying and understanding some of the negative impacts of manufacturing processes and of the configuration of specific global value chains (GVCs) or global production networks (GPNs) should be central to all manufacturing research.

Third, human civilization faces major risks or societal challenges. Many of these are directly or indirectly linked to production systems. Carbon-intensive production systems and carbon-intensive lifestyles are the primary drivers behind anthropogenic climate change. The ongoing intensification of globalization, including the fragmentation of value chains, has produced a socio-economic system that is overtly reliant on the physical movement of raw materials, products, people, money and expertise between places. The world economy has become transformed into a complex set of flows. This comes with many benefits, but there are risks. On the one hand, COVID-19 has highlighted that with enhanced global connectivity, disease anywhere is now potentially disease everywhere. On the other hand, there is a tension between the design of GPNs to enhance profitability based on managing out costs and the configuration of carbon-intensive GPNs (IMO, 2020). A primary research challenge is the decarbonization of production systems and of supply chains.

Fourth, the complexity of production systems requires the development of new methodologies and theories with a focus on advancing understanding to inform policy in order to reduce the negative societal impacts of manufacturing and to contribute to more sustainable approaches to the configuration of GPNs and manufacturing production processes.

This chapter engages with some of the core building blocks that should underpin any research on manufacturing. The aim is to encourage a research dialogue that will reframe existing approaches to manufacturing research, to facilitate the emergence of new research agendas. The chapter is divided into eight sections. The second section explores the tensions between research on manufacturing that is positioned around firms, and understanding firm behaviour, compared with a focus on products. In the third section, attention is given to exploring the variegated nature of the manufacturing sector. The fourth section builds on the concept of variegated manufacturing by exploring the diversity of approaches to monetarization developed by manufacturing companies, including financialization. Scale, and the challenge of applying a multi-scalar approach to manufacturing, is explored in the fifth section. The sixth section focuses on exploring manufacturing paradoxes and the emergence of new forms of risk. In the seventh section, a discussion of manufacturing research and developing a socially responsibility research agenda is explored. The eighth and final section provides an overview of this book.

Firms versus products

The history of research into economic activities is one in which different scholars and disciplines study the same object, but there is no agreement regarding the definition of core terms or the application of theories, concepts or methods. Different scholars respond to different societal challenges, paradoxes or enigmas by defining the object of study in very different ways. This is a major challenge for exploring manufacturing research and for developing new research agendas.

The continued development of disciplinary silos ensures that transdisciplinary research is challenging and often impossible. Yet, the societal challenges and enigmas that need to be addressed cut across disciplinary boundaries as well as policy and stakeholder silos. There are perhaps four critical challenges that need to be addressed: climate change, inclusion including reductions in inequality and poverty, decent work for all, and developing global solutions for global problems including international trade, biosecurity and the climate crisis. All these critical challenges require transdisciplinary research.

Defining and developing agreement on the object of study is critical. For manufacturing research this is especially challenging. Is the object of research the firm, the product, or the process, or all of these? Is the focus on firms and processes in place and across space? Is the focus on product, process and/or employee? Is the focus on operations and/or strategy? Is the focus on people and/or flows of money, including financialization? Is manufacturing severed from other production processes, for example, finance, logistics and services including retailing? For many academics, the starting point is the firm (Dicken and Thrift, 1992; Taylor and Asheim, 2001; Goldstein and Newell, 2019). Some would argue that 'theorizing the firm in economic geography is fundamental to understand how local economies and communities function and evolve in globalising economic environments' (Taylor, 2006: 3). It is hard to disagree with this statement. Nevertheless, research projects that prioritize firms as the object of study tend to focus on understanding the configuration of global value chains or global production networks, highlighting processes connected to efficiency and competitiveness. The firm rather than the service product or good perhaps appears to be the object of study, but the paradox is that the focus of much of this research is not on firms, but on goods/services or on production processes configured to produce a specified product. Most firms manufacture many different varieties of product and each product may have a specially configured production system. Thus, a core research challenge is to develop more holistic approaches to understanding the multiple ways in which value is produced by firms and their related production and service processes.

In some accounts, the firm is taken to be the 'phenotype' or the smallest unit of analysis (Maskell, 2001; Taylor and Asheim, 2001). But for more complex firms, the phenotype might not be the firm, but some subunit, for example, a division or a subsidiary. Too many academics perhaps confuse research that is undertaken at the level of a subsidiary, division or plant with the complete firm. There are many challenges in defining the object of study as the firm. The primary challenge is the definition that is deployed. In some accounts, the firm is taken for granted and no attempt is made to define the firm. Nevertheless, every academic, policymaker and practitioner will have a slightly different definition of firms. Different approaches to defining firms will include firms as the loci of a set of timeless processes that include:

- Profit maximization.
- Decision-making under uncertainty.
- Rules, rituals, routines, habits and conventions.
- Learning, knowledge creation and transfer, and innovation.
- Employee recruitment, training and performance management.
- Corporate activity systems: operations management, sales and marketing, accounts, human resource management, procurement, supply chain management, corporate governance, and so on.
- Improvization under uncertainty.
- Bounded rationality and information asymmetry.
- Path dependency linked to sunk costs.
- Risk versus reward.

All these timeless processes are positioned around definitions of firms which highlight that they operate as mechanisms for coordinating, motivating and assessing individuals in the context of some form of value creation process. Motivation is important in this context, as a primary role played by firms is to 'direct and align perception, understanding, and evaluation by the people connected with it' (Nooteboom, 2000: 71).

People play a central role in firms. This includes exploitation of others, including being directly or indirectly complicit in modern-day slavery, or the severe exploitation of other people for commercial gain, with sexual abuse and sexual harassment against women, and all types of discrimination and exclusionary behaviour. In 2016, the International Labour Organization (ILO) estimated that 40 million people were victims of modern slavery, with 25 million in forced labour; there were 5.9 adult victims of modern slavery for every 1000 adults in the world, and 4.4 child victims for every 1000 children (ILO, 2017: 5). Too many GPNs are configured around severe labour exploitation combined with environmental pollution.

Within firms, there is a small group of people involved in strategic decision-making, a much larger group involved in the management of everyday operations, and an even larger group that is removed from having any significant input to organizational decisions. Organizational decision-making reflects trade-offs that are negotiated between senior managers. This is a political process that is also shaped by external influences including shareholders, competitors, politicians and the media, including social media. Very little research has been undertaken that has focused on understanding the negotiation of trade-offs in the context of manufacturing research. This is an important research gap, as the configuration of a GPN is one outcome of these types of negotiation processes. This is a complex process, as negotiations result in decisions that are then layered on top of decisions that have been made in the past. This process of layering produces symbiotic and perverse or unexpected outcomes.

An alternative approach to defining firms is based on identifying key characteristics. These include the firm as a:

- controller and coordinator of assets;
- negotiator and enforcer of contracts;
- set of relationships between people and other organizations;
- collective of individuals who have come together to achieve some common purpose;
- legal entity that can negotiate and agree written and unwritten contracts for which it is legally accountable;
- tax entity and tax collector;
- locus where societal needs are aligned with production processes to create use and exchange values.

Different scholars will emphasize some of these characteristics over others. There are perhaps surprising omissions in the literature. Very few papers explore how contracts are negotiated and enforced as well as the contribution contracts make to procurement processes, the configuration of GPNs and to path dependency (Mulhall and Bryson, 2013, 2014). There has been a significant emphasis placed on trust in interorganizational relationships, but these relationships are underpinned by written and unwritten contracts. These contracts might be underpinned by trust or the reputational damage that would result from any threat of contract enforcement (Bryson and Taylor, 2010; Taylor and Bryson, 2006).

Treating the firm as the object of study then highlights three critical activities. First, all firms are goal-directed, but not all firms are driven by a sole focus on profit maximization. Different firms have different motivations and very disparate drivers, including a triple bottom line approach or market maximization. Goal-direction does not mean that decisions made by a firm will be rational and will not result in perverse consequences including organizational failure. With very few exceptions, all firms eventually fail, and failure is the result of some balance between exogenous and endogenous factors. For some firms, failure is due to poor decision-making. Understanding failure is a critical research area and is one that is too often neglected. Second, a firm is a legal entity, and this highlights that a core function is in maintaining and clearly demarcating the boundary between a firm and other firms. The legal boundary is clearly defined as the governance structure that has the right to agree contracts and against which legal proceedings can be instituted. In operational terms, the boundary of a firm is much more complex, as many firms can only operate through a multiple array of interlocking arrangements with other organizations, but all such arrangements are regulated by contract law. Third, a firm is the locus within which a set of activity systems have been established that include accessing information, knowledge creation, product design, sourcing and procuring raw materials, recruitment and training employees, and creating service products or goods that can be monetarized in some way.

A GPN is not a firm, but a collection of firms. Each firm will be goal-directed, but there will be very many different types of goals. For some firms, involvement in a particular GPN will be business-critical, and for other firms it will represent a minor part of their business activities. There is an interesting tension in the GVC and GPN literatures between firms, networks and products. Much of the research is focused on products and the ways in which their GPNs are configured by a lead firm. But these lead firms will be configuring many different forms of good/product GPNs; the interactions between different forms of configuration within the same firm are perhaps as important as the configuration of any specific good/product GPN. This includes different forms of joint ventures and strategic partnerships with various partners and with different modes of governance. This is an important research gap that requires further attention.

Decisions regarding the object of study illuminate some processes and place other processes in darkness. There are two points to consider here. On the one hand, it is important not to isolate one aspect of a firm from the firm's wider context. Thus, focusing on one product, activity system or GVC or GPN is to separate a process from a much more complex set of processes and decisions. On the other hand, displacing the firm as the object of study with a good/service product, or some combination, focuses the analysis on processes, decisions and outcomes that are required to close the gap between the demand and supply of some good or service product. The type of good/service product raises interesting research questions that should be central to the manufacturing research agenda. These include alternative ways of designing a product to increase fabrication efficiency, to reduce good/product-related environmental pollution, including decarbonizing operational processes, or to increase good/product societal inclusion. Too much emphasis has been placed on understanding offshoring and reshoring, and capital substitution for labour (Urry, 2014; Peck, 2019), and too little research emphasis has been placed on the implications of the redesign of operational procedures combined with good/product redesign (Vanchan et al., 2018). This is a call for a good/product-informed, or good/product-centric, understanding of both firms and GVCs and GPNs (Bryson and Rusten, 2011). Nevertheless, this is only one entry point to understanding manufacturing that must also be positioned within an analysis of labour exploitation, environmental impacts and the variegated nature of manufacturing.

Variegated manufacturing

The manufacturing sector is extremely heterogeneous. These differences range from companies involved in the production of comparatively simple products that involve very few inputs, to goods that contain over 1 million components. Every physical good is the outcome of a distinctive production process that involves the configuration of machines and production tasks. These tasks might be completely mechanized with employees overseeing the process, focusing on supervision and maintenance. All tasks may be located at the same site, or the complete good might be the outcome of a production process that has been fragmented via the application of a spatial division of labour leading to some form of GVC or GPN. The manufacture of a good might be extremely labour-intensive with limited application of technological solutions to the performance of tasks. The heterogeneity of manufacturing takes three forms: by type of firm, the configuration of the production processes and good/service product combinations.

The degree of heterogeneity implies that manufacturing research is an exercise in identifying and understanding the variegated nature of manufacturing or production systems. All theories developed to explain some aspect of manufacturing must be able to engage with the variegated nature of manufacturing. This includes theory that can be applied to complex, highly fragmented production systems, or GPNs, and manufacturing processes which are predominantly localized and which are only indirectly linked to GVCs or GPNs. It is important to consider the three processes that sit behind manufacturing's variegation.

First, there are an infinite variety of firms involved in manufacturing goods and in configuring manufacturing processes. These include international or global businesses. An analysis of the largest manufacturing companies by revenue highlights the continued importance of automotive companies and the dominance of American, Japanese and German companies in the global rankings of the largest manufacturing companies (Table 1.1). Nevertheless, these extremely large manufacturing companies are unusual, with most companies involved in manufacturing being small and medium-sized enterprises (SMEs) (Gallemore et al., 2019; Wang, 2019). The national context is important here. A comparative analysis of firm size and employment growth between Japanese and United Kingdom (UK) manufacturing firms between 1972 and 1991 identified significant differences between these countries; over this period in the UK both the total stock of small manufacturing firms and employment increased, but there was no increase in employment amongst Japanese firms (Doi and Cowling, 1998). There is no question that manufacturing firms of different sizes and ages play different roles in terms of employment, growth, innovative activities and wider socio-economic impacts (Ge et al., 2020). There is an important research agenda here that should focus on the relationships between firm size, place, production network, and wider socio-economic contributions.

The variegated nature of manufacturing firms includes transnational to small single-site family businesses, branch plants to complete corporations, joint ventures and subsidiaries, franchisees to subcontractors, sole proprietorships to listed companies, for-profit and not-for-profit companies, and companies held in various forms of employee ownership scheme (Fernández-Esquinas et al., 2017). The last of these may be 100 per cent employee-owned. Employee ownership alters the relationship between employee and employer by blending capitalism with communitarianism (Sauser, 2009). Some of these are large firms that make important products (Table 1.2). These firms challenge existing practices and represent an important research area, but one that has been neglected. Employee-owned firms may be juxtaposed against sweatshops, or factories and workshops with employees on very low wages, working long hours and often in unsafe conditions. Many GPNs have hidden within them these types of manufacturing firms that are based on labour exploitation. The variegated nature of manufacturing firms also includes state-owned enterprises (SOEs) that may operate in very different ways to other types of firms. A SOE may operate in the same way as other companies, but there may also be important differences that need to be identified and acknowledged. There is a further complication in that the form of governance that exists in the host state will impact on the operation of a SOE. A SOE may be at arm's length from the government owner or may be a corporate vehicle intended to advance some political objective.

Table 1.1   Largest manufacturing companies by revenue, 2020

Rank	Company	Industry	Revenue (US$m)	Employees	Headquarters
1	Volkswagen Group	Automotive	282 760	671 205	Germany
2	Toyota Group	Engineering, various	275 288	359 542	Japan
3	Samsung Electronics	Electronics, various	197 705	287 439	South Korea
4	Daimler	Automotive	193 346	298 655	Germany
5	Hon Hai Precision Industry (Foxconn)	Electronics	172 869	757 404	Taiwan
6	Ford	Automotive	155 900	190 000	United States
7	Honda	Automotive	137 332	218 674	Japan
8	General Motors	Automotive	137 237	164 000	United States
9	Mitsubishi	Engineering, various	135 940	86 098	Japan
10	Huawei	Tele-communications equipment, Electronics	124 316	194 000	China
11	China Railway and Engineering Group	Engineering	123 324	302 394	China
12	SAIC Motor	Automotive	122 071	151 785	China

Source: Adapted from Fortune (2020).

Second, similar manufactured goods can be produced by the application of a different configuration of machines, labour inputs and configurations of supply chains. These differences are ignored in much of the literature, but they will become increasingly critical. We need to know much more about alternative approaches to manufacturing similar products, with a focus on reducing environmental impacts and enhancing recyclability and sustainability. These differences include goods that have been redesigned in response to the monomaterials challenge. The very near future will be associated with a radical shift, from products that are designed to incorporate a variety of raw

Table 1.2   Majority employee-owned American manufacturing
companies, 2020

Rank	Company	Business	Date of establishment	Employees
1	Amsted Industries	Industrial components	1986	18 000
2	W.L. Gore & Associates	Manufacturing	1974	10 800
3	Challenge Manufacturing Company	Automotive manufacturing	1987	3 000
4	EVAPCO Inc.	Manufacturing	1984	3 000
5	Krueger International, Inc.	Furniture Manufacturing	1991	3 000
6	S&C Electric	Electrical equipment	1989	2 600
7	Jasper Engines & Transmissions	Engine and transmission remanufacturing	2010	2 400
8	Bradford White Water Heaters	Water heaters	1992	2 300
9	Columbia Forest Products	Plywood	1977	2 100
10	Airborn Inc	Electronic connectors	1996	1 500

Source: Adapted from NCEO (2020).

materials, to monomaterial products. Monomaterial products facilitate 100 per cent material recycling. Monomaterial products will emerge across all sectors, with perhaps one of the lead sectors being packaging (Nguyen et al., 2020). By 2030, all plastic packaging used within the European Union (EU) must be recyclable and reusable (Boz et al., 2020). This requires companies within all GVCs and GPNs to redesign goods and related packaging (Skoda, 2019). A good example is the environmentally friendly monomaterial baseball cap made by Atlantis. This includes a QR (quick response) code that when scanned provides access to the Atlantic tracking system, which provides information about the product's supply chain journey from the place of manufacture to the point of consumption; the QR code includes details of the production location, inland transportation, departure and arrival ports and vessel's name. These baseball caps are made from 100 per cent recycled fabric as well as including near-field communication (NFC) technology which enables information embedded in the cap to be shared with devices equipped with an NFC chip.

A primary corporate and academic challenge relates to the decarbonization of manufacturing processes and related supply chains (Dangelico and Pujari, 2010). This involves both product and production process redesign, but also identifying and removing processes and tasks that are carbon-intensive. This includes both the decarbonization of operations and logistics combined with waste reduction and recycling. In other words, this is about the development of zero-waste and zero-emissions manufacturing production processes and related products. Manufactured goods will increasingly be differentiated not on price but on environmental credentials. In any case, the production of some goods will no longer be permitted on environmental grounds. Clothing supply chains will increasingly engage with the food production system with innovations in the conversion of food by-products into textiles. Thus, Piñatex has emerged as a fruit-based vegan leather made from waste pineapple leaf fibres that cannot be eaten, and 'Orange Fiber' is created from waste orange peel discarded during the manufacture of orange juice. An alternative is recycling waste plastic into new fabric. Olas leggings, for example, are designed and made in England from Italian fabric from 78 per cent recycled polyester and 22 per cent Lycra. The laundry advice for this product is to hand wash using a green detergent and to deposit the used water in the soil to avoid microfibres polluting oceans. This highlights an important paradox: eco-friendly products also create environmental pollution.

The ecological aspects of manufacturing will become an extremely important new research agenda. This will include decarbonization linked to direct and indirect energy embedded in products, but also recycling and reuse. A good example are the products made for the Girlfriend Collective. This company's packaging is 100 per cent recycled and recyclable. The firm's leggings are made from 79 per cent recycled polyester, with a pair of leggings made from 25 recycled post-consumer bottles, and a bra from 11 bottles. Their range of LITE leggings are made from 83 per cent recycled fishing net, and other waste, and the company's T-shirts are made from the waste left by the cotton industry, with the yarn made in a zero-waste, zero-emissions facility in Japan. The Girlfriend Collective has also introduced the 'recycle, reuse and reGirlfriend' scheme. When a customer is finished with an old Girlfriend product then they can purchase a shipping label from the company's website. On receipt, the polyester is separated from the spandex and new fibres formed to make new Girlfriend pieces. The consumer receives a $15 store credit towards the purchase of a new item of clothing. The company's fabrics are designed to enhance recyclability.

Third, manufacturing has changed and continues to change. This includes the blurring of the boundaries between manufactured goods and service products (Daniels and Bryson, 2002). It has become increasingly difficult to isolate the production and consumption of goods from service products. There are product hybrids that combine both physical goods and services, for example, smartphones and laptops; and also goods that have been converted into services (Bryson et al., 2020). In the latter case, consumers no longer purchase the good, but purchase service inputs. Good examples are companies that provide mobility services rather than selling vehicles, or firms that provide pumping hours rather than selling industrial pumps. The conversion of a good into a service comes with many advantages. Selling a good includes one profit realization moment, whilst converting a good into a service provides the producer with a continual stream of profit realization moments. There are also sustainability advantages as the producer is completely responsible for product maintenance and for recycling. A key challenge for research on manufacturing is to develop a holistic approach that explores companies producing and selling similar goods, but using different channels to market and different configurations of production network and approaches to monetarization. This type of holistic approach would require more research that placed the analysis of a GPN within the context of the complete firm. Each channel will have very different characteristics including different forms of competitiveness, and each will have a different environmental footprint.

Monetarization, financialization and manufacturing

At the centre of all manufacturing processes is a monetarization process that is focused on converting something into money. Monetization requires a much broader critical discussion regarding value (Bryson and Vanchan, 2020). An important manufacturing research agenda involves developing a critical debate on value: for whom, for what, and from what. Too often, value is assumed or taken for granted. Value includes monetized and non-monetized values and different blends of these forms of value (Bryson et al., 2018). Value may include economic prosperity, inclusive economic prosperity, environmental protection and social justice.

Too often it is assumed that companies adopt similar approaches to the monetization of value. Thus, a research agenda may only focus on monetized value based on the assumption that the primary role of a firm involves minimizing costs and maximizing revenues and profitability. Anything that is assumed within a social science research agenda must be challenged. Different firms will operate to very different margins, and this reflects different governance structures including ownership, but also decisions related to product differentiation. Some products compete solely on price and other products compete on non-price-based characteristics (Bryson and Ronayne, 2014). For some products there is a direct relationship between production cost and the final sales price, and for similar products there may be a very different relationship between costs versus sales price. Further research is required into the relationship between monetarization and different approaches to configuring goods/service product combinations and their production networks. Monetization is a very complex issue as contributions to product profitability may emerge across a GPN. This is an under-researched area. There are two important points to consider.

First, is the analysis of monetarization and manufacturing made at the level of the firm or product? A product line may be a loss leader, or profitability may be hidden through the application of various forms of financial engineering including transfer pricing. For a product, profit may emerge via the application of a spatial division of labour that underpins the configuration of a GPN, and this might include labour exploitation. Contributions to product profitability may rest on effective negotiation of procurement contracts in which order size might be used to transfer margins from suppliers to the procurer. Effective negotiation might be good business, but it might also reflect socially irresponsible business practices. Monetarization might not be directly related to the manufacture of a product. A product may be manufactured to a low or break-even margin, as the primary monetarization moment might be focused on the sale of consumables. A classic example of a revenue-based monetarization model is found in the 'razor–razor blade' model. This operates by 'pricing razors, or computer printers, inexpensively but placing higher margins on consumables – razor blades or printing ink' (Bryson et al., 2020: 51). Monetarization may also include data monetarization in which information is acquired from consumers and then repackaged and sold as data-related products. This also includes the monetarization of websites through the development of revenue-based models. Another form of product-related service monetarization is found in the sale of products that are supported by the provision of finance packages including appliance insurance policies and extended warranties. Automotive companies prefer not to sell vehicles outright, but instead encourage consumers to take out finance packages.

At the corporate rather than the product level, monetarization includes financialization (Christophers, 2015). In a review of the history and definition of financialization, Greta Krippner uses the term to refer to a 'pattern of accumulation in which profit-making occurs increasingly through financial channels rather than through trade and commodity production' (Krippner, 2004, p. 14). Financialization includes companies that allocate a proportion of their profits to share buybacks in order to increase share prices. This is a process that also impacts upon the value of executive stock options and corporate pay. In this case, profit is invested to increase the value of a company without investing in process or product innovation that would contribute directly to value creation over a long period. Mazzucato's analysis of value is especially useful in exploring this process. She notes that:

> In the 2000s … the US arm of Ford made more money by selling loans for cars than by selling the cars themselves. Ford sped up the car's transformation from physical product to financial commodity by pioneering the Personal Contract Plan (PCP), which allowed a 'buyer' to pay monthly instalments that only covered the predicted depreciation, and trade up to a new model after two or three years. (Mazzucato, 2018: 162)

The development of PCPs and their adoption by car manufacturers led to another financial innovation. The PCP contracts could be bundled together, securitized, and then resold as a financial product. In essence, financialization involves the action of money on money to produce additional value. The key question is the relationship between this type of financial value and the wealth created by manufacturing goods. Financialization is also applied by manufacturing companies to intellectual property and to trade in innovation (Clark, 2013).

Financialization is found in all sizes of manufacturing companies. Small companies may extract funds to invest in real estate, or other financial assets, as part of a strategy to create assets to underpin owners' pension plans. For larger companies, their GVCs and GPNs cannot be understood without detailed analysis of corporate financialization. This includes depositing money in offshore banks to avoid taxation, and making 'more money than ever before by simply moving money around … from purely financial activities, such as trading, hedging, tax optimizing, and selling financial services, than they did in the immediate post-World War II period' (Foroohar, 2016: 5). Hedging is commonly applied by manufacturing companies to reduce their exposure to risks related to price volatility and access to raw materials including energy inputs (Mulhall and Bryson, 2013, 2014). For manufacturing companies hedging is a process based around taking purchasing positions to reduce exposure to price movements. This can take two forms: with physical hedging, a supplier agrees to lock in a price for a period with a manufacturer; with financial hedging, the manufacturer uses an intermediary, for example a bank, to agree a locked-in price. The latter type is much more complex as the manufacturer would need to meet the accountancy standards associated with hedging activities and derivative instruments. These accountancy standards do not apply to physical hedging. Nevertheless, one advantage of financial hedging is that the price lock-in would be supported by a large financial institution rather than perhaps a much smaller provider of production inputs.

Over the last two decades, perhaps the most productive line of enquiry for research on the global economy, within the critical social sciences, should have focused on the fact that the 'biggest and brightest companies have started to act like banks' (Foroohar, 2016: 4) rather than manufacturing companies. This includes selecting locations for production and assembly plants based on financial rather than operational grounds, including accessing government subsidies.

Second, corporate profitability is often directly or indirectly linked to the exploitation of people, and the environment. This also includes tax avoidance, which is a form of indirect labour exploitation. In this case, a company benefits from taxes invested in education and related services in a national or regional context, but minimizes its own contribution and is thus indirectly subsidized by other taxpayers. These other taxpayers will be companies as well as low-income workers. This is a complex and under-researched issue and is complicated by approaches to financial engineering, including financialization, developed by companies and consultancy firms. Highly profitable companies may be heavily reliant on strategies that include exploitation of people and environmental pollution. A core critical social science research agenda involves identifying how and where manufacturing firms are directly and indirectly engaged in such strategies. This includes designing and fabricating manufactured projects that are impossible to recycle. It also includes products with GPNs configured to maximize profitability, but which exploit people and, at the same time, maximize environmental pollution. All this highlights that further research is required to explore manufacturing as a set of linked multi-scalar processes that engage directly and indirectly with the wider social and physical environments.

The challenge of scale and production processes

For manufacturing, geography matters: the place, or places, of production matter combined with the places in which product recycling occurs (Lee and Luca, 2019). The question of scale plays a central role in the configuration of manufacturing production processes. A primary research challenge is to develop a much more sophisticated approach to scale. Currently, manufacturing research relies on applying a multi-scalar approach based on allocating production processes to local, regional, national or international/global scales. There are two problems with this approach.

First, at a regional level, regions are defined based on established political, religious or administrative boundaries. These are socially constructed boundaries that often have no meaning for companies. Thus, a focus on understanding the functioning economic geographies of a politically defined region – for example, the West Midlands (UK) – could result in a distorted analysis as economic activity crosses over these socially constructed regional boundaries (Salder and Bryson, 2019). The terms 'international' and 'global' are too often applied to products and companies that operate using a much more restricted geography. One research challenge involves identifying the small number of firms that operate globally rather than internationally. There are no reliable lists of truly global companies. The current lists of global companies use size as a proxy measure, but size does not equate with companies having a global rather than an international footprint (Table 1.1).

Second, scale involves places and flows between places. These flows include people, money, raw materials, components, complete products, services, information, knowledge, environmental pollutants and disease. Connections between places are no longer measured based on geographic distance, but on travel time and, ideally, on carbon footprint. A core challenge for manufacturing research is to develop a much more sophisticated approach to exploring scale. The current approach needs to be problematized, as it has become taken for granted.

The starting point for the problematization of scale is to consider how a local versus a regional company is defined or identified. Do local manufacturing firms exist? Do manufacturing firms exist that operate regionally? The problem is that the definition of local and regional is too often assumed or based on existing socially constructed definitions that are overlaid on to manufacturing companies. These socially constructed definitions are based on established administrative boundaries that, in some contexts, reflect decisions that were made in the far distant past. Thus, the West Midlands is a region defined not on the basis of some objective assessment or appreciation of the area's functioning economic geography. This region is defined based on historic decisions that can be traced back to the emergence of Anglo-Saxon territories around 500 AD and the identification of ten regions by Oliver Cromwell's Protectorate in the 1650s. These types of regions are too often applied to explore firm behaviour and the operation of 'regional' economies. This approach needs to be turned on its head. The alternative approach is based on appreciating that scale at the corporate level is socially constructed based on processes of enactment. The implication is that every manufacturing firm will have enacted its own local and regional scales of activities, and these scales may have no relationship with existing administration boundaries. In this account, scale is an experiential process. A research process must be applied to identify a company's local and regional geography, and this may be idiosyncratic. The same approach must be applied to identifying and defining a company's enacted definition of the 'international' or 'global' scale. The national scale is different, as there is a legal definition based on national jurisdictions. Thus, the local, regional, international and global scales are experiential, whilst the national reflects a legal boundary.

The approach to treating scale as a multi-scalar process must be transformed. This approach is too rigid, as it is based on a simplistic account and set of assumptions regarding the complex interrelationships between organizations or individuals, place and space. Multi-scalar processes are in reality experienced and constructed in a much more fluid manner, with constant interactions between different forms of place-based interactions. The relationships between organization and scale are better conceptualized as being based around 'scalar-plasticity' in which there are multiple interlayered geographical relationships between different places that have different characteristics. These relationships involve different types of intensity, including duration, but also some of these inter-place-based interactions are strategic, some emotional and some circumstantial (Salder and Bryson, 2019). This new concept of scalar-plasticity replaces the multi-scalar approach by recognizing that every individual and organization constructs and enacts their own applied or practice definition of scale(s). This makes comparative research much more challenging, as simple unproblematized definitions of local, regional and international/global are replaced by an approach to scale that is framed within the terms set by the individuals and organizations engaging with place and space.

This approach must be applied to international or global processes as they relate to production processes. Every company will enact its own applied definition of international/global through performance and practice. The implication is that there are perhaps as many corporate configurations of the local, regional and global scales as there are companies. There will be a balance between that which is particular to a firm and that which is perhaps more universal, but this requires considerable further research (Sayer, 1982). In this context, it is important to appreciate that there continues to be a considerable Anglophonic bias in manufacturing research. Different cultures will have very different approaches to enacting and defining scale in practice. An important new research agenda involves problematizing scale and developing a more practice-orientated approach that will also require methodological innovation. This research agenda must also include comparative research to explore the relationships between culture and scale as a practice-defined process.

There is a danger that research on manufacturing, production networks and scale focuses on the state, firms, and national and global policy. All these are important, but it is also important to remember the role that consumption decisions made by individuals and households play in shaping economic outcomes. Too often consumers are considered to be relatively unimportant as the emphasis is on understanding production processes in isolation from consumption. This is surprising, as supply is considered in isolation from demand. Recently, Clark has noted that it is important 'to consider the local and the household scales which are increasingly sites of policy action – both from the bottom up and the top down' (Clark, 2019: 1179).

There is another complication regarding scale. There is a tendency amongst some social sciences to overemphasize the importance of scale or geography. This is becoming a major constraint on manufacturing research in these disciplinary contexts. In these disciplines, journal editors desk-reject papers that are not positioned within an account of scale. In 1984, Massey developed an important distinction between spatial and aspatial processes. The danger is that overemphasizing spatial processes relegates aspatial processes. Critical economic geography urgently needs to appreciate that aspatial and spatial processes are interlinked in complex ways and that sometimes an analysis must focus on the aspatial aspects of a process. The current overemphasis on spatial processes in economic geography, for example, explains the emphasis placed on clusters and GPNs and the neglect of research on operational management and processes. This is a major problem that can be highlighted via an example.

In February 2021, Mondelēz International announced plans to invest £15 million (US$20.5 million) in the company's Bournville site in Birmingham, UK. This site was described as the 'heart and home' of Cadbury (Ferrer, 2021). This investment includes £11 million to create a production line for Cadbury Dairy Milk chocolate bars (tablets) as part of a strategy to consolidate the majority of tablet production on the Bournville site. This new production line would increase annual capacity by 125 million Cadbury Dairy Milk (CDM) chocolate bars and would come with additional capacity for future growth. The company also planned to invest £4 million to increase the site's chocolate-making capacity. Since 2014, the company had invested over £80 million (US$109.5 million) on plant modernization to enhance efficiency. In 2016, production costs at Bournville were three times that of similar factories in Germany and other European markets, but the investments increased production efficiency by more than 30 per cent at Bournville since 2014. Bournville is supported by two other UK-based satellite sites. The 2021 planned increase in production capacity involves no additional employment. This is an example in which aspatial and spatial processes are combined. The investment in a new production line reflects a place-based enhancement to operational capacity. This additional capacity could have been located elsewhere. How is this decision explained? In cost terms, there are perhaps locations that would be cheaper and would require reduced investment in technology. Nevertheless, part of this strategy is based on enhancing plant-based productivity by investing in technology rather than hiring people. This is partly about technological substitution for people via operational enhancement.

There is another important aspect to this strategy. Bournville plays an important non-price-based role in this company's competitiveness; CDM was invented in Bournville. There are important place-based associations between this place and the product (Rusten et al., 2007). This site is also the location for Mondelēz International's Global Centre of Excellence for Chocolate Research and Development, including the company's innovation kitchen where all Cadbury products across the globe are invented. There is a paradox here, in that non-cost-based factors may underpin investment and strategic decisions regarding adjustments to the configuration of an existing GPN. In this case, Bournville has important associations for some consumers, but this site also plays an important role in this company's corporate culture. This is a form of corporate emotional attachment to the place that encourages the company to apply a technological substitution strategy to enhance productivity, rather than a spatial strategy based on identifying the cheapest location to produce these products. All this highlights that further research is required to explore the relationships between technological innovation, and related investment strategies, and the spatial configuration of production.

Manufacturing paradoxes and new forms of risk

Manufacturing is replete with many paradoxes and contrasts, including inertia and rapid change. The word 'manufacture' is a paradox in its own right. This word comes from the Latin *manu factum* or the action or process of making something by hand. This term was applied to the making of products by physical labour, or mechanical power, in the seventeenth century (Bryson and Rusten, 2011: 164). Manufacturing includes highly automated systems as well as labour-intensive production processes. It includes, for example, synthetic fibres that are created chemically and woven using highly automated machines, with integrated drive operations facilitated by industrial network architecture to facilitate the flow of data around a plant and international business (Bryson and Ronayne, 2014). Nevertheless, it also includes Harris Tweed®, which is the only fabric in the world governed by its own Act of Parliament, the 1993 Harris Tweed Act. Harris Tweed is 'hand-woven by the islanders at their homes in the Outer Hebrides, finished in the Outer Hebrides, and made from pure virgin wool dyed and spun in the Outer Hebrides' (Platman, 2011: 24).

One of the paradoxes of manufacturing is related to the emergence of new forms of risk. Both Beck (1992) and Giddens (1998) have explored the emergence of a new risk society. Manufacturing is associated with new technological solutions that are intended to transform everyday living, reducing risk. Nevertheless, the strange paradox here is that 'risk might in fact be increasing due to technology, science and industrialism rather than being abated by scientific and technological progress' (Jarvis, 2007: 23). There are many explanations for this paradox.

On the one hand, everyday living is supported by complex assemblages of manufactured products. Any component breakdown may result in widespread systemic failure. A 'cyber-energy-production plexus' has formed around multiple connections between telecommunication, energy and production networks (Bryson et al., 2021). Across manufacturing, industrial control systems (ICSs) have been developed that integrate hardware with software through network connectivity. ICSs underpin critical infrastructure within production systems. Historically, production equipment was isolated or air-gapped from the outside world. The cyber-energy-production plexus includes directly or indirectly linking ICS components to the internet and these expose core operational systems to cyberattacks. An excellent example is the extensive cybersecurity attack on Norsk Hydro, one of the largest producers of aluminium in the world, with smelting plants, factories and offices in 40 countries. On 19 March 2019, a classic ransomware cyberattack affected information technology (IT) systems in most business areas. The company's worldwide IT network went down, and the company had to switch its ICS from automated to manual. The company did not pay a ransom, but the cyberattack cost at least £300 million Norwegian kroner (£25.6 million). Every local factory manager was tasked with maintaining customer orders, and the company instigated an incident representation response plan that included a temporary website. Microsoft employees and representatives from cybersecurity firms were flown in to assist the company. Full recovery was estimated to take months (Beaumont, 2019). Cyberattacks have become one of the primary risks facing all ICSs that are linked to the internet.

On the other hand, the ongoing development of the cyber–energy–production plexus is associated with the creation of tightly coupled systems. Charles Perrow (1984) made important contributions to understanding the emergence of new forms of risk in tightly coupled systems. He identified two factors that enhance system susceptibility to risk. First, risk emerges in the ways in which different parts of a system interact with one another. Some systems are linear, making any failure immediately obvious; whilst other systems are much more complex, with different parts of the system interacting with one another in unexpected ways. Much that occurs in complex systems is hidden. The second factor in Perrow's theory is based on how much slack exists in a system. This concept of slack comes from the engineering literature on tight coupling or system optimization. In this account of engineering systems, tight coupling is associated with limited slack, or buffering, existing between different parts of the system. The opposite of tight coupling is loose coupling, in which slack exists in a system, with the result being that any failure of one part of a system can be covered by the slack that exists elsewhere. Loose coupling enables a system to respond to shock, as sufficient additional capacity, including alternative routeways, may be available during times of crisis. The danger is that GPNs which are configured around cost control and profitability also tend to be tightly coupled networks in which decision-making has focused on system optimization rather than system resilience.

Another manufacturing paradox is the relationship between a focus on enhancing productivity in production processes and risk. All production-orientated theory must include a focus on understanding the drivers behind the race to enhance productivity, and the perverse consequences of this process. Productivity is a measure of the ratio of inputs to outputs in a production process. Some manufacturing firms are fixated with a concern to enhance productivity. This includes identifying tasks to relocate to low-cost labour locations, combined with substituting labour with machines. Productivity can be a measure of team or plant performance as well as being applied nationally as part of a comparative assessment of national productivity differentials (McCann, 2009).

In 1994, Paul Krugman proclaimed that: 'Productivity isn't everything, but in the long run it is almost everything. A country's ability to improve its standard of living over time depends almost entirely on its ability to raise its output per worker' (Krugman, 1994: 13). This quotation has become a cliché to support debates on the importance of productivity in national and regional economies (McCann, 2009: 280). Krugman's statement is both correct and misleading and: 'should be rewritten: "Invention and innovation isn't everything, but in the long run it is almost everything in facilitating productivity improvements".

The problem is one of causality: productivity improvements are an output of invention and innovation' (Bryson et al., 2020: 35–36).

Nevertheless, the application of invention and innovation to manufacturing companies in order to increase productivity involves system optimization, and this includes tight coupling; tight coupling enhances exposure to risk and reduces corporate resilience. A major challenge facing all manufacturing companies is the need to balance system optimization against risk to ensure that sufficient loose coupling or organizational slack exists (Cyert and Marsh, 2001). Identifying risk and developing approaches to ameliorating societal risks should be at the centre of all socially responsible social science, and it is to this topic that we now turn our attention.

Manufacturing research and socially responsible social science

The term 'critical human geography' emerged in the mid-1990s as part of a debate in Anglophonic geography that engaged with a broader debate on critical social science. Critical human geography represents 'a diverse set of ideas and practices linked by a shared commitment to a broadly conceived emancipatory politics, progressive social change, and the use of a range of critical socio-geographic theories' (Berg, 2010: 617). At one level, this is a purely academic project with analysis placed in the context of a call for progressive social change; but at another level, this is a call for applied and action-oriented research that is intended to make a difference (Martin, 1999, 2001; Massey, 2000; Pollard et al., 2000). The challenge for critical human geography is to develop a dialogue between geographical research and ongoing debates on the ethical challenges related to socially responsible science. The literature on socially responsible science highlights that 'scientists have a responsibility to address the social implications of their research' (Resnik and Elliott, 2016: 31). This is a complex process, since 'acknowledging one's social responsibilities as a scientist is only the beginning of dealing with the value implications of one's work, since responsibility requires one to address the moral, political, social, and policy issues at stake' (Resnik and Elliott, 2016: 32). The definition of social responsibility is context-specific as every topic will have a different set of related social implications. This could include engaging with the 17 Sustainable Development Goals (SDGs) identified by the United Nations in 2015 (UN General Assembly, 2015).

The manufacturing research agenda must be positioned within a debate on socially responsible research. There is a tension here. On the one hand, all researchers are consumers; every time we consume, we support employment, create employment and destroy jobs, whilst also supporting and contributing to all types of environmental pollution. Social scientists should engage in socially responsible consumption. Defining this represents a critical research agenda, and enacting this as everyday behaviour is challenging. On the other hand, deciding not to consume is impossible, but selective and socially responsible consumption is perfectly possible. An avenue for research revolves around approaches to balancing the tensions between consumption and social responsibility.

For the academic this is about recognizing 'the value implications of one's research [as] an important first step towards exercising social responsibility' (Resnik and Elliott, 2016: 37). Ignoring this is not an option, as this would be to act irresponsibility, 'because behaving responsibly requires one to deal with the implications of one's conduct' (Resnik and Elliott, 2016: 37). For those involved in manufacturing research, social responsibility involves identifying the perverse consequences of manufacturing and then working to address these consequences. This includes identifying products and GPNs that incorporate any form of labour exploitation, including modern-day slavery. This includes labour exploitation that sits across a GPN, including raw material inputs and those involved in logistics and recycling. It also includes identifying those parts of a GPN that are carbon-intensive or which contribute to environmental pollution.

It used to be the case that academics conducted rigorous and robust research and that social responsibility was passed onto policymakers, politicians, journalists and the public, whose roles included dealing with the consequences of new knowledge. This is no longer the case. It has become increasingly unacceptable for academics to adopt a value-free approach, but instead, where appropriate, research agendas must include a concern with social responsibility. This is an important point for journal editors to consider. Editors and reviewers should be asked to assess a paper based on academic rigour combined with social responsibility. Authors should be encouraged, where appropriate, to provide a social responsibility statement that, for example, aligns their paper's contribution to the SDGs. Such a statement would highlight the wider societal implications of the research and would include an impact statement. All social science journals should clearly acknowledge the critical importance of adopting and enacting effective approaches to supporting and encouraging socially responsible social science. This includes three dimensions:

1. Problem selection.
2. Data sharing and open access publication.
3. Public engagement.

We will consider each of these in turn.

First, problem selection requires careful reflection regarding the comparative importance of a research challenge. This includes an assessment of the number of people and non-humans who would be impacted upon by a process that is selected as the object of research. Thus, some problems challenge the life chances of many millions of people, and then there are other problems that impact on one or two individuals or non-humans. Socially responsible social science requires a justification for focusing time and resources on one research challenge compared to another.

Second, publication must be considered carefully. Too frequently, the place of publication is based on citations, journal impact scores or journal rankings. A socially responsible publication strategy would include due consideration regarding the wider societal relevance of a publication. Across the social sciences, an overemphasis on the theoretical contribution that a paper makes has emerged. Thus, for many journals the decision to publish a paper is not based on societal relevance combined with social responsibility, but on the contribution a paper makes to academic theory. There are perverse consequences of this approach. It means that papers might be rejected that identify pathways to create better societal outcomes, on the grounds that they do not make a theoretical contribution. A key debate that is urgently required is the tension between theoretical versus socially responsible research contributions.

Third, socially responsible social science involves more than publishing for career advancement. An important question concerns the assessment of the quality of a publication. Do we use proxy measures, including the publisher's reputation or the impact factor or ranking of a journal? To Kennedy (1999: 192), 'in the end the judgments of peers – often after a substantial lapse of time – will yield the most reliable verdict'. Kennedy was writing in 1999, and times have moved on. The judgement of peers would suggest that research and publication is targeted at other academics rather than the wider society. The final judgement regarding the quality of a paper should be based on wider societal relevance. This includes authors engaging in public engagement activities to ensure that the implications of a research project are addressed. This includes direct and indirect public engagement activities. Indirect activities include incorporating new knowledge into university courses; teaching becomes an important element in socially responsible social science. Direct activities include press releases, social media, blogs, providing expert testimony, publicly advocating for change via media interviews and public speeches, and direct intervention. Direct intervention includes establishing not-for-profit companies to address private and public sector failure, and whistleblowing regarding unethical and irresponsible activities.

Conclusions

This book is intended to contribute towards identifying a research agenda for manufacturing. It is important that all involved in manufacturing research periodically stand back from their everyday practices and reflect on what they are trying to achieve. This period of reflection should also consider the social relevance of their research and teaching contributions.

This raises the question of what contribution social science should make to society. This might be defined in the terms of critical commentary combined with a socially responsible research agenda that is intended to enhance societal outcomes. For manufacturing-orientated research this raises some interesting questions:

1. Is the objective enhanced understanding of manufacturing processes as an end in itself to inform a predominantly academically orientated discussion?
2. Is the objective focused on research that is intended to improve company performance?
3. Is the objective focused on labour and the conditions of employment with a focus on trying to produce better outcomes for people?
4. Is the emphasis on research that is intended to reduce negative environmental consequences of manufacturing processes including recycling and waste?
5. Is the objective about identifying different ways in which policy can shape outcomes?
6. Is the objective to develop understanding to inform teaching on the understanding that better-informed graduates will make better decisions?

These questions are critical, but too frequently ignored. There is a real danger that an overemphasis on academically focused research, as well as theoretically focused research, undermines the perceived contribution that social science makes to society. There must be some perceived and actual broader societal contribution.

The chapters in this book set out a series of thematic, theoretical and methodological contributions that inform the development of manufacturing research agendas. In Chapter 2, Chloe Billing and John Bryson explore the emergence of new industries as a process that challenges existing conventions. This chapter sets out a legitimacy-building framework for exploring emerging industries. This approach to emerging industries provides the backdrop for Jennifer Johns's (Chapter 3) analysis of a research agenda framed within a discussion of additive manufacturing including three-dimensional (3D) printing. This chapter identifies four key research directions for research on additive manufacturing. Developments in production technologies underpin some of the aspects of a new research agenda for research on the automotive industry that is explored by Godfrey Yeung in Chapter 4. In this analysis, he identifies disruptive megatrends that are creating new automotive companies and even new automotive subsectors. This includes artificial intelligence (AI) and autonomous driving that is blurring the boundaries between software and hardware. Part of the context of this chapter is highlighting the need for further research that will explore resilience and supply chain management.

Emerging industries and disruptive innovation are linked to alternations in labour markets and in the skills that support manufacturing. In Chapter 5, Anne Green and Abigail Taylor explore the changing skills and policy requirements for manufacturing. This includes the challenge of replacement demand in local labour markets linked to skills gaps and skills underutilization. This discussion of policy provides an entry point into Chapter 6 by William Graves and Harrison Campbell, Jr. This chapter focuses on the automotive industry and the impacts that policy has had on reshaping the geography of the American automotive industry. This is positioned within an account of the evolution of clustering strategies and highlights that there is an important research agenda that focuses on policy, place and manufacturing. This requires the application of a holistic approach to explore the wider impacts of policy on companies, place, labour markets and the wider society.

The analysis then shifts to focus on SMEs and manufacturing. Intermediaries play an important role in regional and national economies. In Chapter 7, Ronald Kalafsky and Douglas Gress focus on one type of intermediary: trade fairs. This chapter highlights the ways in which research on trade fairs is one entry point to explore the export dynamics and learning networks of SME manufacturers. Everyday living is supported by an ever-increasing array of devices that rely on electronics. The production of these devices is based on a complex and evolving set of GPNs. These GPNs are supported by SMEs, and trade shows are important intermediary spaces that facilitate the development of new GPNs and products. In Chapter 8, David Chan and Chun Yang explore the transformation of Asian electronics production networks as a pathway to identifying new research agendas on manufacturing in general and the electronics industry in particular. Production is underpinned by production management and operations and supply chain management. Chapter 9, by Donato Masi and Janet Godsell, explores approaches to undertaking research on operations and supply chain management, with an emphasis on rigour and relevance. Rigour comes from embedding empirical research within a theoretical framework, but research should also be relevant, and this includes encouraging alterations in company behaviour.

Research that is rigorous and relevant must be underpinned by an appropriate research design and related methods. The focus of Chapter 10 by John Bryson et al. is on corporate interviewing as a methodological tool, but the emphasis is on accessing corporate elites. This chapter develops a framework for accessing corporate elites that draws upon the experiences of four PhD students who completed research on manufacturing companies. The framework includes an analysis of the role social media and networking tools may play in accessing corporate elites.

The final chapter of this edited collection, Chapter 11 by John Bryson, outlines and develops an approach to reading businesses to inform practice, research and policy. This approach includes identifying 28 key questions that should underpin any attempt to read a business. This reading business approach is then applied to develop a research agenda for manufacturing research. This includes further research on value, operations, care and responsibility, including diversity, risk and uncertainty, products and scale, including the development and application of the scalar-plasticity approach to the scale question. This is positioned within a broader argument regarding the emergence of a new epoch in the ongoing evolution of capitalism. We have entered the period of Jenga Capitalism, in which system convergence, combined within increased global connectivity, produces domino effects that ripple across the globe, enhancing inequalities, and disrupting global production networks and national economies.

Currently, humanity faces five critical challenges:

1. Climate change and the race to decarbonize production and consumption, including minimizing the environmental and societal impacts of supply chains and production/consumption processes.

2. Inclusive prosperity that is truly inclusive and sustainable.
3. Risks related to system convergence and optimization including cybersecurity.
4. Risks related to biological hazards and pandemics.
5. The impacts of developments in artificial intelligence (AI) and robotics on manufacturing, employment, consumption, governance and lifestyles.

These are five cross-cutting themes that will result in the emergence of new industries, technologies, production processes and lifestyles. Life as we know it will change radically over the next decade as production processes and lifestyles increasingly decarbonize. There will also be important implications for labour markets and skills. All these five themes will play an important role in the manufacturing research agendas that will emerge over the next decade.

References

BBC (2021), 'BP staff set to work from home two day a week', *BBC News*, accessed 8 March 2021, available at https://www.bbc.co.uk/news/business-56319623.

Beaumont, K. (2019), 'How Lockergoga took down Hydro – ransomware used in targeted attacks aimed at big business', accessed 10 February 2021, available at https://doublepulsar.com/how-lockergoga-took-down-hydro-ransomware-used-in -targeted-attacks-aimed-at-big-business-c666551f5880.

Beck, U. (1992), *Risk Society: Towards a New Modernity*, London: SAGE.

Berg, L. (2010), 'Critical human geography', in Warf, B. (ed.), *Encyclopedia of Geography*, London: SAGE Publications, pp. 617–621.

Boz, Z., Korhonen, V. and Koelsch C.S. (2020), 'Consumer considerations for the implementation of sustainable packaging: a review', *Sustainability*, 12(6): 2192. https://doi.org/10.3390/su12062192.

Bryson, J.R., Andres, L., Ersoy, A. and Reardon, L. (2021), 'A year into the pandemic: shifts, improvisations and impacts for people, place and policy', in Bryson, J.R., Andres, L., Ersoy, A. and Reardon, L. (eds), *Living with Pandemics: Places, People and Policy*, Cheltenham, UK and Northampton, MA, USA: Edward Elgar Publishing, pp. 2–34.

Bryson, J.R., Mulhall, R.A., Song, M., Loo, B., Dawson, R.J. and Rogers, C.D.F. (2018), 'Alternative-substitute business models and the provision of local infrastructure: alterity as a solution to financialization and public-sector failure', *Geoforum*, 95: 25–34.

Bryson, J.R. and Ronayne, M. (2014), 'Manufacturing carpets and technical textiles: routines, resources, capabilities, adaptation, innovation and the evolution of the British textile industry', *Cambridge Journal of Regions, Economy and Society*, 7(3): 471–488.

Bryson, J.R. and Rusten, G. (2011), *Design Economic and the Changing World Economy*, London: Routledge.

Bryson J.R., Sundbo, J., Fuglsang, L. and Daniels, P. (2020), *Service Management: Theory and Practice*, London: Palgrave Macmillan.

Bryson J.R. and Taylor, M. (2010), 'Mutual dependency, diversity and alterity in production: cooperatives, group contracting and factories', in Fuller D., Jonas A.E. and Lee R. (eds), *Interrogating Alterity*, Farnham: Ashgate, pp. 75–94.

Bryson, J.R. and Vanchan, V. (2020), 'COVID-19 and alternative conceptualisations of value and risk in GPN research', *Tijds. voor econ. en Soc. Geog.*, 111: 530–542.

Christophers, B. (2015), 'The limits to financialization', *Dialogues in Human Geography*, 5(2): 183–200.

Clark, J. (2013), *Working Regions: Reconnecting Innovation and Production in the Knowledge Economy*, London: Routledge.

Clark, J. (2019), 'Remodeling capitalism: a return to scale', *Environment and Planning A: Economy and Space*, 51(5): 1178–1180

Cyert, R.M. and Marsh, J.G. (2001), *A Behavioural Theory of the Firm*, Oxford: Blackwell.

Dangelico, R.M. and Pujari, D. (2010), 'Mainstreaming green product innovation: why and how companies integrate environmental sustainability', *Journal of Business Ethics*, 95: 471–486.

Daniels, P.W. and Bryson, J.R. (2002), 'Manufacturing services and servicing manufacturing: knowledge-based cities and changing forms of production', *Urban Studies*, 39(5–6): 977–991.

Dicken, P. and Thrift, N. (1992), 'The organization of production and the production of organization: why business enterprises matter in the study of geographical industrialization', *Transactions of the Institute of British Geographers*, New Series 17: 279.

Doi, N. and Cowling, M. (1998), 'The evolution of firm size and employment share distribution in Japan and UK manufacturing: a study of small business presence', *Small Business Economics*, 10: 283–292.

Fernández-Esquinas, M., van Oostrom, M. and Pinto, H. (2017), 'Key issues on innovation, culture and institutions: implications for SMEs and micro firms', *European Planning Studies*, 25(11): 1897–1190.

Ferrer, B. (2021), 'Cadbury to return to Bournville with US$20.5M investment in Dairy Milk tablets production', *Food Ingredients 1st*, accessed 17 February 2021, available at https://www.foodingredientsfirst.com/news/cadbury-to-return-to-bournville-with-us205m-investment-in-dairy-milk-tablets-production.html.

Foroohar, R. (2016), *Makers and Takers: The Rise of Finance and the Fall of American Business*, New York: Crown Business.

Fortune (2020), Global 500, accessed 16 February 2021, available at https://fortune.com/global500/2020/search/.

Gallemore, C., Nielsen, K.R. and Jespersen, K. (2019), 'The uneven geography of crowdfunding success: spatial capital on Indiegogo', *Environment and Planning A: Economy and Space*, 51(6): 1389–1406.

Ge, C., Zhang, S.-G. and Wang, B. (2020), 'Modeling the joint distribution of firm size and firm age based on grouped data', *PLoS ONE*, 15(7): e0235282. https://doi.org/10.1371/journal.pone.0235282.

Giddens, A. (1998), *The Third Way: The Renewal of Social Democracy*, Cambridge: Polity Press.

Goldstein, B. and Newell, J.P. (2019), 'Why academics should study the supply chains of individual corporations', *J. Ind. Ecol.*, 23(6): 1316–1327, 10.1111/jiec.12932.

ILO (2017), *Global estimates of Modern Slavery*, ILO: Geneva.

IMO (2020), *Reduction of GHG Emissions from Ships: Fourth IMO GHG Study 2020*, London: IMO.

Jarvis, D.S.L. (2007), 'Risk, globalisation and the state: a critical appraisal of Ulrich Beck and the world risk society thesis', *Global Society*, 21(1): 23–46.

Kennedy, D. (1999), *Academic Duty*, Cambridge, MA: Harvard University Press.

Krippner, G. (2004), 'What is financialization', mimeo, Department of Sociology, UCLA.

Krugman, P. (1994), *The Age of Diminishing Expectations*, Boston, MA: MIT Press.

Lee, N. and Luca, D. (2019), 'The big-city bias in access to finance: evidence from firm perceptions in almost 100 countries', *Journal of Economic Geography*, 19(1): 199–224.

Martin, R.L. (1999), 'The "new economic geography": challenge or irrelevance?', *Transactions, Institute of British Geographers*, 24: 387–391.

Martin R. (2001), 'Geography and public policy: the case of the missing agenda', *Progress in Human Geography*, 25(2): 189–210.

Maskell, P. (2001), 'The firm in economic geography', *Economic Geography*, 77(4): 329–344.

Massey, D. (1984), *Spatial Division of Labour: Social Structures and the Geography of Production*, London: Palgrave.

Massey, D. (2000), 'Practising political relevance', *Transactions, Institute of British Geographers*, 24: 131–134.

Mazzucato, M. (2018), *The Value of Everything*, London: Allen Lane.

McCann, P. (2009), 'Economic geography, globalisation and New Zealand's productivity paradox', *New Zealand Economic Paper*, 43(3): 279–314.

Mulhall, R. and Bryson, J.R. (2013), 'The energy hot potato and governance of value chains: power, risk and organizational adjustment in intermediate manufacturing firms', *Economic Geography*, 89(4): 395–419.

Mulhall, R.A. and Bryson, J.R. (2014), 'Energy price risk and the sustainability of demand side supply chains', *Applied Energy*, 123: 327–334.

NCEO (2020), 'The Employee Ownership 100: America's largest majority employee-owned companies', National Center for Employee Ownership, accessed 16 February 2021, available at https://www.nceo.org/articles/employee-ownership-100.

Nguyen, Anh Thu, Parker, L., Brennan, L. and Lockrey, S. (2020), 'A consumer definition of eco-friendly packaging', *Journal of Cleaner Production*, 252: 119792.

Nooteboom, B. (2000), *Learning and Innovation in Organisations and Economies*, Oxford: Oxford University Press.

Peattie, K. and Crane, A. (2005), 'Green marketing: legend, myth, farce or prophesy?', *Qualitative Market Research*, 8(4): 357–370.

Peck, J. (2019), *Offshore: Exploring the Worlds of Global Outsourcing*, Oxford: Oxford University Press.

Perrow, Charles (1984), *Normal Accidents: Living With High Risk Technologies*, Princeton, NJ: Princeton University Press.

Platman, L. (2011), *Harris Tweed: From Land to Street*, London: Francis Lincoln.

Pollard, J., Henry, N., Bryson, J. and Daniels, P. (2000), 'Shades of grey? Geographers and policy', *Transactions, Institute of British Geographers*, 24: 243–248.

Resnik, D.B. and Elliott, K.C. (2016), 'The ethical challenges of socially responsible science', *Accountability in Research*, 23(1): 31–46.

Rusten, G., Bryson, J.R. and Aarflot, U. (2007), 'Places through products and products through places: industrial design and spatial symbols as sources of competitiveness', *Norsk Geografisk Tidsskrift*, 61(3): 133–144.

Salder, J. and Bryson J.R. (2019), 'Placing entrepreneurship and firming small town economies: manufacturing firms, adaptive embeddedness, survival and linked enterprise structures', *Entrepreneurship and Regional Development*, 31(9-10): 806–825.

Sauser, W.I (2009), 'Sustaining employee owned companies: seven recommendations', *Journal of Business Ethics*, 84: 151–164

Sayer, A. (1982), 'Explanation in economic geography: abstraction versus generalization', *Progress in Human Geography*, 6(1): 68–88.

Skoda, E. (2019), 'The monomaterials challenge', Packaging Europe, accessed 16 February 2021, available at https://packagingeurope.com/the-monomaterials-challenge/.

Taylor, M. (2006), 'Fragments and gaps: exploring the theory of the firm', in Taylor, M. and Oinas, P. (eds), *Understanding the Firm: Spatial and Organizational Dimensions*, Oxford: Oxford University Press, pp. 3–31.

Taylor, M. and Asheim, B. (2001), 'The concept of the firm in economic geography', *Economic Geography*, 77(4): 315–328.

Taylor, M. and Bryson, J.R. (2006), 'Guns, firms and contracts: the evolution of gun-making in Birmingham', in Taylor, M. and Oinas, P. (eds), *Understanding the Firm: Spatial and Organizational Dimensions*, Oxford: Oxford University Press, pp. 61–84.

UN General Assembly (2015), *Transforming our World: The 2030 Agenda for Sustainable Development*, A/RES/70/1, accessed 13 March 2021, available at: https://www.refworld.org/docid/57b6e3e44.html.

Urry, J. (2014), *Offshoring*, Cambridge: Polity.

Vanchan, V., Mulhall, R. and Bryson, J. (2018), 'Repatriation or reshoring of manufacturing to the US and UK: dynamics and global production networks or from here to there and back again', *Growth and Change*, 49: 97–121.

Wang, Q. (2019), 'Gender, race/ethnicity, and entrepreneurship: women entrepreneurs in a US south city', *International Journal of Entrepreneurial Behavior and Research*, 25(8): 1766–1785.

2 Theoretical and methodological approaches to understanding emerging industries

Chloe Billing and John R. Bryson

Introduction

This chapter argues that an important part of the future of research on manufacturing industries in the global economy must focus on exploring the emergence of new industries and the legitimacy-building process that allows this to occur. Emerging industries are 'industrial sectors, typically based on new products, services, technologies or ideas, which are in early-stage development and are characterised by high growth rates and market potential' (Europa, 2012). The development of a new industry challenges existing conventions including those linked to regulations and consumer behaviour (Ross, 2016). New projects and their companies must become accepted, and this acceptance process includes legitimisation. Legitimacy is defined, in the context of organisational management, as 'a generalized perception or assumption that the actions of an entity are desirable, proper, or appropriate within some socially constructed system of norms, values, beliefs, and definitions' (Suchman, 1995: 573). Building legitimacy is a social process, involving several different stakeholders (including innovators, investors and regulators) and institutions, working at different spatial scales.

This chapter outlines the theoretical and methodological approaches required for understanding the legitimacy building processes of emerging industries, using the example of the United Kingdom (UK) space sector. Over the past decade, there has been significant disruptive innovation and regulatory change to the space industry, which has led to the emergence of 'New Space' or Space 2.0 (Pyle, 2019). New Space, or Space 2.0, are terms used to describe the emergence of a new private sector space industry led by space entrepreneurs or 'astropreneurs'. These technologies focus on developing 'faster, better, and cheaper access to space' and include small satellites, mega-constellations and new launch vehicles (Quintana, 2017).

There is consensus across the academic and grey literature on the importance of emerging industries, given the impact of new industries on economic development. For example, in recent decades the emergence of biotechnology and internet-related industries have catalysed significant economic development (Agarwal and Tripsas, 2008). Similarly, the emergence of electrical lighting and automotive industries decades earlier accelerated economic growth. Nevertheless, 'the processes by which new industries emerge are not sufficiently explained by current theories, concepts, research strategies, and empirical accounts in economic geography' (Steen, 2016: 1607). Future research on manufacturing industries must work to address the gap, as understanding these processes is necessary for identifying strategies on how best to support emerging industries. To help guide this research agenda, this chapter will outline the theoretical and methodological approaches for researching emerging industries

The chapter begins by introducing Space 2.0. The chapter then outlines the challenge of defining an emerging industry from a data point of view. It explores the European Cluster Observatory research classification system as one route to defining an emerging industry, and demonstrates the challenge of researching a sector such as Space 2.0 without a fixed Standard Industrial Classification (SIC) code. This highlights the importance of qualitative research to test data assumptions and to understand the complexities behind the emergence of new manufacturing industries. The chapter then outlines the multi-scalar structures and processes that led to legitimacy-building in the establishment of Space 2.0. Finally, the chapter reflects on the COVID-19 pandemic and the impact that this is likely to have on the emergence of new business models and industry sectors.

Space 2.0

The chapter is based on research on the UK space sector. The focus on the UK is deliberate as despite cancelling its rocket launch programme in 1971, the UK has remained a leading international contributor to the production of satellite-enabled services (it has built a quarter of the world's largest communication satellites), and is the global leader in the production of small satellites which typify Space 2.0. The space value chain is structured by:

- Space manufacturing – design and manufacture of space components, subsystems, launch vehicles, satellites/spacecraft and infrastructure.
- Space operations – launch and operation of satellites and spacecraft.
- Space applications – applications of satellite/spacecraft signals, data and services.
- Ancillary services – specialised services that support manufacture, operations and applications.
- Users – those not directly involved in space-related activities but reliant upon satellite/space data, signals and services.
- Non-users – those who are not reliant upon space data/services but indirectly benefit from space-related activities.

Over the last decade, the space industry has undergone a sustained period of change. Technological advancement and new manufacturing, launch and operation capabilities have led to the reconfiguration of value chains and market disruption. The commercial space industry has been reinvented by new companies, such as SpaceX, Virgin Galactic, Blue Origin, One Web, Kymeta and Planet, which in turn is driving change within the incumbents, such as Lockheed Martin, Airbus, Boeing and Northrop Gruman. Key technologies that have driven change include:

- Lower-cost and more capable launch vehicles and services, significantly improving the accessibility of space.
- Lower-cost ground antenna systems capable of satellite tracking, enabling commercial use/operation of new low Earth orbit (LEO) small and cube satellite constellations.
- Advanced digital coding systems, enabling enhanced transmission capabilities, use of new spectrum frequencies and improved efficiencies.
- New (small) satellite production capabilities, utilising advanced manufacturing processes (such as, additive manufacturing), standardised components and integrated quality testing, enabling faster and lower-cost manufacture of satellites at higher volume.

Space 2.0 has a very different set of technologies compared to Space 1.0 and thus involves a very different mix of firms and related regional geographies. Space 2.0 is so far removed from the traditional space sector that it classifies as a new industry. This presents a research challenge, since emerging industries are difficult to empirically study and measure, as discussed in the following section.

Defining industries

The standard definition of an 'industry' is a group of firms producing closely substitutable products. To measure the size, scale and geography of an industry, researchers draw on industrial classification codes of firms and products. Industrial classification codes organise 'activities and companies into industrial groupings based on similar production processes, similar products, or similar behaviour in the markets' (Europa, 2012). A wide variety of industry classification systems are in use across the world, sponsored by different countries or organisations, and based on different criteria. They include the ISIC12 (International Standard Industrial Classification of All Economic Activities), NAICS13 (North American Industry Classification System) and NACE14 (European Classification of Economic Activities). To measure the size, scale and geography of Space 2.0 in the UK, the UK's Standard Industrial Classification (SIC), 2007 revision, can be used, which is consistent with the United Nations' (UN) International Standard Industrial Classification of all Economic Activities (ISIC). Regional data on employment and firm count can be derived from the Office for National Statistics (ONS) Business Register and Employment Survey, and UK Business counts. The former is a representative survey of 80 000 enterprises providing employment information by Standard Industrial Classification (SIC), 2007 revision, while the latter is an excerpt from the Inter-Departmental Business Register (IDBR), which is a registry of firms covering more than 90 per cent of UK economic activity.

All standard classification systems face several 'key limitations with regards to the identification and full representation of emerging industries' (Europa, 2012: 16). These limitations are as follows:

- They are based upon the observation of economic activities that exist at the time of their construction or revision; while emerging industries are in their early stages of development and their existence can be difficult to observe in some cases.
- They only account for categories of activities that can be defined precisely and present sufficient stability over time; while emerging industries are the result of a continuous creation and innovation process and therefore 'emerge', develop, transform and mutate all the time.
- Industry classifications are built upon categories of activities that are meant to be homogeneous and mutually exclusive, and therefore cannot constitute appropriate tools to identify and classify new activities that emerge from the combination and cross-fertilisation of different types of activities and sectors.

- In most cases, emerging industries result from cross-sector spillovers between related but distinct sectors that transform, evolve and combine or sometimes even merge into new industries. This process cannot be captured by statistical classification systems.

For example, the SIC codes relevant to 'upstream manufacturing' in Space 2.0 include 30.3: Manufacture of air and spacecraft and related machinery; 33.16: Repair and maintenance of aircraft and spacecraft; and 51.22: Space Transport. However, the complexity of operations within Space 2.0 suggests that solely focusing on these SIC codes underestimates the size and importance of the sector. Nevertheless, this is preferred to including related SIC codes, such as engineering or satellite telecommunication providers, which would skew the analysis by incorporating satellite broadcasters and consultancy services. This outlines the challenge of researching a sector such as Space 2.0 without a fixed SIC code. To test the data assumptions, quantitative and qualitative insights should be combined to obtain a more accurate picture of the evolution and dynamics of an industry. This follows Forbes and Kirsch's (2011: 590) argument that to understand emerging industries, scholars must 'work with qualitative and historical data to a greater extent than they have in the recent past'. Industrial classifications often hide emergent industries by placing firms and activities that are impossible to classify in a miscellaneous category of activities that are not elsewhere classified. These miscellaneous categories are too often overlooked by academics and policymakers. Bryson and Taylor explored this category for the West Midlands, UK, and noted that the analysis of this category was one way of exploring the geographies of emerging industries (Bryson and Taylor, 2006; Taylor and Bryson, 2012). The same approach has been applied to identifying emerging service industries that are hidden in miscellaneous categories (Keeble et al., 1991).

The European Cluster Observatory (ECO III) proposed four further approaches for identifying and determining the scope of emerging industries (Europa, 2012). These approaches address some of the above shortcomings in the process of establishing a classification system for emerging industries, and should be considered for future research on emerging manufacturing industries. The suggested approaches were informed by the observatory's review of different approaches for identifying and determining the scope of emerging industries, from which they concluded that 'no single approach is sufficient to identify and classify emerging industries' (Europa, 2012). These approaches were based on the following assumptions and types of data:

- Approach 1: Firms in emerging industries attract risk capital (classification based on firm capital-raising data).

- Approach 2: Firms in emerging industries attract interest from companies from previously unrelated sectors (classification based on cross-sector deal data).
- Approach 3: Firms in emerging industries are highly innovative (classification based on firm patenting data).
- Approach 4: Firms in emerging industries grow fast (classification based on sector growth potential).

Full details of the four approaches can be found in the Emerging Industries Report (Europa, 2012).

New industrial path development and legitimacy-building

The economic geography and industry studies literature provides a detailed understanding of new industrial path development. This has followed the seminal work of Martin and Sunley (2006: 429) and their call to 'know much more about how local economic paths emerge, develop, become rigidified and are eventually destroyed'. The literature distinguishes between the continuation of existing industrial paths based only on incremental innovation, the upgrading of existing industries based on major changes to an industrial path, diversification into a new related or unrelated industry, and the emergence and growth of an entirely new industry. The emergence and growth of entirely new industries is the most radical form of these changes and is based on new technologies and organisational processes (Grillitsch et al., 2018). Nevertheless, like all technology, industry and institutional pathways, they are often based on existing assets, resources and competencies of established companies and institutions (Jolly and Hansen, 2021).

Future research on new industrial path development, including the emergence and growth of entirely new industries, must consider the complex processes of legitimacy-building involved. Legitimacy-building is broadly characterised as the matching of new technologies with market demand and regulatory institutional structures. Any technological mismatch would need to be overcome for a new industry to emerge from another. However, the construct does not always relate to technology; for example, legitimacy can be ascribed to different kinds of entities, including individuals, organisations and business models (Markard et al., 2016). Once established, legitimacy is both a resource in its own right but also a route to acquiring other critical resources, such as finance (Vestrum et al., 2017). To Binz et al. (2016) 'legitimacy is actively built up through the interplay of different actor groups in the early stage of a new technology and industry'. These actor groups include firms, regulators, customers, investors, regulators and knowledge institutions (Bitektine and Haack, 2015). Our analysis of the emergence of Space 2.0 highlights that the emergence of a new industry requires a complex multi-level understanding of legitimacy-building and the role of actors and institutions.

Emerging industries must develop three forms of legitimacy. First, their products must match market demand. Second, regulators, insurers and investors must accept their products. Third, firms must develop reputations within industry networks as legitimate contributors. Collectively, these different forms of legitimacy provide the foundations for the establishment of a new industry. The following subsections will outline the multi-scalar structures and processes that led to legitimacy-building in the establishment of Space 2.0. In the discussion section, a conceptual framework is contextualised that has been designed to guide future research on legitimacy-building and emerging industries.

Disruptive innovations

Space 2.0 companies have introduced disruptive innovations, which have met the market demand for there to be 'faster, better and cheaper access to space' (Fahey, 2019). This shift is the product of a new technological innovation system (TIS). A TIS is defined as a 'set of interrelated actors and institutional structures in a specific technological domain that contribute to the development of a focal technology' (Markard et al., 2016). Legitimacy increases as technological domains (a particular area of knowledge or competence, or a specific type of product or service) align with contextual structures. Contextual structures include consumer demand, as well as broader societal values such as political and economic support mechanisms. The TIS for Space 2.0 is characterised by: (1) low-cost launch providers; and (2) the miniaturisation and standardisation of production processes (Billing and Bryson, 2019). Universities, as well as entrepreneurs, have played a central role in the development of disruptive innovations by generating expert knowledge on a range of topics relevant to UK satellite companies.

First, the cost of launching satellites has fallen significantly over the last ten years (London Economics, 2019). Formed in 2002, the American launch company SpaceX has been at the forefront of this, by dramatically reducing costs with innovations in reusable rocket technology, off-the-shelf components, and in-house production of 70 per cent of its spacecraft (reducing dependency on expensive suppliers). SpaceX charges $4653 per kilogram to launch a telecommunications satellite into orbit, while traditional aerospace companies charge up to $39 000 per kilogram. The emergence of more affordable launch options opened the market for smaller-scale satellite manufacturers, who innovated in miniaturisation and the standardisation of production processes to reduce product costs.

The miniaturisation and the standardisation of production processes has involved utilising advanced manufacturing processes (such as additive manufacturing), standardised components and integrated quality testing. This has reduced 'total manufacturing costs' (costs incurred to produce a product over a given period), and the outcome has been a new product – smaller satellites – that can be positioned in lower Earth orbits. This standardised approach contrasts with the manufacture of more expensive satellites (Space 1.0) which typically have no concept of a production line. It has become feasible for these smaller satellites to be launched into low Earth orbit because of the development of lower-cost ground antenna systems capable of satellite tracking, as well as advanced digital coding systems, enabling enhanced transmission capabilities and the use of new spectrum frequencies. It is significant that these satellites can operate in low Earth orbit (400–1200 km above Earth), since the lower altitude allows for improved latency and accuracy of signals travelling between the Earth and the satellites (Quintana, 2017). The combination of cost-effective launch solutions and the increasing affordability of mass-producing thousands of small satellites means that new companies are entering the market to test out new business models around mega-constellations (up to 1000 satellites).

Regulatory change and government support

Regulative legitimacy concerns how 'a new venture works and develops according to rules, regulations, and expectations created by powerful actors in the environment' (Vestrum et al., 2017: 1724). In some cases, regulatory change provides the legitimacy that supports the emergence of a new industry, but in other cases, regulations lag behind firm-level innovations. Both forms occurred in the case of Space 2.0.

The 1967 Outer Space Treaty (OST) is the principal treaty for regulating activities in outer space, and outlines the core principles guiding UN member states concerning their actions in space. One of the key principles of the OST is the 'registration of space objects'. Consequently, all satellites intended for launch must first be registered and allocated an orbital slot (if a geostationary satellite), and a coordinated radio frequency spectrum. Additionally, a space licence is required before a satellite can launch and these are awarded by national space agencies. In the UK, as part of the licensing process, operators are required to obtain minimum liability insurance of €60 million. This protects the satellite operator and the UK. This is an example where regulation lags behind firm-level innovation, as for mega-constellations such insurance costs are unaffordable. Consequently, the UK Space Agency is currently examining new approaches to licensing mega-constellations.

Conversely, an example of where a regulatory change in the UK space sector has supported the emergence of Space 2.0 is the Space Industry Act 2018, which allows for spaceflight activities to take place from the UK. This is the first significant step towards establishing a UK launch market to low Earth orbit. In addition to the regulatory framework being in place, a list of potential UK spaceports has been identified, and 'over £31.5 million in grant funding … made available to help establish launch services' (Fahey, 2019). A UK Spaceport would support potential cost savings, the removal of export control issues, and simplify logistics for the launch of smaller UK satellites. It would reduce time to launch, as currently 'operators wishing to launch satellites weighing more than 50 kg often need to wait between six and nine months to secure a launch contract' (Quintana, 2017). These steps have led to the emergence of launch operators in the UK (Reaction Engines, Skyorra, Orbex), as well as attracting manufacturers of smaller satellites.

Additionally, the government-funded Innovate UK and the Satellite Applications Catapult have invested significant grants in emerging Space 2.0 technologies. This financial support has been part of the renaissance of UK government interest in the UK space sector since 2012. These grants have enabled Space 2.0 firms to develop in ways which they otherwise could not because of limited financial resources, or because of pressure for a very high return on investment from other lenders. Government grants are justified by expected rates of return from future tax payments, and the 'public good' from satellite-enabled applications.

Industry networks

The geography of Space 2.0 consists of regional agglomerations and also dispersed firms. Interfirm networking has been a primary driver behind legitimacy-building across Space 2.0, as through interacting and collaborating with other firms it has maximised the resources available to Space 2.0 firms.

At the same time, new relationships have formed supporting technological innovation, and innovations have become accepted through discussion and debate. Partnerships with firms also create opportunities for gaining intelligence or information on other firms and market demand, which is valuable when developing competitive strategies. Collaboration with other firms is particularly valuable for smaller and younger firms (which is common to Space 2.0), as it broadens their limited resource base, offsetting 'some of their fragility' (Atterton, 2007: 230). These networks both form strategically to address a particular need, or emerge randomly from social interactions (Jones and Craven, 2001). However, it is difficult to distinguish between strategic and random network formation, as there are overlaps, such as the case of the network formation at the Harwell space cluster.

The Harwell space cluster is situated south of Oxford and is home to 110 Space 2.0 companies, the Satellite Applications Catapult, the Rutherford Appleton Laboratory research and test facility, the European Space Agency's (ESA) European Centre for Space Applications and Telecommunications (ECSAT), and ESA's space business incubator (which supports start-up companies with funding and workspace). This concentration of satellite organisations provides networking opportunities for the companies based there permanently, and for firm representatives visiting this cluster. Network formation is supported by opportunities for frequent face-to-face meetings and the exchange of tacit knowledge. Additionally, geographic proximity increases the chance of 'unexpected and spontaneous encounters' occurring (Bathelt and Turi, 2011: 525). These chance encounters are particularly valuable to start-up companies, leading to increasing return effects. Consequently, for the companies based in Harwell, their location is an important part of their networking routine. However, it is important not to overemphasise the role that Harwell plays and underestimate the contribution of external or extra-local connections. For instance, distant relationships are maintained by 'e-mail, Skype and video-conferencing', which can 'cross time zones', permitting the transfer of codified knowledge (Bathelt and Turi, 2011: 526). LinkedIn is also very popular amongst the satellite community as an 'inexpensive tool for networking' (Witzig et al., 2012: 118); industry actors use this social media platform to interact with others using discussion feeds.

Furthermore, alternative opportunities for network formation include events organised by the Satellite Applications Catapult and UK Space Agency. These organisations are responsible for annual and often monthly meetings and conferences. These events vary in purpose and participant composition, but generally serve as platforms for exchanging knowledge, generating ideas, forming new relationships, and creating and projecting legitimacy. These events are a specific type of temporary cluster (Henn and Bathelt, 2015: 105). The bringing together of industry actors and encouragement of face-to-face interactions between them supports the formation of new networks and strengthens existing ties. These events also present firms and individuals with opportunities to generate interest in their products, as well as the chance to interact with other delegates and form networks with actual or potential customers and collaborators. Consequently, attending networking events is a strategic investment, with Space 2.0 companies expecting new transactions to develop.

Discussion and conclusions

The COVID-19 pandemic has led to worldwide economic, political and social disruption. Research has shown that in past crises, grand challenges serve as triggers for the emergence of new industries (Moeen, 2020). This occurs as the disruption encourages knowledge exchange and collaboration between groups of public and private sector stakeholders, including representatives from industry, universities, government agencies and other public institutions. Meanwhile, firms develop new business models and implement organisational changes to absorb short-term shocks, and ensure long-term sustainability and growth (Santiago et al., 2020). For example, there has been increased servitisation and the acceleration of digital transformations. Additionally, manufacturers have increased the adoption of the flexible production models of Industry 4.0, to reduce their dependence on international supply chains. These concurrent processes of collaboration and process innovation will accelerate the emergence of new industries that might have taken too long to arise, or would not have arisen otherwise (Moeen, 2020).

Consequently, this chapter argues that an important part of the future of research on manufacturing industries in the global economy will be in exploring the emergence of new industries. This is important because existing theories, concepts, and theoretically-informed empirical accounts in economic geography do not sufficiently account for the processes which sit behind the emergence of new industries. Therefore, future research on manufacturing industries must work to address this gap to inform policymakers on appropriate business support strategies. In response to this, the chapter outlined the European Cluster Observatory Research classification system for defining an emerging industry, and demonstrated the challenge of researching an emerging sector without a fixed SIC code. The chapter is based on research on the UK space sector and specifically the emergence of Space 2.0. Space 2.0 has a very different set of technologies compared to Space 1.0 and thus involves

Table 2.1   Legitimacy-building and multi-scalar actors

Legitimacy-building	Examples	Geography/stakeholders involved
Disruptive innovation	New technological innovation system Reduction in total manufacturing costs	Firm-level innovation Regional: determined by the local skills mix, and higher education institutions have a role in capability-building
Regulatory change and government support	Government grants and contracts – helping firms to overcome technological lock-in	National and international institutions Regulators, government agencies, investors, business support
Industry networks	Legitimacy-building via networks formed in localised clusters or via processes of temporary clustering	Regional, national and international Networking facilitators; online and in person events

a very different mix of firms and related regional geographies. Space 2.0 is so far removed from the traditional space sector that it should be classified as a new industry.

The chapter also highlights how an important part of this future research agenda needs to be on understanding multi-scalar structures and processes of legitimacy-building. The chapter highlights how emerging industries must develop three forms of legitimacy: (1) their products must match market demand; (2) regulators, insurers and investors must accept their products; and (3) firms must develop reputations within industry networks as legitimate contributors. To approach future analysis of the legitimacy-building process of emerging manufacturing industries the following conceptual framework can be applied (Table 2.1). This is based on the interplay between technological innovation, alterations in market demand, and regulatory change, which were identified as the key drivers behind the emergence of Space 2.0. Networks also play an important role in this process as they secure inputs, outputs and new opportunities for firms. These processes are multi-scalar and involve both public and private sector actors.

COVID-19 is a cultural inflection point and a discontinuity. As a cultural inflection point it has accelerated the application of existing technologies by companies, and their acceptance by consumers. The pandemic accelerated processes of legitimacy-building that sit behind the application and accept-ance of new innovations. As a discontinuity, the pandemic displaced policy and corporate attention away from existing societal challenges. Pandemic recovery will see a return to the ongoing decarbonisation of lifestyles, supported by major alterations in the economy including the emergence of new industries. It is important to appreciate that the economy is the outcome of an extremely complex and ever-changing delicate network of interdependencies. One industry's outputs are inputs to support incremental or disruptive innovation in other sectors. Space 2.0 represents one form of cross-sector disruption, as innovations in the provision and functionalities of satellites are catalysing innovations in other sectors. The same is also the case in terms of innovations in additive manufacturing, digital manufacturing, and developments in algorithm applications to manufacturing and everyday living. It is important that further research focuses on the acceptance, spread and legitimisation of cross-sector innovations that transform existing industries and facilitate the emergence of new industries.

Acknowledgements

This chapter is based on an unpublished PhD thesis undertaken at the University of Birmingham, sponsored by an Economic and Social Research Council (ESRC) Scholarship Grant (ES/J50001X/1). We thank the interviewees and also the participants at the stakeholder events who gave their time to discuss this topic. The usual disclaimers apply.

References

Agarwal, R., and Tripsas, M. (2008). Technology and industry evolution. In Shane, S. (ed.), *The Handbook of Technology and Innovation Management*, Vol. 1, Chichester: John Wiley & Sons, 3–55.

Atterton, J. (2007). The 'strength of weak ties': social networking by business owners in the Highlands and Islands of Scotland. *Sociologia Ruralis*, 47(3), 228–245.

Bathelt, H., and Turi, P. (2011). Local, global and virtual buzz: the importance of face-to-face contact in economic interaction and possibilities to go beyond. *Geoforum*, 42(5), 520–529.

Billing, C.A., and Bryson, J.R. (2019). Heritage and satellite manufacturing: firm-level competitiveness and the management of risk in global production networks. *Economic Geography*, 95(5), 423–441.

Binz, C., Harris-Lovett, S., Kiparsky, M., Sedlak, D.L., and Truffer, B. (2016). The thorny road to technology legitimation – institutional work for potable water reuse in California. *Technological Forecasting and Social Change*, 103, 249–263.

Bitektine, A., and Haack, P. (2015). The 'macro' and the 'micro' of legitimacy: toward a multilevel theory of the legitimacy process. *Academy of Management Review*, 40, 49–75. doi:10.5465/amr. 2013.0318.

Bryson, J.R., and Taylor, M. (2006). *The Functioning Economic Geography of the West Midlands*, Birmingham: West Midlands Regional Observatory.

Europa (2012). Emerging Industries Report. Available from: https://ec.europa.eu/research/industrial_technologies/pdf/emerging-industries-report_en.pdf.

Fahey, C. (2019). Space 2.0 Regulating Growth in the Space Industry. Available from: https://www.scl.org/articles/10494-space-2-0-regulating-growth-in-the-space-industry.

Forbes, D.P., and Kirsch, D.A. (2011). The study of emerging industries: recognizing and responding to some central problems. *Journal of Business Venturing*, 26(5), 589–602.

Grillitsch, M., Asheim, B., and Trippl, M. (2018). Unrelated knowledge combinations: the unexplored potential for regional industrial path development. *Cambridge Journal of Regions, Economy and Society*, 11(2), 257–274.

Henn, S., and Bathelt, H. (2015). Knowledge generation and field reproduction in temporary clusters and the role of business conferences. *Geoforum*, 58, 104–113.

Jolly, S., and Hansen, T. (2021). Industry legitimacy: bright and dark phases in regional industry path development. *Regional Studies*, 1–14.

Jones, O., and Craven, M. (2001). Expanding capabilities in a mature manufacturing firm: absorptive capacity and the TCS. *International Small Business Journal*, 19(3), 39–55.

Keeble, D., Bryson, J.R., and Wood, P. (1991). 'Small firms, business services growth and regional development in the United Kingdom', *Regional Studies*, 25, 439–457.

London Economics (2019). *Industry 4.0 and the Future of UK Space Manufacturing*. Available from: https://londoneconomics.co.uk/blog/publication/industry-4-0-and-the-future-of-uk-space-manufacturing-july-2019/.

Markard, J., Wirth, S., and Truffer, B. (2016). Institutional dynamics and technology legitimacy – a framework and a case study on biogas technology. *Research Policy*, 45(1), 330–344.

Martin, R., and Sunley, P. (2006). Path dependence and regional economic evolution. *Journal of Economic Geography*, 6(4), 395–437.

Moeen, M. (2020). How new industries could grow out of the fight against Covid-19. Entrepreneurship and Innovation Exchange, 28 May. Retrieved 16 June 2020 from https://eiexchange.com/content/how-new-industries-could-grow-out-of-the-fight-against-covid-19.

Pyle, R. (2019). *Space 2.0: How Private Spaceflight, a Resurgent NASA, and International Partners are Creating a New Space Age*, Dallas, TX: BenBella Books.

Quintana, E. (2017). The new space age: questions for defence and security. *RUSI Journal*, 162(3), 88–109.

Ross, A. (2016), *The Industries of the Future*, New York: Simon & Schuster.

Santiago, F., Dachs, B., and Peters, B. (2020). Foster recovery from COVID-19 through science, technology and innovation. Industrial Analytics Platform. Available from: https://iap.unido.org/articles/foster-recovery-covid-19-through-science-technology-and-innovation.

Steen, M. (2016). Reconsidering path creation in economic geography: aspects of agency, temporality and methods. *European Planning Studies*, 24(9), 1605–1622.

Suchman, M.C. (1995). Managing legitimacy: strategic and institutional approaches. *Academy of Management Review*, 20(3), 571–610.

Taylor, M., and Bryson J.R. (2012). West Midlands (UK) regional planning (1999–2012), functioning economic geography and the E3I belt: coping with uncomfortable truths. In Stimson, R. and Haynes, K.E. (eds), *Studies in Applied Geography and Spatial Analysis*, Cheltenham, UK and Northampton, MA, USA: Edward Elgar Publishing, 196–216.

Vestrum, I., Rasmussen, E., and Carter, S. (2017). How nascent community enterprises build legitimacy in internal and external environments. *Regional Studies*, 51(11), 1721–1734.

Witzig, L., Spencer, J., and Galvin, M. (2012). Organizations' use of LinkedIn: an analysis of nonprofits, large corporations and small businesses. *Marketing Management Journal*, 22(1), 113–121.

3 Transforming manufacturing? An additive manufacturing research agenda

Jennifer Johns

Introduction

In the search for the future of manufacturing, three-dimensional (3D) printing has been allocated an important role by policymakers (Schwab, 2017; Eurofound, 2019). The general public discourse around our capacity to use 3D printing technologies heralds a new, distributive era in which production and consumption are collapsed in time and geography. 3D printing technologies are a combination of general-purpose technologies that build a product layer-by-layer based on its digital representation (Berman, 2012). With these technologies, a computer-aided design (CAD) model can be directly transformed into a 3D object, built layer-by-layer, in a relatively short time and with low cost, avoiding the long processes of conventional methods of production[1] (Culmone et al., 2019). 3D printing is part of a wider set of machine tools that apply digital-based processes. These 3D printing technologies are heralded as transformative, marking a radical departure in how goods are designed and manufactured. They have been classified as 'revolutionary' (Goulding et al., 2013), 'disruptive' (Berman, 2012; D'Aveni, 2015; Hyman, 2011; Rylands et al., 2016), 'game-changing' (Kothman and Faber, 2016), as creating an era in which 'everything becomes science fiction' (Lipson and Kuman, 2013), and are claimed to be 'bringing about a revolution in manufacturing' (Winnan, 2012: 1).

Positive futuristic visions permeate much of our conception of the technology and perpetuate a set of hyped myths about the potential of the technology to impact on how goods are made, transported and consumed. These myths include the assertions that we will all have domestic 3D printers at home, that 3D printing will replace traditional manufacturing techniques, and that production will be relocalised and distributed. There are also some underlying assumptions about the technology that obfuscate better understandings of the technology and its potential.

This chapter focuses on additive manufacturing (AM), the term generally adopted within manufacturing to describe the use of 3D printing in industrial settings, and to differentiate these manufacturing activities from distinct, but interrelated, domestic and hobbyist 'maker movement' activities involving digital technologies (Anderson, 2012; Carr and Gibson, 2016; Johns and Hall, 2020). The chapter does three things in turn. First, it contextualises the hype around additive manufacturing, identifying the key drivers of the current political and economic focus on these technologies. Second, it discusses the scope of existing work and highlights the paucity of empirical work on AM. Third, the chapter identifies the key issues that require academic attention in order to understand AM, its impact on manufacturing and its place within the manufacturing sector, which proposes a research agenda for AM. The final section draws conclusions.

Hype and politicisation of AM technological futures

By the end of 2018, the global additive manufacturing market was estimated to have reached $9.3 billion. This figure, which encompasses hardware, software, materials and services, represented 18 per cent growth from the previous year (SmarTech, 2019). Wohlers (2019) reported that the growth and sales of industrial AM systems (defined as those priced at €5000 or more) have increased year on year, but in 2018 desktop 3D printing systems (priced under €5000) saw a significant decline in annual growth as well as several equipment manufacturer firm failures. AM is not a 'new' technology – stereolithography was invented by Chuck Hall in 1986 – it has simply become more widely publicised, gaining increasing attention over the last two decades due to the potential offered by its approach to designing and manufacturing. Additive techniques offer different applications to those of subtractive methods (such as turning, drilling and milling). It is defined as 'a process of joining materials to make objects from 3D model data, usually layer upon layer, as opposed to subtractive manufacturing technologies' (ASTM, 2012). AM techniques allow more complex structural geometries to be produced that can offer new efficiencies through design, materials and performance, and meet demands for customisation and flexibility (Weller et al., 2015). As no tooling or traditional machining is required, it becomes possible to have single lot sizes at affordable cost. This is significant when applied to spare and legacy parts (reducing warehousing and logistics costs). Other cost advantages are foreseeable in production processes with efficiencies impacting on manufacturing set-up, waste, quality control and labour; however, efficiencies are also impactful in distribution, with the reduction or elimination of final product inventories and freight, and in consumption, with the ability for individuals to mass produce customised products (Bak, 2003).

There are multiple different types of 3D printing technologies: material extrusion, vat photopolymerisation, powder bed fusion, binder jetting, material jetting, directed energy deposition and sheet lamination. These process a variety of materials: polymers, metals, ceramics and composites (Guo and Leu, 2013), creating a highly fragmented market with a diversity of applications rather than one universal 3D printing technology. Since the development of the different techniques in the 1980s and 1990s, the greatest significant uptake in the use of AM has been in prototyping across manufacturing. There are some limitations of the technology that tend to escape the media coverage, and present some challenges for the adoption of AM beyond its core role in proto-typing. For final-version products AM has high costs (using current 'high-end' contender technologies) compared to conventional processes such as injection moulding and machining (Baumers et al., 2016), not only in production but in post-production (finishing), which is currently labour-intensive.[2] There are increasing numbers of applications in which AM is used for final production, and there is debate within the sector around the degree to which AM is ready for high-volume production (Johns, 2020a).

Having established that AM is a diverse and potentially useful tool in creating cost and other efficiencies, the contemporary focus on the technologies by policymakers and national governments is explained by their understandings of the potential of AM rather than a realistic assessment of the capabilities of AM (Johns, 2020b). This potential is articulated through discourses on the role of AM, and it often plays a catalysing role in roadmaps and scenarios of the future of manufacturing (Birtchnell and Urry, 2015; Potstada and Zybura, 2014; Tucker et al., 2014). This is due to the capacity of AM to contribute to, or even drive, transformative change that suits the agenda of those policymakers and politicians. There are two significant policy areas in which AM is expected to play an important role.

First, in the public and often the policymaking imaginary, 3D printing is included as part of a vaguely understood part of Industry 4.0 and the 'Factory of the Future'. As a consequence, the value and future trajectory of additive manufacturing is bound up with narratives of all different kinds of technological progress, including AI and big data (Ghobakhloo, 2018; Haleem and Javaid, 2019). For those in the AM industry, who certainly view AM as having a significant role in the Factory of the Future, this can obscure the identifica-tion of the change dynamics and particular industry and policy demands of the sector. The current rhetoric around 'Industry 4.0'[3] is driving many national government strategies around technology in manufacturing, and the move towards full automation of production lines and factories. In 2019 the World Economic Forum met in Davos to discuss 'Globalisation 4.0: Shaping a Global Architecture in the Age of the Fourth Industrial Revolution'. The agenda discussed how countries can respond to and shape changes in how goods are produced, distributed and consumed, based on the concept of the 'fourth industrial revolution' (Schwab, 2017), where a new wave of technological progress will launch us into a new era of globalisation. The world's leaders are pinning their hopes for economic growth on technological leaps, of which AM is expected to be one (Johns, 2019). These global discussions are mirrored with national initiatives such as the widely mimicked German Industry 4.0 strategy, the United Kingdom's (UK) Industrial Strategy, and the Chinese action plans around technology development.

Second, a related theme is the relocalisation of supply chains and 'reshoring' of manufacturing from low-cost economies back to advanced economies. AM is expected by many to transform not only how products are made but also where they are manufactured, as the technology has the potential to radically change the geographies of where products are designed, prototyped, produced and distributed by greatly reducing supply chain length and delivery times (Gress and Kalafsky, 2015; Laplume et al., 2016). Reshoring is intimately linked to the rhetoric around Factories of the Future, which are located in advanced economies in the collective imagining. The drive to reshore manufacturing has been pushed by several national governments and within industry, exemplified by the UK's Reshoring Advisory Service and the United States' (US) Reshoring Initiative. The intersection of advanced manufacturing and reshoring is a core feature of most, if not all, national government policies, with a focus on the potential for AM to facilitate and enable the reshoring of manufacturing activ-ities back to advanced economies (Berman, 2012; D'Aveni, 2015).

Through the combination of these two fields of policymaking interest and public media interest in 3D printing as a futuristic technology, AM is sur-rounded by a high degree of hype. The development of new technologies is often accompanied by hype, a phase characterised by an upsurge of public attention and high rising expectations about the potential of the innovation (Ruef and Markard, 2010). Hype has surrounded AM for several decades and has 'overshot', the term used by Van Lente et al. (2013) to describe the waves of high rising expectations that have become too positive. This hype has become particularly intense as 3D printing has received much attention in the battle to resolve shortages of immediate need items such as medical personal protection equipment (PPE), ventilators and face masks during the COVID-19 crisis. This chapter will argue that the technological development and future potential of AM is embedded within a broader set of expectations and visions. This refers to images of the future where technical and social aspects are tightly intertwined (Borup et al., 2006), and the outcomes for the AM industry are not wholly positive. Therefore, to fully understand the contemporary AM sector and its likely future trajectory, a social science perspective is required that can integrate technical, economic and political change dynamics.

Disciplinary perspectives on AM

The majority of academic work on AM has been conducted within engineering and materials science, focusing on innovation of the technology, its materials and applications. These contributions are highly technical, but there are some examples of work that is reaching a broader audience through a focus on the contribution of the technology to broader systems (for example, the circular economy; see Despeisse et al., 2017). Outside engineering, work on AM has tended to focus on supply chain management (Holmström et al., 2010, 2016; Khajavi et al., 2018; Roca et al., 2019; Strong et al., 2018, 2019), global value chains and production networks (Rehnberg and Ponte, 2018; Gress and Kalafasky, 2015), socio-economic impacts (Birtchnell and Urry, 2016) and international business (Laplume et al., 2016; Hannibal and Knight, 2018; Hannibal, 2020). Of these bodies of work, the most significant contribution by volume is from supply chain management, where the focus has been on the potential for AM (more typically called 3D printing in this context) to change supply chain configurations. Several sophisticated models have been developed that seek to consider the variables involved in these configurations and the consequential impact on supply chain relationships (for example, the number of supply chain actors) (see, e.g., Sasson and Johnson, 2016; Khajavi et al., 2018; Emelogu et al., 2019) and related issues such as sustainability and environmental implications (Bag et al., 2018; Ford and Despeisse, 2016; Rejeski et al., 2018).

Khajavi et al. (2018) contribute to debates around distributed manufacturing, modelling 3D printer machine costs, original equipment manufacturer (OEM) locations, supplier and customer locations, to determine the optimum scale of distributed manufacturing of spare parts using AM. Here they argue that machine cost and speed determine the most efficient manufacturing locations, but hesitate to make firm predictions, noting the debate within industry regarding the speed of progress towards faster, more efficient AM machines. Their analyses are based on a flat, uniform concept of space, providing an idealised model of AM distributive manufacturing that would need to be placed within a geographical (real-world) context. At present, the majority of modelling has taken place in advanced economies, most notably the US. These supply chain management perspectives offer quantitative analysis of AM manufacturing and provide useful modelling of how distributive manufacturing using AM might look in the future.

Contributions from geography, sociology and international political economy have directly engaged with broader debates around the socio-economic impact of AM technologies. This work is grounded primarily in discussions of 3D printing, covering both domestic and industrial 3D printing, but with a firm privileging of the former (due in part to the focus of media and the availability of primary and secondary data). Birtchnell and Urry (2015, 2016) provide background information on the development of 3D printing and consider various affordances and limitations on 3D printing. The embeddedness of their discussions of 3D printing within consideration of how society conceptualises its future offers valuable insights that relate to the positioning of AM within Industry 4.0. There are several contributions (Gress and Kalafsky, 2015; Rehnberg and Ponte, 2018; Laplume et al., 2016; Hannibal and Knight, 2018) that consider the impact of 3D printing on manufacturing in general, typically using secondary data to conceptualise the ways in which 3D printing could generate systematic changes in how goods are manufactured and distributed. All adopt global value chain, global production network and global factory approaches in order to posit their arguments about how 3D printing could transform product design, production and distribution, and the geographies of that production. Hannibal and Knight (2018) highlight that shifts in the global location of economic activity have been dramatic in the factory paradigm (Buckley, 2009; Buckley and Strange, 2015) and that AM is set to likely shift the location of economic activity again as it gains momentum (Petrick and Simpson, 2013). They argue that AM will cause the re-localization of production at the level of individuals and firms (rather than nations), but that some aspects of traditional manufacturing will continue, as economies of scale tend to favour traditional dispersed mass production of many types of goods. Interestingly, while the impacts of AM are increasingly acknowledged to be far from universal, and given the importance placed on its future role in manufacturing and ways of living and working (Birtchnell and Urry, 2016), it is surprising that there is a paucity of social science research into the AM industry itself. Less is known about how the industry is evolving and the ways in which it engages with other manufacturing technologies, customers and consumers (Johns, 2020c).

At present existing academic research on AM is firmly positioned within two silos: quantitative, technology-focused approaches (engineering, materials science, supply chain management) versus qualitative social science approaches that theorise the impacts of 3D printing technology. These works rarely engage with each other. Social science would benefit from a stronger grasp of the intricacies of the technology, the diversity of applications, and a more realistic understanding of the challenges facing the sector and the limitations of the discourses of the technologies. In contrast, science, technology, engineering and maths (STEM) could benefit from a broader perspective and understanding of how technologies fit together in a broader innovation system, and of the potential impacts of the technology. The industry itself is both seduced by the glamour and worthiness of particular applications (printing body parts such as hearts was particularly in vogue pre-COVID-19) but also quite self-deprecating in terms of what has been achieved. This modesty is fuelled perhaps by the lack of a combined set of industry objectives and goals, as the sector is still experiencing high-intensity competition between firms as it begins to mature. Therefore, there are many dynamics around the AM industry and its position vis-à-vis other societal stakeholders that have not been explored by existing literature, as the majority of work in social science is on 3D printing rather than the specific use of the technology in industrial applications.

Charting a future research agenda

There is still much work to do in relation to understanding additive manufacturing and its impacts. Given the paucity of existing work and lack of primary empirical data collection on industrial AM across the social sciences, there is plenty of scope for future research. STEM subjects such as engineering and material sciences will continue to push technological and application boundaries over time. Those working in the social sciences who wish to know more about the contemporary AM industry, the likely impact of AM on manufacturing and society in general, and the role of AM in broader discourses such as Industry 4.0 and reshoring, are currently challenged by two restrictions.

First is the lack of verified quantitative data on the sales of AM technology and adoption levels within manufacturing due to poor data collection and widespread distrust of the annual Wholers Report which firms have to pay to be included in. While competitiveness overrules collaboration within AM, the collection and collation of quantitative data is likely to be limited. This also applies to the materials needed for 3D printing, most commonly plastics, resins and metal powders, which have their own complex supply chains.

Second is the repeated tendency of existing work to fall into traps offered by the hype surrounding AM. This chapter therefore proposes four complementary areas of future research that could steer research on industrial 3D printing in a more critical direction: (1) questioning the degree to which AM will 'transform' manufacturing; (2) moving beyond the framing of AM within Industry 4.0 policy debates; (3) interrogating (and not necessarily assuming) the role of AM in shifts in the geographies of production, specifically reshoring; and (4) initial reflections on AM in the context of the COVID-19 pandemic and resulting impacts and pressures on manufacturing globally.

First, there should be growing awareness that AM is not a new technology that will not replace traditional manufacturing and cannot single-handedly revitalise manufacturing in advanced economies. The use of AM is in complement to traditional manufacturing techniques in the vast majority of sectors, contrary to the hype around replacement. There are some niche sectors in which AM has almost entirely replaced traditional methods – such as hearing aids (Sandström, 2016) and dental implants (Dawood et al., 2015) – but these are small items that are individually customised by necessity. There is little discussion within AM about the technology replacing subtractive techniques in their entirety in other manufacturing sectors (Johns, 2020b). This is due in part to the contemporary focus on the shift of AM from prototyping to volume manufacturing, which is understood as a process rather than as an abrupt, disruptive act. For example, in several manufacturing sectors, there is an evolution from prototyping to using AM to print jigs and fixtures for the production line, before considering AM for production parts (often in polymers before metals). This learning curve reflects the barriers to entry for the use of AM, as increasing levels of investment in expertise, machines and infrastructure can be lower in the earlier stages of AM adoption (often utilising resources of existing prototyping departments before investing in AM for production). The challenges of new technology adoption in manufacturing are often understated or even misunderstood in existing social science literature.

A much more detailed understanding of the manufacturing process and context are needed by those seeking to research the impacts of AM. There is clear scope for greater engagement across the perceived STEM-social science divide, to generate more sophisticated analyses of the impacts of AM as a potentially significant technology. At present, nuanced knowledge of the different 3D printing technologies, their limitations, potential and applications, are produced within STEM subjects, with some translation into supply chain management. However, the diversity of technologies and competing discourses within AM and manufacturing in general, and expertise in manufacturing processes, are not adequately reflected in social science contributions at present. Interdisciplinary approaches, or at the very least, disciplinary approaches grounded in a stronger technical awareness of the AM technologies, would combine the technological and socio-economic aspects of AM. This would better acknowledge that 3D printing is impacting on the production process of existing products as well as opening up new product areas. As such, there is differentiation between different pathways to production and the subsequent types of product.

Second, the tendency for contemporary social science AM research to be situated within Industry 4.0 is understandable, given the compelling and pervasive discourse around manufacturing futures and digitisation. However, the concept of Industry 4.0 is itself often vague and opaque, serving as a catch-all term to describe the Factory of the Future. As such, framing the AM industry within this diffuse label may serve to obscure some of the key dynamics of the sector and place undue attention on those aspects considered most relevant to Industry 4.0, such as the position of technology and its contribution to the factory of the future, degree of automation and big data. At present, AM is a distinct set of technologies that are only just beginning to work alongside other production techniques on the factory floor. In many respects the hype surrounding AM has created a false impression of the maturity of the sector, accelerating its inclusion in a vision of the future that it may not yet be able to contribute to as hoped.

Further, the framing of AM within policymaking and Industry 4.0 does not necessarily reflect the degree to which the sector is receiving specific policy attention. While it is often (but not always) considered to be part of Industry 4.0, it rarely receives individual attention. As such, there is less awareness of the potential contribution of AM to digital manufacturing. Indeed, this prevailing Industry 4.0 vision of high autonomy and integrated production systems can also silence other narratives about other potential manufacturing futures. There is no one future in which all manufacturing sectors are heading, rather multiple possibilities. At present, the AM sector is simultaneously under pressure to conform to the narratives around technological solutions securing our futures, and relatively neglected in terms of national policy focus (with some notable exceptions such as China and Singapore). There needs to be greater attention paid to the directions in which policymaking is directing AM and the consequential influence on how the technology impacts on society, as the Industry 4.0 policy agenda primarily focuses on productivity and supply chain efficiency. Thus, there needs to be greater awareness of both the benefits and the perils of the automatic association between AM and Industry 4.0. AM is part of the digitisation of manufacturing, but this needs to be viewed critically, and the Industry 4.0 project viewed as a political and economic construct with its own agenda and intended outcomes. The focus on productivity and economic outcomes with which Industry 4.0 is often related provides a partial view of the evolution of AM and, in particular, its social impacts.

Third, the highly politicised agenda surrounding the reshoring of manufacturing from low-cost countries back to advanced economies is shaping much of the narrative around the benefits offered by AM. Much of the extant literature on reshoring focuses on defining and positioning the phenomenon (Ellram, 2013; Fratocchi et al., 2014; Gray et al., 2013) and conceptualises the drivers to reshore (Ellram et al., 2013; Foerstl et al., 2016; Fratocchi et al., 2016). There is increasing visibility of the cooling of offshoring (Bailey and De Propris, 2014) and offshoring failures, and acknowledgement that offshoring is not always beneficial (Wiesmann et al., 2017). Within international business, work on reshoring has focused on understanding the drivers for a company's reshoring decision, and as such, transaction cost theory (Williamson, 2008), the resource-based view (Teece et al., 1997), internalisation theory (Buckley and Casson, 1976) and Dunning's eclectic paradigm (Dunning, 1998) have been widely applied (Fratocchi et al., 2016; Grappi et al., 2018). Yet, extant literature on reshoring has so far been unable to interrogate the utility of these existing frameworks (for a critique of the global value chain approach to tackling reshoring, see Vanchan et al., 2018, and Bryson and Vanchan, 2020, for reflections on value chain approaches in relation to value and risk).

The assumption that AM will drive reshoring is therefore problematic for two reasons. First, reshoring as a process is still relatively poorly conceptualised and understood. Second, the purported and potential impact of AM operate across the whole value chain from design ('design for AM'; see Simpson et al., 2017; Thompson et al., 2016) through to production and consumption (Huang et al., 2013; Despeisse et al., 2017; Birtchnell and Urry, 2016), not just production stages. It is therefore less straightforward to examine the immediate impact of AM on traditional supply chains, as the end-point of AM's transformation of manufacturing is constructed as a utopian distributive, localised model. Even if this is a possible future, the journey we will take to get there is not well considered. The most likely scenarios involve uneven and incremental adoption of AM, resulting in a diversity of different outcomes for supply chain geographies and configurations that evolve over time. This also relates to the discussions above around the anticipated level of adoption of AM, and increasing debate about the degree to which AM will replace traditional methods. In a hybrid manufacturing scenario (Strong et al., 2018, 2019) the combination of

AM and traditional methods will result in a multitude of different production geographies. Clearly, much more research is needed on the evolution of AM adoption in different manufacturing contexts, and the resulting impact on where and how goods are manufactured and transported.

Fourth, greater research is needed into the ability of additive manufacturing to provide concrete solutions to supply chain vulnerabilities. The COVID-19 crisis has highlighted the precarity of geographically extensive supply chains, and the failure of firms to build redundancy into their supply relationships, including local ones. The initial period following the emergence and spread of the pandemic witnessed severe pressure on disrupted and permanently ruptured supply chains to deliver immediately needed products, particularly those for the medical sector (for example, ventilators, PPE, swabs). The 3D printing industry has been under a renewed spotlight as it can offer fast, flexible and localised solutions to supply chain problems, and both domestic 3D printing and industrial additive manufacturing have been playing a role in meeting manufacturing needs. As the pandemic progresses the degree to which 3D printing in general, and AM specifically, can address longer-term issues that result from COVID-19 is still unclear, especially as 3D printing is also dependent on its own supply chain, particularly materials such as polymers, resins and metal powders. During a time of crisis, speed and deliverability are favoured over cost, enabling industrial AM to replace more elements of traditional manufacturing. For critical-need PPE, for example, 3D printed parts have provided a crucial stop-gap supply while critical mass manufacturing efforts increase their production to the quantities required.

Even before the crisis, we were starting to witness cost-driven supply decisions being questioned by businesses, following the high-profile collapse of many supply relationships (for example, the severe disruption to the global automotive supply chain caused by a CDT chemical factory fire in Germany in 2012, or Boeing's supply chain management issues producing the Dreamliner[4]), and the dependency of many upon transport and logistics infrastructures that are also fragile due to decades of cost-driven pricing. As the outcomes of the COVID-19 crisis become known, it is clear that there is huge opportunity for the technologies to mitigate against some of the likely consequences such as ruptured geographically extensive supply chains, particularly those to the Far East, relocalised sourcing, and repurposing of production lines to meet new and changing demands. AM is most likely to play a significant role in the production of spare and legacy parts (den Boer et al., 2020; Holström et al., 2010), reducing the need for warehousing and enabling on-site printing of required parts. It is also likely to radically change the tooling process for new and adapted production lines. 3D printing enables quicker and cheaper tooling, which could be a significant contribution to the adaptability and flexibility of manufacturing as it faces contemporary and future challenges.

Conclusion

Discussions around the future of manufacturing are of particular contemporary relevance. Manufacturing is receiving renewed attention in terms of the pressure both to produce critical supplies and to reorganise to ensure delivery of essential and everyday consumer items. 3D printing technologies, particularly industrial AM, have a significant part to play in the future of manufacturing in their application in a number of different sectors, likely working alongside traditional manufacturing. There is much that academia can offer in terms of developing our understandings of both the technologies themselves and their application (and therefore their impact on businesses, workers, consumers and communities). Several key research questions remain only partially unanswered around the barriers to the adoption of AM and the degree to which sectoral differences matter; the realistic (rather than hyped) business models underpinning the use of AM; the role of AM in Industry 4.0 (whatever that now looks like, following COVID-19); and the role of AM in responding to, and reshaping, our responses to the challenges of the new world order post-COVID-19. There is a clear role for the social sciences in answering these important questions, particularly through offering critical perspectives that unpick the logic and rationale of AM, and step outside the predominately transformationalist and positive rhetoric surrounding 3D printing. The AM industry itself clearly calls for AM to be considered as one tool in the suite of manufacturing options (Johns, 2020a). Any future research agenda around AM should aim to combine engineering and materials science technical know-how with social science insights into business models, supply chain configurations and the socio-economic impacts of the adoption of the technology.

Notes

1. Traditional methods of production are either subtractive (removing material to form a shape, for example using milling machines) or formative (for example, injection moulding where a material is poured into a mould).
2. The AM industry is now starting to make significant progress in the automation of post-production finishing (Johns, 2020b).
3. 'Industry 4.0' is the term used to describe the fusion of technologies that is blurring the line between the physical and the digital. It is based not just on digitisation but

also on the integration of new and emerging technologies such as robotics, artificial intelligence, big data and 3D printing. These will combine into the 'Factories of the Future', which are wholly automated (Johns, 2019).
4.   Boeing moved to 70 per cent of parts outsourced (up from 30 per cent) and experienced severe production line problems as a result. https://www.supplychaindigital.com/scm/boeing-787-dreamliner-tale-terrible-supply-chain-management.

References

Anderson, C. (2012) *Makers: The New Industrial Revolution*. London: Random House.
ASTM (2012) *ASTM F2792-12a: Standard Terminology for Additive Manufacturing Technologies*. West Conshohocken, PA: ASTM International.
Bag, S., Telukdarie, A., Pretorius, J.H.S. and Gupta, S. (2018) Industry 4.0 and supply chain sustainability: frameworks and future research directions. *Benchmarking: an International Journal* 28 (5): 1410–1450.
Bailey, D. and De Propris, L. (2014) Manufacturing reshoring and its limits: the UK automotive case. *Cambridge Journal of Regions, Economy and Society* 20 (1): 66–68.
Bak, D. (2003) Rapid prototyping or rapid production? 3D printing processes move industry towards the latter. *Assembly Automation* 23: 340–345.
Baumers, M., Tuck, C., Wildman, R., Ashcroft, I. and Hague, R. (2016) Shape complexity and process energy consumption in electron beam melting: a cast of something for nothing in additive manufacturing. *Journal of Industrial Ecology* 21 (S1): 157–167.
Berman, B. (2012) 3D printing: the new industrial revolution. *Business Horizons* 55: 155–162.
Birtchnell, T. and Urry, J. (2015) The mobilities and post-mobilities of cargo. *Consumption, Markets and Culture* 18 (1): 25–38.
Birtchnell, T. and Urry, J. (2016) *A New Industrial Future?* London: Routledge.
Borup, M., Brown, N., Konrad, K. and Van Lente, H. (2006) The sociology of expectations in science and technology. *Technology Analysis and Strategic Management* 18 (3/4): 285–298.
Bryson, J.R. and Vanchan, V. (2020) COVID-19 and alternative conceptualisations of value and risk in GPN research. *Tijdschrift voor Economische en Sociale Geografie* 111 (3): 530–542.
Buckley, P.J. (2009) Internalisation thinking: from the multinational enterprise to the global factory. *International Business Review* 18: 224–235.
Buckley, P.J. and Casson, M. (1976) *The Future of the Multinational Enterprise*. London: Macmillan Press.
Buckley, P.J. and Strange, R. (2015) The governance of the global factory: location and control of world economic activity. *Academy of Management Perspectives* 29: 237–249.
Carr, C. and Gibson, C. (2016) Geographies of making: rethinking materials and skills for volatile futures. *Progress in Human Geography* 40 (3): 297–315.
Culmone, C., Smit, G. and Breedveld, P. (2019) Additive manufacturing of medical instruments: a state-of-the-art review. *Additive Manufacturing* 27: 461–473.
D'Aveni, R. (2015) The 3D printing revolution. *Harvard Business Review* May.
Dawood, A., Marti Marti, B., Sauret-Jackson, V. and Darwood, A. (2015) 3D printing in dentistry. *British Dental Journal* 219: 521–529.

den Boer, J., Lambrechts, W. and Krikke, H. (2020) Additive manufacturing in military and humanitarian missions: advantages and challenges in the spare parts supply chain. *Journal of Cleaner Production* 257: 1–11.

Despeisse, M., Baumers, M., Brown, P., Charnley, F., Ford, S.J., et al. (2017) Unlocking value for a circular economy through 3D printing: a research agenda. *Technological Forecasting and Social Change* 115: 75–84.

Dunning, J.H. (1998) Location and the multinational enterprise: a neglected factor? *Journal of International Business Studies* 29: 45–66.

Ellram, L.M. (2013) Offshoring, reshoring and the manufacturing location decision. *Journal of Supply Chain Management* 49 (2): 3–5.

Ellram, L.M., Tate, W.L. and Petersen, K.J. (2013) Offshoring and reshoring: an update on the manufacturing location decision. *Journal of Supply Chain Management* 49 (2): 14–22.

Emelogu, A., Chowdhury, S., Marufuzzaman, M. and Bian, L. (2019) Distributed or centralized? A novel supply chain configuration of additively manufactured biomedical implants for southeastern US States. *CIRP Journal of Manufacturing Science and Technology* 24: 17–34.

Eurofound (2019) *The Future of Manufacturing in Europe.* Luxembourg: Publications Office of the European Union.

Foerstl, K., Kirchoff, J.F. and Bals, L. (2016) Reshoring and insourcing: drivers and future research directions. *International Journal of Physical Distribution and Logistics Management* 46 (5): 492–515.

Ford, S. and Despeisse, M. (2016) Additive manufacturing and sustainability: an exploratory study of the advantages and challenges. *Journal of Cleaner Production* 137: 1573–1587.

Fratocchi, L., Ancarani, A., Barbieri, P., Di Mauro, C., Nassimbeni, G., et al. (2016) Motivations of manufacturing reshoring: an interpretative framework. *International Journal of Physical Distribution and Logistics Management* 46 (2): 98–127.

Fratocchi, L., Di Mauro, C., Barbieri, P., Nassimbeni, G. and Zanoni, A. (2014) When manufacturing moves back: concepts and questions. *Journal of Purchasing and Supply Management* 20 (1): 54–59.

Ghobakhloo, M. (2018) The future of manufacturing industry: a strategic roadmap toward Industry 4.0. *Journal of Manufacturing Technology Management* 29 (6): 910–936.

Goulding, C. G., Bonafe, A. and Saell, G. (2013) The R&D tax credits and the US 3D printing initiative. *Corporate Business Tax Monthly* 15 (1): 207–15.

Grappi, S., Romani, S. and Bagozzi, R.P. (2018) Reshoring from a demand-side perspective: consumer reshoring sentiment and its market effects. *Journal of World Business* 52 (2): 194–208.

Gray, J.V., Skowronsky, K., Esenduran, G. and Rungtudanatham, M.J. (2013) Reshoring phenomenon: what supply chain academics ought to know and should do. *Journal Supply Chain Management* 49 (2): 27–33.

Gress, D.R. and Kalafsky, R.V. (2015) Geography of production in 3D: theoretical and research implications stemming from additive manufacturing. *Geoforum* 60: 43–52.

Guo, N. and Leu, M.C. (2013) Additive manufacturing: technology, applications and research needs. *Frontiers of Mechanical Engineering* 8 (3): 215–243.

Haleem, A. and Javaid, M. (2019) Additive manufacturing applications in Industry 4.0: a review. *Journal of Industrial Integration and Management* 4 (4): 1–23.

Hannibal, M. (2020) The influence of additive manufacturing on early internationalisation: considerations into potential avenues of IE research. *Journal of International Entrepreneurship* 18 (4): 473–491.

Hannibal, M. and Knight, G. (2018) Additive manufacturing and the global factory: disruptive technologies and the location of international business. *International Business Review* 27: 1116–1127.

Holmström, J., Holweg, M., Khajavi, S.H. and Partanen, J. (2016) The direct digital manufacturing (r)evolution: definition of a research agenda. *Operational Management Research* 9: 1–10.

Holmström, J., Partanen, J., Tuomi, J. and Walter, M. (2010) Rapid manufacturing in the spare parts supply chain: alternative approaches to capacity deployment. *Journal of Manufacturing Technology Management* 21 (6): 687–697.

Huang, S.H., Liu, P., Mokasdar, A. and Hou, L. (2013) Additive manufacturing and its societal impact: a literature review. *International Journal of Advanced Manufacturing Technology* 67: 1191–1203.

Hyman, P. (2011) Ten disruptive technologies. *Communications of the ACM* 59 (9): 20.

Johns, J. (2019) Davos: leaders talk about globalisation as though it's inevitable – when it isn't. *Conversation* 22 January. Available at: https://theconversation.com/davos-leaders-talk-about-globalisation-as-though-its-inevitable-when-it-isnt-110216.

Johns, J. (2020a) Current perspectives on metal AM: hype, volume manufacturing and the geographies of production. *Metal AM* Spring edition: 123–133. Available at: https://www.metal-am.com/wp-content/uploads/sites/4/2020/03/Metal-AM-Spring-2020-sp-1.pdf.

Johns, J. (2020b) *Insights on Additive Manufacturing: Value, Volume and Reshoring*. Available at: https://issuu.com/home/published/additive_manufacturing_industry_report.

Johns, J. (2020c) A glimpse into which future? COVID-19, 3D printing and work. *Futures of Work* 15(July). Available at: https://futuresofwork.co.uk/2020/07/13/a-glimpse-into-which-future-covid-19-3d-printing-and-work/.

Johns, J. and Hall, S.M. (2020) 'I have so little time [...] I got shit I need to do': critical perspectives on making and sharing in Manchester's FabLab. *Environment and Planning A*. Available online first: https://doi.org/10.1177/0308518X19897918.

Khajavi, S.H., Holmström, J. and Partanen, J. (2018) Additive manufacturing in the spare parts supply chain: hub configuration and technology maturity. *Rapid Prototyping Journal* 24 (7): 1178–1192.

Kothman, I. and Faber, N. (2016) *Supply Chain Management: Processes, Partnerships, Performance*, 4th edn. Sarasota, FL: Supply Chain Management Institute.

Laplume, A., Petersen, B. and Pearce, J.M. (2016) Global value chains from a 3D printing perspective. *Journal of International Business Studies* 47 (5): 595–609.

Lipson, H. and Kuman, M. (2013) *Fabricated: The New World of 3D Printing*. Indianapolis, IN: John Wiley.

Petrick, I.J. and Simpson, T.W. (2013) 3D printing disrupts manufacturing: how economies of one create new rules of competition. *Research-Technology Management* 56: 12–16.

Potstada, M. and Zybura, J. (2014) The role of context in science fiction prototyping: the digital industrial revolution. *Technological Forecasting and Social Change* 84: 101–114.

Rehnberg, M. and Ponte, S. (2018) From smiling to smirking? 3D printing, upgrading and the restructuring of global value chains. *Geoforum* 18 (1): 57–80.

Rejeski, D., Zhao, F. and Huang, Y. (2018) Research needs and recommendations on environmental implications of additive manufacturing. *Additive Manufacturing* 19: 21–28.

Roca, J.B., Vaishnav, P., Laurejs, R.E., Mendonca, J. and Fuchs, E.R.H. (2019) Technology cost drivers for a potential transition to decentralized manufacturing. *Additive Manufacturing* 28: 136–151.

Ruef, A. and Markard, J. (2010) What happens after a hype? How changing expectations affected innovation activities in the case of stationary fuel cells. *Technology Analysis and Strategic Management* 22 (3): 3170338.

Rylands, B., Bohme, T., Gorkin III, R., Fan, J. and Birtchnell, T. (2016) The adoption process and impact of additive manufacturing on manufacturing systems. *Journal of Manufacturing Technology Management* 27 (7): 969–989.

Sandström, C.G. (2016) The non-disruptive emergence of an ecosystem for 3D printing – insights from the hearing aid industry's transition 1989–2008. *Technological Forecasting and Social Change* 102: 160–168.

Sasson, A. and Johnson, J. (2016) The 3D printing order: variability, supercentres and supply chain configurations. *International Journal of Physical Distribution and Logistics Management* 46 (1): 82–94.

Schwab, K. (2017) *The Fourth Industrial Revolution*. New York: Crown Publishing Group.

Simpson, T.W., Williams, C.B. and Hripko, M. (2017) Preparing industry for additive manufacturing and its applications: summary and recommendations from a National Science Foundation workshop. *Additive Manufacturing* 13: 166–178.

SmarTech (2019) *2019 Additive Manufacturing Market Outlook and Summary of Opportunities*. Available from: https://www.smartechanalysis.com/reports/2019 -additive-manufacturing-market-outlook/, accessed 16 March 2020.

Strong, D., Kay, M., Conner, B., Wakefield, T. and Manogharan, G. (2018) Hybrid manufacturing – integrating traditional manufacturers with additive manufacturing (AM) supply chain. *Additive Manufacturing* 21: 159–173.

Strong, D., Kay, M., Conner, B., Wakefield, T. and Manogharan, G. (2019) Hybrid manufacturing – locating AM hubs using a two-stage facility location approach. *Additive Manufacturing* 25: 469–476.

Teece, D.J., Pisano, G. and Shuen, A. (1997) Dynamic capabilities and strategic management. *Strategic Management Journal* 18 (7): 509–533.

Thompson, K., Moroni, G., Vaneker, T., Fadel, G., Campbell, I., et al. (2016) Design for additive manufacturing: trends, opportunities, considerations and constraints. *CIRP Annals* 65 (2): 737–760.

Tucker, K., Tucker, D., Eastham, J., Gibson, E., Varma, S. and Daim, T. (2014) Network based technology roadmapping for future markets: case of 3D printing. *Technology and Investment* 5 (3): 137–156.

Van Lente, H., Spitters, C. and Peine, A. (2013) Comparing technological hype cycles: towards a theory. *Technological Forecasting and Social Change* 80: 1615–1628.

Vanchan, V., Mulhall, L. and Bryson, J. (2018) Repatriation or reshoring of manufacturing to the US and UK: dynamics and global production networks or from here to there and back again. *Growth and Change* 49 (1): 97–121.

Weller, C., Kleer, R. and Piller, F.T. (2015) Economic implications of 3D printing: market structure models in light of additive manufacturing revisited. *International Journal of Production Economics* 164: 43–56.

Wiesmann, B., Snoei, J.R., Hilletofth, P. and Eriksson, D. (2017) Drivers and barriers to reshoring: a literature review on offshoring in reverse. *European Business Review* 29 (1): 15–42.

Williamson, O.E. (2008) Outsourcing: transaction cost economies and supply chain management. *Journal of Supply Chain Management* 44 (2): 5–16.

Winnan, C.D. (2012) *3D Printing: The Next Technology Gold Rush: Future Factories and How to Capitalise on Distributed Manufacturing.* CreateSpace Independent Publishing.

Wohlers (2019) *Wohlers Report 2019: 3D Printing and Additive Manufacturing: State of the Industry.* Fort Collins, CO: Wohlers Associates.

4 Megatrends and new research agendas in the automotive industry

Godfrey Yeung

Introduction

Not all innovations have a tangible impact on consumer markets; revolutionary innovations may not be visible to or accepted by consumers. Disruptive innovation, however, has a profound impact on market dynamics as it creates new applications and reshapes or even produces new business models or markets for the product in question (Bower and Christensen, 1995). A typical example of disruptive innovation is Ford's adoption of assembly line technology to mass produce affordable passenger vehicles. The launch of the Ford Model T car in 1908 created a new market segment as passenger vehicles were no longer a niche product.

The literature on innovation covers humongous topics and disciplines, from the meanings of innovation (Hobday, 1998; Carlsson et al., 2002) and its related concepts (Landry and Bianchini, 1995), how to measure it (Humphrey and Memedovic, 2003; Kaplinsky and Morris, 2001), to the role of institutional proximity (Lundvall and Johnson, 1994; Morgan, 1997) and industrial policies (Humphrey and Schmitz, 2002), including the national innovation system (NIS) (Freeman and Lundvall, 1988; Lundvall, 1992; Nelson, 1993). In the automotive industry, researchers have shown strong interest in examining the relationship between car manufacturers and parts suppliers (Sturgeon et al., 2008, 2009; Schmitt and Van Biesebroeck, 2013; Bollhorn and Franz, 2016). Researchers, however, should not be focused on a specific industrial sector excessively, as significant innovation in related sectors could be disruptive and thus have a profound impact on the existing competitive dynamics of the automotive industry.

The electrification of powertrains, digitalization of vehicle control systems, and autonomous driving are the emerging megatrends in the automotive industry.[1]

Using the three emerging megatrends in the automotive industry as a case study, this chapter investigates the potential challenges technological innovation poses for the passenger vehicle sector and how changing competitive dynamics in the automotive industry can affect researchers' conceptualization of potential research topics within manufacturing. Although it is premature to judge whether these emerging megatrends could be disruptive innovations, and mainstream customers have so far been reluctant to accept such technologies, no one can deny the potential direct and indirect socio-economic and environmental impacts of such developments in the automotive industry.

The automotive industry is one of the most globalized industrial sectors, since each passenger vehicle model contains tens of thousands of parts made and assembled by various suppliers in plants all over the world. The development of the automotive industry is closely interrelated with a number of complementary sectors, from iron and steel to petrochemicals, electrical and electronics. The megatrends in automotive could thus have profound impacts on industrial development and subsequent socio-economic impacts. For example, car manufacturers employ about 8 million people worldwide and many more are employed by their parts suppliers (*New York Times*, 6 June 2019). This is especially a concern in countries where car manufacturers play an important role in their economies, for example, Germany, France, Italy, Japan, the United States (US), South Korea and China.

The pertinent literature on innovation is reviewed briefly in the next section, before an examination of three megatrends in the automotive industry. I then discuss two potential research agendas that could emerge from such megatrends, before concluding the chapter.

Innovation, upgrading and industrial development

Innovation is defined as an interactive process involving the generation, adoption, implementation and incorporation of new ideas and practices by an actor (Carlsson et al., 2002; Lundvall, 1992). Innovation can occur through open or closed channels. Open innovation utilizes the open inflows and outflows of knowledge when company boundaries are permeable for the transfer of knowledge that can promote innovation (Chesbrough, 2003); while closed innovation relies on in-house resources for innovative activities (Docherty, 2006).

Innovation is related to a number of pertinent concepts, especially creativity and upgrading. Creativity involves non-evaluative divergent thought processes that generate ideas, while innovation encompasses convergent processes involving the selection and implementation of ideas (Landry and Bianchini, 1995: 13). Adopting the product-oriented approach, Amabile (1988: 126) argued that 'creativity is the production of novel and useful ideas by an individual or small group of individuals working together. Innovation is built on creative ideas as the basic element. Organizational innovation is the successful implementation of creative ideas within an organization.' Innovative activity within a firm is an interactive process characterized by the technological interrelatedness of various processes (Teece, 1996; Hobday, 1998), from concept generation, product development to production technology, and so on. In other words, the key to innovation is the innovator's capability to spot an opportunity, develop a solution that has economic value, and then utilize the minimum necessary resources (vis-à-vis the big budget strategy, as highlighted by Radjou et al., 2012) to bring it about.

Industrial upgrading is a related but arguably more measurable concept than innovation. Researchers have identified four types of industrial upgrading: product upgrading, process upgrading, functional upgrading and chain upgrading (Humphrey and Schmitz, 2002; Humphrey and Memedovic, 2003; Kaplinsky and Morris, 2001; Sturgeon et al., 2008). Product upgrading refers to a move to more sophisticated and higher-value product lines; process upgrading occurs through the deployment of sophisticated modes of production, and new technologies may be involved; functional upgrading is achieved through entrance into a new, higher-value-added function or level in the value chain, such as developing own brands; chain upgrading means moving into a higher-value sector by acquiring new competences.

Proximity is normally credited as being the catalyst for innovation. Although spatial and institutional proximity and network relations enable face-to-face interaction that could facilitate design and engineering development (Camagni, 1991; Becattini, 1992; Lundvall and Johnson, 1994; Freeman, 1995; Cooke et al., 1997; Morgan, 1997), these are arguably not sufficient conditions for innovation. The absorption capacity of engineers is determined by how much codified knowledge they are able to internalize and their ability to acquire the relevant tacit knowledge, either through informal socialization and/or involving (formal) sessions of knowledge exchange with other engineers (Lagendijk, 2006).[2] Cognitive proximity is used to explain the development trajectory of specific industrial sectors in regions that share a complementary set of skills and competences pertaining to a common knowledge base. A similar and related concept is technological proximity, a concept based on the traditions of industrial organization. Both technological and cognitive proximity explain how similarities in cognitive maps can enhance the transfer of knowledge across space. Technological proximity focuses on the effective transfer of knowledge on the basis of similarities of specialization in industrial economic activities; while cognitive proximity reconciles the existence of knowledge diffusion, whereby people share the same scientific language (that is, the same technological paradigm) even if they are in different technological or industrial sectors according to conventional classification (Orlando, 2004; Jaffe and Trajtenberg, 1999).

In the automotive industry, competitive advantages in thermal efficiency technologies and scale economies allow a few international automobile giants to play an instrumental role in connecting competent local suppliers to the global production networks (Clark and Fujimoto, 1991; Coe and Yeung, 2015).[3] A number of pertinent studies in the automotive industry are specific to either a region and/or a car manufacturer. The former focus on the impacts of automotive in regional development; while the latter are about the relationships between car manufacturers and their Tier I suppliers. For instance, Schmitt and Van Biesebroeck (2013) estimated that Asian brand-named manufacturers are 2.5 times more likely to establish a supply contract with Asian component suppliers in the automotive industry. The relationship between car manufacturers and their parts suppliers has gathered strong interest from researchers. The previously vertically integrated car manufacturers have created top spin-off firms for parts manufacturing since the 1990s; for example, Delphi from the GM, and Visteon from Ford (Sadler, 1998; Humphrey, 2003; Carrillo, 2004; Herrigel, 2004). Sturgeon et al. (2008, 2009) highlighted the dominance of a few powerful lead firms, while Bollhorn and Franz (2016) portrayed car manufacturers as the visible tip of an iceberg in an asymmetrical power relationship dominated by lead firms.

Other studies have highlighted the importance of knowledge transfer from the global automobile giants to ensure good quality standards of the outputs from their suppliers (Ernst and Kim, 2002; Humphrey and Schmitz, 2004), and have pointed out that the effectiveness of knowledge transfer depends on the specificities of knowledge and the suppliers' absorption capacities and social networks. Ivarsson and Alvstam (2005) pointed out the importance of spatial proximity for knowledge transfer to Volvo's local suppliers in China, India and Brazil; while Contreras et al. (2012) reported the roles of spin-offs, socio-professional networks and market relations for the emergence of knowledge-intensive local suppliers in Ford's automotive cluster in Mexico. Despite the involvement of suppliers in design and product development tasks, car manufacturers still dictated the specific type of upgrade that could be opened up to their local suppliers in Turkey (Özatağan, 2011). The changing global competitive dynamic and local development conditions have led to changes in interfirm and intra-firm relationships between global lead firms and latecomer manufacturers (Liu, 2017).

All of these studies have enhanced our understanding of innovation and upgrading in general, and their impacts on the automotive industry, specifically. By highlighting the importance of proactive industrial policies for the establishment of new production networks in battery electric vehicles (BEVs), however, Yeung (2019) has argued that such asymmetrical power relationships between global lead firms and local suppliers could be challenged by the electrification of powertrains in automotive industry. The emerging megatrends in the automotive industry could demand a refocus of our research.

Hype and reality of megatrends in the automotive industry

The three emerging megatrends in the automotive industry are driven by a combination of push (largely regulatory) and pull (largely market demand) factors. One could argue that these megatrends are about mobility (of people) as a service rather than assembling and selling vehicles as in the conventional automotive industry.

Electrification and digitalization

The global trend towards increasingly stringent emission controls for vehicles with internal combustion engines (ICEs) pushes the automotive industry towards electrification and digitalization. This is especially the case in the European Union (EU) with the launch of 'Euro 2' environmental standards in 1996 and the subsequent more stringent and comprehensive emission standards to include hydrocarbons, nitrogen oxide and particulate matter in petrol engines. Car manufacturers specialize in the energy efficiency of ICEs and transmissions, but the increasingly stringent emission standards call for wider use of microelectronic control systems to reduce the emission of harmful gases (such as carbon monoxide, nitrogen oxides) and particles (especially from diesel engines).

The massive push of European countries to adopt new energy vehicles (NEVs) facilitates the phasing-out of ICE-driven vehicles. A number of (European) countries have announced that they are banning the sale of new vehicles with ICEs by 2025–40, after Norway took the initiative in 2016 (Wappelhorst and Cui, 2020). The drive towards electrification was accelerated by the launch of the Worldwide Harmonised Light Vehicles Test Procedure (WLTP)[4] in 2015 and the emissions scandal of diesel-fuelled engines. The WLTP, effective on 1 September 2018, demands a more rigorous test on fuel consumption and a much higher level of emission control of pollutants for all new passenger vehicles. Specifically, the EU stipulates that all car manufacturers must keep their average new passenger vehicle fleet emissions to less than 95 grams/ km of carbon dioxide (CO_2) by 2021. Importantly, the fuel consumption and emission tests have to be conducted in every configuration of powertrain, from the least to the most economical specifications. In the case of Volkswagen Aktiengesellschaft (hereafter: Volkswagen), the new regulation demands it test each of its 260 different motor-gearbox combinations alongside other variations affecting emissions (*Financial Times*, 15 November 2018). No wonder car manufacturers have had to budget €15.5 billion to make their vehicles comply with the EU's average fleet emissions target, according to Evercore ISI estimates (*Financial Times*, 16 April 2019). Automobile giants General Motors (GM) and Ford subsequently announced that they will only sell zero-emission vehicles by 2030-35 (*New York Times*, 17 February 2021).

In addition to the rise in consumers' environmental awareness, the emphasis on passive and active safety systems and passengers' comfort (noise reduction inside the vehicle) increase the weight of a vehicle, and this negates some of the thermal efficiency improvements of ICEs. Car manufacturers are thus forced to include more advanced microelectronic control modules to improve thermal efficiency and reduce emissions, for example, powertrain control module (PCM) with controls solenoids to adjust hydraulic valves in variable camshaft timing (VCT). Car manufacturers' strategies need to strike a delicate balance between emission control and safety, such as the adoption of start-stop system and (plug-in) hybrid powertrains to further facilitate the move towards digitalization.

The rising awareness of safety by potential car buyers promotes digitalization in the automotive sector. The introduction of the European New Car Assessment Programme (Euro NCAP) has had a significant impact, raising potential car buyers' awareness of safety. Euro NCAP is based on the New Car Assessment Program (NCAP), introduced by the US National Highway Traffic Safety Administration in 1979. Initially conceived largely for driver and passenger safety when it was launched in 1997, the Euro NCAP has incorporated elements of active safety into the NCAP Advanced reward scheme since 2010.

To secure the top rating of NCAP Advanced reward, an important business-to-consumer marketing point, car manufacturers have to integrate advanced microelectronics devices in the form of advanced driver assistance systems (ADAS) in passenger vehicles; for example, blind spot monitoring, lane support systems, adaptive cruise control, autonomous emergency braking with post-collision assist systems, a vision enhancement system, and so on. As a consequence, an average high-end vehicle has seven times more code in its 11–14 computers than a Boeing 787 (Gao et al., 2014: 7; Chatelain et al., 2018: 15).

Autonomous driving

Furthermore, the environmental consciousness of the new/next generation of customers demands mobility of a different nature. Instead of owning their own private vehicles, they demand a much higher level of flexibility concerning the way vehicles are used.[5] To capture the projected loss of sales revenues from ICE-driven vehicles, car manufacturers adjust their business models towards electrification, digitalization and (subscription-based) car-sharing, and autonomous driving.

In addition to the established Waymo (the autonomous vehicle unit of Alphabet, the parent company of Google), major car manufacturers and a number of ride-hailing companies, such as Uber and Lyft, and other venture capitalists, have been investing heavily in autonomous driving since 2016. For instance, General Motors acquired Cruise with US$1 billion in 2016, and Honda also injected capital into that unit in 2018. Ford invested US$1 billion in a start-up (Argo AI) and this was followed by another pledge of the same amount from Volkswagen. It is estimated that car manufacturers and start-ups invested about US$80 billion in autonomous driving between 2014 and 2017 (Kerry and Karsten, 2017). The wide adoption of autonomous vehicles is expected to accelerate the shift of mobility as a service in the automobile sector, that is, car manufacturers have to transform themselves into providers of mobility services rather than simply sell vehicles as in the conventional business model.

China could be at the forefront of the mass deployment of autonomous vehicles, partly due to their higher acceptance level among the general public, at 38 per cent (10–20 percentage points higher than the US, Japan and Germany), according to the Global Automotive Consumer Study conducted by Deloitte (Vitale et al., 2017; Pizzuto et al., 2019). Importantly, the new generation of information technology and intelligent connected vehicles are two specific sectors outlined in the ambitious government initiative, Made in China 2025.[6] Chinese internet giants Alibaba, Tencent and Baidu have all invested in BEV start-ups with autonomous capabilities and formed partnerships with car manufacturers; for example, Baidu and Tencent are venture investors in NIO and Alibaba has invested in Xpeng Motors. One of the most high-profile firm actors is Apollo, the autonomous vehicle unit of Baidu, which launched its 'robo-taxi' service with a fleet of 45 autonomous vehicles in Changsha, the capital of Hunan province, in 2019, available for public customers in April 2020 (*China Daily*, 18 May 2020).

Optimistic projections for autonomous driving have led to some rosy forecasts in the pertinent sectors. IHS Markit forecasts the automotive semiconductors market will reach US$57.6 billion by 2022, an increase of 51 per cent from 2017 (*Financial Times*, 9 September 2018). McKinsey estimates that autonomous vehicles will account for 40 per cent of market share and reach US$0.9 trillion of sales value, and mobility services will generate another US$1.1 trillion of revenue, by 2040 (Pizzuto et al., 2019).

Changing competitive dynamics

However, such rosy future projections are in stark contrast to reality. With the exception of digitalization, where a number of automotive-grade semiconductor manufacturers have long-standing business associations with automotive and other major firms, actors are generating revenues from non-automotive businesses, and none of the firm actors working solely on BEVs and autonomous driving are profitable.

In BEVs, almost all pure BEV makers are losing money to capture market share, partly due to the high costs of electric vehicle batteries. This is the case in China, the largest BEVs market in the world. NIO is one of the most high-profile and well-known pure BEV makers in China as it possesses proprietary technology on BEVs, from the deployment of powertrains on its supercar (EP9 holds a few track records) to battery swapping stations. NIO, however, has been losing money every quarter since its establishment in 2014. Other major firm actors, notably SAIC (including SAIC-GM-Wuling) and BAIC, could sell their entry-level BEVs at a price close to cost parity with ICE-driven vehicles, partly because of cross-subsidization with the profits from millions of ICE-driven vehicles (Yeung, 2019).

In the autonomous vehicle and driving market, all firm actors, especially start-ups, are haemorrhaging capital due to the heavy research and development expenses while generating zero revenue. None of the firm actors are able to resolve the expected and unexpected technical difficulties encountered for completely autonomous driving (level 5) where no driver is required under all circumstances; that is, the best prototypes so far still have an unacceptably high rate of disengagement that requires human driver intervention at level 4 of autonomous driving.[7]

But these gloomy financial balance sheets are unlikely to derail the megatrends in the automotive sector, due to the significant potential synergies in the connected and smart society; that is, BEVs with autonomous driving are just one of the instruments in the Internet of Things (IoT) platforms through vehicle-to-vehicle and vehicle-to-infrastructure 5G communication. Chinese local governments (including Chongqing and Hefei) awarded contracts to one of the Chinese internet giants, Baidu, to construct a smart transport infrastructure in March 2020.

All the top automobile giants are investing heavily in these megatrend areas as part of their long-term investment plans. The electrification of powertrains eliminates the core competitive advantage of car manufacturers on ICE, and thus car manufacturers need to change their business models. To stay afloat in the major automobile markets, all the major automobile giants have been electrifying their powertrains, from the adoption of 'mild hybrid' with 48-volt systems to fully electrified powertrains in BEVs. Volkswagen is a typical example of such a massive readjustment to the business model, with its investment of €33 billion in the MEB chassis, designed specifically for the more than 50 models of BEVs to be launched by 2025. In addition to investing €1.1 billion to acquire 26 per cent equity of Guoxuan High-tech, one of the largest electric vehicle battery makers in China, Volkswagen injected another €1 billion to increase its equity in JAC-Volkswagen (its key BEV joint venture in China) from 50 to 75 per cent in May 2020 (*Financial Times*, 30 January 2019 and 29 May 2020).

Importantly, such industrial megatrends change the relationship between car manufacturers. To lower development costs and increase adoption for the economy of scales, Ford has become the first global car manufacturer to license Volkswagen's MEB platform for its own brand of BEVs in Europe (*Automotive News*, 12 July 2019). Instead of using ICE powertrains to differentiate between vehicles, the main components of BEVs, such as motors and batteries, have become commodified. This could be the same for chassis in the future. Car manufacturers therefore have to compete with each other in terms of the driver and passenger experience, and connectivity could be the key. For instance, the electronic control unit embedded in the MEB platform connects the car to Volkswagen's Automotive Cloud (in partnership with Microsoft), which enables vehicle-to-vehicle connectivity and paves the way for autonomous driving in the smart city.

Volkswagen is not the only automobile giant to respond to the challenge of megatrends by transforming itself from manufacturer into mobility service provider. FCA admitted that the competitive pressure and rapid transformation of the automotive industry, particularly in areas like connectivity, electrification and autonomous driving, expedited its decision to merge with PSA to form the Stellantis (*The Economist*, 9 January 2021). Mr Akio Toyoda, chief executive officer of Toyota, said in May 2019: 'My true mission is to completely redesign Toyota into a mobility company … [and provide] all kinds of services related to mobility' (Bloomberg, 1 August 2019).

New research agendas in the automotive industry

The three emerging megatrends in automobile production generate fresh agendas for research, especially – but not exclusively – the intersection and competitive dynamics between sectors, and local versus global production networks.

Intersections and the competitive dynamics between sectors

Electrification, digitalization and autonomous driving are reshaping the competitive dynamics in the automotive sector by disrupting the current division of sales and component supply between different industrial sectors, which in turn makes obsolete the existing conceptualization and classification of industrial sectors themselves. Currently, this is based on how the different sectors are perceived and classified: car manufacturers for making and selling vehicles; transportation and logistics companies for providing mobility services; technology actors for supplying parts and bespoke software to car manufacturers.

Software and (big) data constitute the competitive advantages of autonomous driving and there are signs that car manufacturers are crossing over to other sectors: car manufacturers can integrate vertically by developing software in-house or engaging in the mobility service directly. For instance, BMW, Audi and Daimler acquired HERE (a major mapping and location-based services provider) in a US$3.1 billion deal in 2015, to bring the development of mapping services in-house, while BMW and Daimler formed a US$1 billion car-sharing joint venture by merging DriveNow and car2go in 2019.

The megatrends have thus promoted a high level of intersection and reshaping of the competitive dynamics between sectors, which demands the expertise to integrate microelectronic monitor and control modules and their related software into the powertrain control systems. This then provides opportunities for firm actors to specialize in microelectronics and/or software systems and so pay an increasingly important role in the aspects that distinguish different brands of cars, as the core competency is moving from powertrains to software and electronics. For instance, the Chevrolet Bolt, BEV's powertrain, contains US$580 worth of semiconductors, which is 6–10 times more than in an average comparable car with an ICE, for example the VW Golf (UBS, 2017: 8). IHS Markit forecasts that the automotive chip market could reach US$57.6 billion by 2022 (*Financial Times*, 9 September 2018).

Moreover, other firm actors can create synergies using their existing micro-electronic products and thus benefit from the megatrends in automobile production. Notable examples of autonomous driving are the producer oligopolies in graphics processing units (GPUs) (especially Nvidia's Xavier as the onboard computing platform), radar, light detection and ranging (LIDAR), camera and systems integrators (*The Economist*, 3 March 2018). Intel acquired Mobileye, a leading supplier of cameras, sensors and software for autonomous driving, in a US$15.3 billion deal in 2017. Intel-Mobileye is working with BMW, Volkswagen and Renault-Nissan-Mitsubishi on autonomous driving (*New York Times*, 8 August 2017).

Furthermore, technology actors could disrupt the traditional divisions of production and supply by acquiring vehicles from car manufacturers, and providing mobility services to customers and capturing the value-added directly. No wonder Mr Akio Toyoda, the chairman of Toyota, recently proclaimed that car manufacturers are facing a 'life-or-death battle … [against their] new rivals … in an era of profound transformation' (*Daily Telegraph*, 18 May 2018).

These megatrends are disruptive as they not only blur the boundaries between industrial sectors as used in trade and manufacturing statistics – Standard International Trade Classification (SITC), Harmonized System (HS) and the United Nations International Standard Industrial Classification (ISIC) codes – but are also creating new players (microelectronics and battery makers are becoming Tier I suppliers) or even 'new sectors' (such as ride-hailing and car-sharing). For instance, the World Customs Organization's HS Nomenclature (2017 edition) is one of the most commonly used classifications of traded commodities – it is used in the United Nations (UN) Comtrade. It is relatively straightforward to identify passenger vehicles in chapter 87.03, but the classification of parts of ICE passenger vehicles, largely grouped under chapters 84, 85 and 87, results in overestimation of ICE passenger vehicle value and volumes since it includes parts for commercial vehicles as well (Table 4.1). The margin of error increases significantly should one want to estimate the economic impacts of electrification: there is no specific classification for BEVs, or parts specifically for BEVs, as chapters 85.01 and 85.06 include motors and batteries for other uses. The quantitative estimate of the impacts of autono-

mous driving has an even high margin of error. For instance, LIDAR is classified in a single category in chapter 9015 as surveying equipment, but it is one
of the three necessary devices (along with cameras and radar) for full autonomous driving.[8] Under the existing nomenclature, the best that researchers can
achieve is a (very) rough estimate of the quantitative impacts of the emerging
megatrends in the regional economy. Researchers are facing a herculean
task should they use the Standard International Trade Classification (SITC,
revision 4, 2007). Automobiles and their parts are listed under division 78 of
SITC, but the latest version was launched back in 2007 when the megatrends
had yet to gain traction in the automotive industry.[9] An update is crucial as
the UN Comtrade is an important source of data for researchers to conduct
cross-country and time-series quantitative analysis.

The potential impact of artificial intelligence (AI) on autonomous driving
muddles the distinction between software and hardware in manufacturing
even further. To understand the roles and importance of various actors in
automotive innovation, researchers not only have to understand different
firms actors' interdependence, especially non-conventional automotive suppliers, but they also need to reconceptualize how to (re)classify and research
manufacturing by industrial sector. This demands the reclassification of
industrial outputs and international trade data, and possible revised ways of
collecting the corresponding data and research methods in manufacturing.

Global or local production networks?

The automotive industry is one of the most globalized manufacturing sectors.
Although the bulky chassis is normally manufactured near the assembly plant,
the tens of thousands of key parts and components are made by specialized
suppliers located all over the world. The globalized production networks
demands a high level of resilience in the just-in-time (JIT) and just-in-sequence
(JIS) supply chains to minimize the disruption that could derail the efficient
assembly plants' operating systems. As economies of scale are essential for
cost maintenance and competitiveness in passenger vehicle assembly, any
prolonged disruption to the supply chain, whether local or global, is very costly
to car manufacturers.

Localized disruption to the supply chain does happen occasionally, and the
supply chain management of car manufacturers is normally robust enough to
resume assembly at capacity within a short period of time. This is illustrated by
the recent week-long stoppage at BMW's assembly plants in Germany, China
and South Africa. A production bottleneck at Albertini Cesare, an Italian
subcontractor of aluminum castings for electronic steering systems, delayed

Table 4.1   Selected HS nomenclature (2017 edition) on passenger vehicles

HS code	Description
Passenger vehicles:	
87.03	Motor cars and other motor vehicles principally designed for the transport of persons (other than those in chapter 87.02), including station wagons and racing cars
Passenger vehicle parts (including commercial vehicles):	
8706.00	Chassis fitted with engines, for motor vehicles in chapter 87.01 to 87.05
87.07	Bodies (including cabs), for motor vehicles in chapter 87.01 to 87.05
87.08	Parts and accessories of the motor vehicles in chapter 87.01 to 87.05 (including drive shafts, clutches, etc., but excluding engines)
ICEs parts:	
8408.20	Diesel engines of the kind used for the propulsion of vehicles of chapter 87
8409.91	Parts suitable for use solely or principally with spark-ignition internal combustion piston engines
8502.20	Generating sets with spark-ignition for internal combustion piston engines
8503.00	Parts suitable for use solely or principally with the machines, in chapter 85.01 or 85.02
8507.10	Lead-acid of the kind used for starting piston engines
85.11	Electrical ignition or starting equipment of the kind used for spark-ignition or compression-ignition internal combustion engines
8512.20	Other lighting or visual signalling equipment
8512.30	Sound signalling equipment
8512.40	Windscreen wipers, defrosters and demisters
8512.90	Other parts
8544.30	Ignition wiring sets and other wiring sets of the kind used in vehicles, aircraft or ships
For BEVs parts (Not automotive specific):	
85.01	Electric motors and generators
85.06	Primary cells and primary batteries

HS code	Description
For autonomous driving (Not automotive specific):	
85.42	Electronic integrated circuits
8526.10	Radar apparatus
9015	Surveying (including photogrammetrical surveying), hydrographic, oceanographic, hydrological, meteorological or geophysical instruments and appliances, excluding compasses; rangefinders
9006.59	Other (non-cinematographic) cameras
9013.20	Lasers other than laser diodes

Source: Compiled from the World Customs Organization (2017).

a Bosch shipment to BMW. Bosch subsequently acquired the Italian subcontractor to ensure stability of supply (*Automotive News*, 31 May and 1 June 2017). Other stoppages are due to contract disputes between car manufacturers and suppliers. For instance, Volkswagen had to halt the assembly of its Golf and Passat models in ten German plants, as deliveries were interrupted from the only supplier of its seats (CarTrim) and its cast iron parts for gearboxes (ES Automobilguss). UBS estimates that a one-week production stoppage at Volkswagen's Wolfsburg headquarters would result in US$113 million gross profit losses (*Financial Times*, 23 August 2016).

Globalized disruption to supply chains, although rare, could be devastating for car manufacturers. No volume assemblers are vertically integrated car manufacturers, and none have a robust enough supply chain management to withstand a prolonged disruption on a global scale. The 2011 floods in Thailand led to the collapse of a 6 metre high dike in Nikom Rojna Industrial Estate, which housed major manufacturing plants (including Honda). The disruption to the supply chain led to a 5 per cent reduction in global car output and lost sales of US$5 billion (*Financial Times*, 29 May 2020). The ongoing COVID-19 pandemic caused by the highly infectious virus ruptured the supply chains of all global car manufacturers within a month. The automotive industry suffered an unprecedented supply chain shock after the lockdown of Wuhan in China from late January till April 2020, and the subsequent outbreak of COVID-19 worldwide. A major wiring harness supplier stopped production after one of its workers became infected, which resulted in different levels of stoppage on all five assembly plants in South Korea within two weeks: Hyundai Motor and Ssangyong Motor suspended all production in February for a week, and Kia Motors reduced its output from its Hwaseong and Gwangju plants (*South China Morning Post*, 16 May 2020).

As Wuhan is one of the key automotive manufacturing bases in the world, the lockdown of Hubei province created a domino effect on the global supply chains.[10] The Hubei lockdown was also highly disruptive for the operations of parts suppliers and car manufacturers, as more than half of the top 20 global parts makers, such as Robert Bosch, Valeo and ZF Friedrichshafen, have production plants in Hubei (*South China Morning Post*, 5 February 2020). In 2019, China exported US$53 billion of automotive parts and ranked fourth in the world, just behind the traditional automotive powerhouses of Germany, the US and Japan (*South China Morning Post*, 3 April 2020). This explains why other major car manufacturers had to suspend their operations at assembly plants in February and March 2020; for example, Nissan had to close a plant in Japan. Jaguar Land Rover had to ask its staff in China to send car parts by air in suitcases to try to keep its three assembly plants in Castle Bromwich, Solihull and Halewood in the UK operational in March 2020 (*Telegraph*, 18 February 2020). The reality is that selected hardware parts (such as suspension ball-joints and bushes) can be made in small volumes through three-dimensional (3D) printing, but not a number of other parts that demand bespoke designs with exact specifications for each model, for example, wire harness. When the outbreak of COVID-19 spread to Europe and then North America, a number of major car manufacturers and parts suppliers had to temporarily close their plants in the US and Europe in the last quarter of 2020. The stoppage and the unexpected rapid recovery of automobile market in China created a severe shortage of automotive semiconductors and this led to a domino effect on car manufacturers: the slowdown or even stoppage of their assembly lines led to an output reduction of 280 000 vehicles, and this figure could be increased to 500 000 as the global shortage of semiconductors continues in 2021 (*Financial Times*, 26 January 2021).

Furthermore, the current trade friction between the US and China, as well as between the US and Europe, in the automotive sector, has already generated certain preconditions for the decoupling and the return (reshoring) of selected manufacturing to the home market. In addition to the high-profile campaigns by the US government to relocate production from China, the Japanese government announced in April 2020 that it would spend US$2 billion to help its firms to move their production out of China. Although it is way too early to evaluate the longer-term impacts, such reshoring policies are not expected to have an immediate impact on the automotive industry, due to the complex and well-developed supply chains in China, from engines and electrical systems to interior fittings and components. Toyota has already openly declared that it has no plans to deviate from its existing investment strategy in China, presumably in order to maintain a presence in the largest automobile market in the world. Moreover, car manufacturers and their major suppliers have already established assembly and supplier networks in Southeast Asia, especially Thailand and Indonesia, as part of their diversification strategies (*South China Morning Post*, 13 May 2020).[11]

Looking to the future, the impact of megatrends in automobile production is not only about the spatial division of production networks, but also about the establishment of specific technical standards and protocols. The crux of such development is whether the recent political economy concerning such megatrends will lead to some forms of 'national champion' and/or globalized technology platforms for autonomous vehicles and their related development. In the former, all actors have to follow the technical parameters outlined by the 'national champion' endorsed by the home government, while the latter could range from an adaptation of a globalized technology platform to suit the specificities of local markets, to a localizing global alliance where the platform has to be embedded in local markets.

Furthermore, there is also concern about the security of supply of raw materials and minerals that could be part of the supply chains of strategic industries. For instance, heavy rare earths (gadolinium, samarium and yttrium) are used in batteries for electric vehicles and in magnets vital to missile guidance systems. One could argue that the suppliers of rare earths and other strategic products could hold hostile importing countries to ransom. In the case of rare earths, China accounted for 70 per cent of global outputs in 2019, and 59 per cent of imported rare earths used in electronics, guidance systems and wind turbines in the US in 2018 (*South China Morning Post*, 22 May 2019).[12]

Will the pandemic push manufacturing towards decentralized and shorter supply chains, with networks of warehouses located in logistics hubs across space? What may be the financial and socio-economic implications of such diversification strategies, in terms of both the competitiveness of an industry and the regional economy (especially the employment in automotive sectors)? What are the challenges for the reorientation from 'just-in-time' to the 'just-in-case' supply chain management on non-strategic and non-essential goods? To what extent are such challenges industry- and/or region-specific? All these developments will surely have profound implications for the development of mobility-related industries and regional development, and are thus fertile ground for research.

Conclusions

Based on the three emerging megatrends in the automotive industry, this chapter examined the potential challenges posed by technological innovation on the passenger vehicle sector, and how the changing competitive dynamics in the industry could impact on the conceptualization of potential manufacturing research topics. Researchers into manufacturing, especially the automotive industry, need to be aware of the interdependence of the two major emerging research agendas: intersections and the competitive dynamics between industrial sectors, and the local versus global production networks with respect to the resilience (or rupture) of supply chains management.

The electrification of powertrains, digitalization of control systems and autonomous driving are reshaping competitive dynamics in the automotive sector by disrupting the current division of supplies and skills by industrial sectors. The electrification of powertrains eliminates the core competitive advantage of car manufacturers of internal combustion engines (ICEs), and digitalization and autonomous driving promote a high level of intersection between sectors, specifically where expertise is required to integrate microelectronic monitor and control modules and their related software systems into the powertrain's control systems. The megatrends can facilitate the change of business model by both incumbent and new firm actors. As software and (big) data are competitive advantages for autonomous driving, there are signs of car manufacturers crossing over to other sectors: car manufacturers may integrate vertically by developing software in-house or engage in the mobility service directly. On the other hand, technology actors could disrupt the traditional division of skills and competences by providing mobility services to customers and capturing value-added directly.

The emerging megatrends disrupt the existing automotive ecosystem and thus have significant socio-economic and environmental impacts on major automotive economies. The drive for electrification and the emerging business model on mobility as a service is replacing the existing automotive ecosystem based on ICEs, and this is likely to lead to structural unemployment on major automotive economies. Electrification and other potential paths for decarbonization sre not pollution-free. The drive for electrification demands the manufacturing of new cars, which itself consumes energy and raw materials, and its supporting infrastructures (especially high-power charging stations). The phase-out of ICE-driven vehicles will release land used by the petrochemical industry for fuel processing and the refuelling stations. Such land has to be decontaminated before used for other purposes. The production of (lithium-ion) batteries is highly polluting and their recycling is very costly. The circular economy aspects of the automotive industry, including the reuse and repurposing of resources, is a crucial research agenda that has profound long-term societal impacts.

Megatrends in the automotive industry are disruptive, as they not only blur the boundaries between the industrial sectors used in trade and manufacturing statistics (HS, SITC), but also generate opportunities for new entrances (such as microelectronics and battery makers, who are becoming Tier I suppliers), or they may even establish new sectors, for example, car-sharing. The potential impact of artificial intelligence (AI) on autonomous driving muddies the distinction between software and hardware in manufacturing. These megatrends demand that researchers reconceptualize how to reclassify and research manufacturing by industrial sectors, requiring the reclassification of industrial outputs and international trade data, and potentially reviewing the corresponding data collection and research methods for manufacturing.

The automotive industry is one of the most globalized manufacturing sectors, with tens of thousands of key parts and components made by specialized suppliers located all over the world. Supply chain management is not simply a matter of the just-in-time and just-in-sequence delivery; it is also about the resilience of the supply chains to exogenous shocks, including geopolitical factors that may affect the national (in)dependence of strategic sectors. The current trade friction between the US and China has already generated the precondition for decoupling. The COVID-19 pandemic has rung alarm bells by rupturing the automotive global supply chains, resulting in the shutdown of assembly plants in different countries temporarily.

Will the recent political economy surrounding these megatrends lead to some forms of 'national champion' and/or a globalized technology platform for autonomous vehicles and their related development? Will the pandemic push manufacturing towards decentralized supply chains with networks of warehouses located in logistics hubs across space? What are the challenges for the 'just-in-case' supply chain management of non-strategic and non-essential goods? What will the economic implications for the globalized world be?

All these issues call for further research into the intersections and the competitive dynamics between sectors, and the resilience of supply chain management, and the potential impacts of localized supply chains, from their logistics to the industrial (re)structuring of regional economies.

Acknowledgement

The author's research is supported by the NUS Strategic Research Grant (R-109-000-183-646).

Notes

1. In addition to product development and innovation, the changing regulatory environment obviously has an impact on the pace of such megatrends (Bryson and Ronayne, 2014).
2. Absorption capacity is the ability of an actor to identify, value, assimilate and exploit knowledge from the environment (Cohen and Levinthal, 1989, 1990). A related concept is technological capabilities, which is about the knowledge, skills and experience required to generate and manage technical change (Bell and Pavitt, 1993; Dosi, 1988).
3. See Yeung (2016) for a critical review on the operationalization of global production networks.
4. For further details about the WLTP, see https://www.wltpfacts.eu/.
5. Sixty-four per cent of US potential car buyers aged 20-30 do not expected to own a vehicle (Vitale et al., 2017). However, the ongoing COVID-19 pandemic appears to be persuading a proportion of the younger generation to own private vehicles to alleviate their concerns about using public transport. This is especially the case in China, where 65 per cent of under-35 consumers were considering purchasing their own vehicles, according to a survey conducted in April 2020. Subscription-based long-term car-sharing is also gaining market traction in countries with high costs of car ownership (*Financial Times*, 20 May 2020).
6. See Yeung (2019) on Made in China 2025, and on how the Chinese government policy is driving the rapid development of BEVs. Whether electrification is the solution to lessen the environmental impact generated by vehicle mobility is questionable.
7. See SAE International (2018) for the classification of autonomous driving from level 0 to 5.
8. LIDAR (light detection and ranging) is a method of measuring distance by illuminating the target with pulsed laser light and measuring the reflected pulses with a sensor. Camera, radar and LIDAR are widely regarded as complementary sensors for autonomous driving (with the exception of Tesla, as it does not use LIDAR): cameras can see road markings but cannot measure distance; radar can measure distance and velocity but is unable to provide detailed images; while LIDAR provides high-resolution 3D maps but is expensive and could be interfered with by snow.
9. Research could use concordance tables to convert HS into SITC and other commonly used systems of nomenclature, but this may create even more noise in the data. One such concordance table is prepared by Jon Haveman, https://www.macalester.edu/research/economics/PAGE/HAVEMAN/Trade.Resources/TradeConcordances.html#FromHS.

10. Wuhan is the fourth-largest automotive manufacturing base after Shanghai, Beijing and Guangzhou in China. Hubei is also the key manufacturing hub for electronics and pharmaceuticals.

11. According to the annual survey conducted by the American Chamber of Commerce in Shanghai, 5.1 per cent of its members with global revenues over US$500 million plan to leave China, while another 57.5 per cent are operating with the strategy of focusing on China (*South China Morning Post*, 9 September 2020).

12. Rare earths consist of 17 elements and are used for various manufacturing processes, from precision polishes and to add special optical properties in glass production (cerium, lanthanum and lutetium), and in manufacturing flat panel display screens (yttrium, cerium, lanthanum, europium and terbium), to removing impurities in steelmaking, and making phosophers used in incandescent and LED lights.

References

Amabile, Teresa M. (1988) 'A model of creativity and innovation in organizations', *Research in Organizational Behavior* 10: 123–167.

Becattini, G. (1992) 'The Marshallian industrial district as a socio-economic notion', in Pyke, F., Becattini, G. and Sengenberger, W. (eds), *Industrial Districts and Inter-Firm Co-operation in Italy*. Geneva: International Institute for Labour Studies, pp. 37–51.

Bell, M. and Pavitt, K. (1993) 'Technological accumulation and industrial growth: contrasts between developed and developing countries', *Industrial and Corporate Change* 2(1): 157–210.

Bollhorn, K. and Franz, M. (2016) 'Production network knowledge as a foundation for resistance – workers influence on a Chinese acquisition in Germany', *Tijdschrift voor Economische en Sociale Geografie* 107: 407–420.

Bower, Joseph L. and Christensen, Clayton M. (1995) 'Disruptive technologies: catching the wave', *Harvard Business Review* 73(1): 43–53.

Bryson, John R. and Ronayne, Megan (2014) 'Manufacturing carpets and technical textiles: routines, resources, capabilities, adaptation, innovation and the evolution of the British textile industry', *Cambridge Journal of Regions, Economy and Society* 7(3): 471–488.

Camagni, R (1991) 'Local milieu, uncertainty and innovation networks: towards a new dynamic theory of economic space', in Camagni, R. (ed.), *Innovation Networks: Spatial Perspectives*, London: Belhaven-Pinter, pp. 121–144.

Carlsson, B., Jacobsson, S., Holmén, M. and Rickne, A. (2002) 'Innovation system: analytical and methodological issues', *Research Policy* 31(2): 233–245.

Carrillo, J. (2004) 'Transnational strategies and regional development: the case of GM and Delphi in Mexico', *Industry and Innovation* 11: 127–153.

Chatelain, A., Erriquez, M., Moulière, P-Y. and Schäfer, P. (2018) 'What a teardown of the latest electric vehicles reveals about the future of mass-market EVs', *Trends in Electric Vehicle Design* 2. https://www.mckinsey.com/industries/automotive-and-assembly/our-insights/what-a-teardown-of-the-latest-electric-vehicles-reveals-about-the-future-of-mass-market-evs (accessed 17 June 2020).

Chesbrough, H. (2003) *Open Innovation: The New Imperative for Creating and Profiting from Technology*. Boston, MA: Harvard Business School Press.

Clark, K.B. and T. Fujimoto (1991) *Product Development Performance: Strategy, Organization, and Management in the World Automobile Industry*. Boston, MA: Harvard Business School Press.

Coe, N. and Yeung, H.W.C. (2015) *Global Production Networks: Theorizing Economic Development in an Interconnected World*. Oxford: Oxford University Press.

Cohen, W.M. and Levinthal, D.A. (1989) 'Innovation and learning: the two faces of R and D', *Economic Journal* 99(397): 569–596.

Cohen, W.M. and Levinthal, D.A. (1990) 'Absorptive capacity: a new perspective on learning and innovation', *Administrative Science Quarterly* 35(1): 128–152.

Contreras, O.F., Carrillo, J. and Alonso, J. (2012) 'Local entrepreneurship within global value chains: a case study in the Mexican automotive industry', *World Development* 40: 1013–1023.

Cooke, P., Gomez Uranga, M. and Etxebarria, G. (1997) 'Regional innovation systems: institutional and organisational dimensions', *Research Policy* 26(4–5): 475–491.

Docherty M. (2006) 'Primer on "open innovation": principles and practice', *Vision PDMA* (Product Development and Management Association) April: 13–17.

Dosi, G. (1988) 'Sources, procedures, and microeconomic effects of innovation', *Journal of Economic Literature* 26(3): 1120–1171.

Ernst, D., and Kim, L. (2002) 'Global production networks, knowledge diffusion, and local capability formation', *Research Policy* 31: 1417–1429.

Freeman, C. (1995) 'The National Innovation Systems in historical perspective', *Cambridge Journal of Economics*, 19: 5–24.

Freeman, C. and Lundvall, B.-Å. (eds) (1988) *Small Countries Facing the Technological Revolution*. London: Pinter.

Gao, P., Hensley, R., and Zielke, A. (2014) 'A road map to the future for the auto industry', *McKinsey Quarterly*, October. https://www.mckinsey.com/industries/automotive-and-assembly/our-insights/a-road-map-to-the-future-for-the-auto-industry.

Herrigel, G. (2004) 'Emerging strategies and forms of governance in high-wage component manufacturing regions', *Industry and Innovation* 11: 45–79.

Hobday, M. (1998) 'Product complexity, innovation and industrial organization', *Research Policy* 26(6): 689–710.

Humphrey, J. (2003) 'Globalization and supply chain networks: the auto-industry in Brazil and India', *Global Networks* 3: 121–141.

Humphrey, J. and Memedovic, O. (2003) *The Global Automotive Industry Value Chain: What Prospects for Upgrading by Developing Countries?* Vienna: UNIDO Sectoral Studies Series.

Humphrey, J. and Schmitz, H. (2002) 'How does insertion in global value chains affect upgrading in industrial clusters?' *Regional Studies* 36(9): 1017–1027.

Humphrey, J. and Schmitz, H. (2004) 'Chain governance and upgrading: taking stock', in ed. Schmitz, H. (ed.), *Local Enterprises in the Global Economy: Issues of Governance and Upgrading*. Cheltenham, UK and Northampton, MA, USA: Edward Elgar Publishing, pp. 349–382.

Ivarsson, I. and Alvstam, C.G. (2005) 'The effect of spatial proximity on technology transfer from MNCs to local suppliers in developing countries: the case of AB Volvo in Asia and Latin America', *Economic Geography* 81: 83–112.

Jaffe, A.B. and Trajtenberg, M. (1999) 'International knowledge flows; evidence from patent citations', *Economics of Innovation and New Technology* 8(1): 105–136.

Kaplinsky, R. and Morris, M. (2001) *A Handbook for Value Chain Research* (Vol. 113). Ottawa: IDRC.

Kerry, Cameron F. and Karsten, Jack (2017) 'Gauging investment in self-driving cars', *Bookings Institution*, 16 October. https://www.brookings.edu/research/gauging-investment-in-self-driving-cars/.

Lagendijk, A. (2006) 'Learning from conceptual flow in regional studies: framing present debates, unbracketing past debates', *Regional Studies* 40(4): 385–399.

Landry, C. and Bianchini, F. (1995) *The Creative City*. London: Demos.

Liu, Y. (2017) 'The dynamics of local upgrading in globalizing latecomer regions: a geographical analysis', *Regional Studies* 51: 880–893.

Lundvall, B-Å. (ed.) (1992) *National Systems of Innovation: Towards a Theory of Innovation and Interactive Learning*. London: Pinter.

Lundvall, B.-Å. and Johnson, B. (1994) 'The learning economy', *Journal of Industry Studies* 1(2): 23–42.

Morgan, K. (1997) 'The learning region: institutions, innovation and regional renewal', *Regional Studies* 31(5): 491–503.

Nelson, Richard R. (ed.) (1993) *National Innovation Systems: A Comparative Analysis*. Oxford: Oxford University Press.

Orlando, M.J. (2004) 'Measuring spillovers from industrial R&D: on the importance of geographic and technological proximity', *RAND Journal of Economics* 35(4): 777–786.

Özatağan, G. (2011) 'Shifts in value chain governance and upgrading in the European periphery of automotive production: evidence from Bursa, Turkey', *Environment and Planning A* 43: 885–903.

Pizzuto, Luca C.T., Wang, A. and Wu, T. (2019) 'How China will help fuel the revolution in autonomous vehicles', *McKinsey & Company*, 25 January. https://www.mckinsey.com/industries/automotive-and-assembly/our-insights/how-china-will-help-fuel-the-revolution-in-autonomous-vehicles.

Radjou, N., Prabhu, J. and Ahuja, S. (2012) *Jugaad Innovation: Think Frugal, Be Flexible, Generate Breakthrough Growth*. New York: Wiley.

Sadler, D. (1998) 'Changing inter-firm relations in the European automotive industry: dependence or enhanced autonomy for components producers?', *European Urban and Regional Studies* 5: 317–328.

SAE International (2018) 'SAE International releases updated visual chart for its "levels of driving automation" standard for self-driving vehicles'. https://www.sae.org/news/press-room/2018/12/sae-international-releases-updated-visual-chart-for-its-'levels-of-driving-automation'-standard-for-self-driving-vehicles.

Schmitt, A. and Van Biesebroeck, J. (2013) 'Proximity strategies in outsourcing relations: the role of geographical, cultural and relational proximity in the European automotive industry', *Journal of International Business Studies* 44(5): 475–503.

SITC revision 4 (2007) https://unstats.un.org/unsd/trade/sitcrev4.htm.

Sturgeon, T.J., Memedovic, O., Van Biesebroeck, J. and Gereffi, G. (2009) 'Globalisation of the automotive industry: main features and trends', *International Journal of Technological Learning, Innovation and Development* 2: 7–24.

Sturgeon, T., Van Biesebroeck, J. and Gereffi, G (2008) 'Value chains, networks and clusters: reframing the global automotive industry', *Journal of Economic Geography* 8(3): 297–321.

Teece, D.J. (1996) 'Firm organization, industrial structure, and technological innovation', *Journal of Economic Behavior and Organization* 31: 193–224.

UBS (2017) 'UBS evidence lab electric car teardown – disruption ahead?' 18 May. https://neo.ubs.com/shared/d1wkuDlEbYPjF/ (accessed 1 January 2018).

Vitale Jr, J., Giffi, C.A., Pingitore, G., Robinson, R., Schmith, S. and Gangula, B. (2017) 'What's ahead for fully autonomous driving', *Deloitte*. https://www2.deloitte.com/cn/en/pages/consumer-industrial-products/articles/fully-autonomous-driving.html.

Wappelhorst, S. and Cui, H. (2020) 'Growing momentum: global overview of government targets for phasing out sales of new internal combustion engine vehicles', *International Council on Clean Transportation (ICCT)*, 11 November. https://theicct.org/blog/staff/global-ice-phaseout-nov2020 (accessed 27 February 2021).

World Customs Organization (2017) *HS Nomenclature (2017 edition)*. http://www.wcoomd.org/en/topics/nomenclature/instrument-and-tools/hs-nomenclature-2017-edition/hs-nomenclature-2017-edition.aspx.

Yeung, Godfrey (2016) 'The operation of global production networks (GPNs) 2.0 and methodological constraints', *Geoforum* 75: 265–269.

Yeung, Godfrey (2019) '"Made in China 2025": the development of a new energy vehicle industry in China', *Area Development and Policy* 4(1): 39–59.

5 Getting the right skills in place for manufacturing: challenges and opportunities

Anne Green and Abigail Taylor

Introduction

Although employment in manufacturing is declining and comprises a minority part of most economies in the Global North, it remains important to consider skills for manufacturing as they relate to broader questions concerning human capital, skills utilisation and uneven regional development. Key questions concerning skills in manufacturing have been explored differently in the economics, education, geography and regional development, and sociology literatures. Core themes developed in economics include human capital and decision-making on training to enhance its development. The sociology literature has focused on work-life balance and precarity within the manufacturing sector. A key theme in the geography and regional development literature is analysis of the spatial division of labour in manufacturing. The education literature examines different configurations of training, raising questions regarding how training and lifelong learning may change in future, including as recovery from the impact of the COVID-19 pandemic progresses. This chapter seeks to build on these literatures by bringing the debates together to offer new insights into critical issues relating to the future of manufacturing.

The importance of manufacturing to national and regional economies varies markedly. According to Organisation for Economic Co-operation and Development (OECD) statistics, the share of gross domestic product (GDP) accounted for by manufacturing in major countries is greatest in South Korea (30 per cent), China (29 per cent), Germany (23 per cent), Japan (21 per cent), Turkey (21 per cent) and India (21 per cent). These shares contrast with much smaller proportions in the United States (US) (12 per cent), France (11 per cent) and the United Kingdom (UK) (10 per cent) (Rhodes, 2020). The medium-term trend is one of a reduction in employment in manufacturing relative to services in many countries and regions, coupled with output and productivity growth. However, the extent of the reduction in employment in manufacturing varies between countries and regions.

This chapter draws mainly on evidence from the UK to illustrate selected broader issues of more generic relevance across countries and regions about skills needs in manufacturing and policies to meet changing skills requirements. The UK experience provides a particularly apt focus for this chapter because it illustrates key challenges faced in getting skills in place in the context of an overall decrease in employment in manufacturing. It shares similarities with the United States of America (USA) and many other European countries in terms of an age profile skewed towards older age groups. This is an issue that China is facing increasingly as a consequence of its one-child policy. This raises the issue of the extent to which technology will continue to replace labour in the years ahead. Germany, the manufacturing powerhouse of Europe, has the highest robot intensity (calculated as the industrial stock of robots by manufacturing value added) among European countries (Duell and Vetter, 2020).

The next section of this chapter provides a contextual overview charting key trends in employment in manufacturing, sets out the persistence of skills deficiencies and highlights key policy interventions aimed at getting skills in place. The third section examines changing skills needs in more detail, focusing on the types and mix of skills required in manufacturing now and in the future. The fourth section outlines key disciplinary perspectives on skills in manufacturing, including from economics, geography and regional development, sociology and education. The fifth section presents a future research agenda, focusing on three key issues relating to skills in manufacturing: making manufacturing an attractive sector, accessing and developing skills for the future and the role of new types of training, and skills utilisation. The final section draws conclusions.

Context

Table 5.1 presents data on employment trends in manufacturing in selected countries in the Global North. It shows that employment in manufacturing has been falling over the past two decades, although a small increase in employment was evident in some countries between 2015 and 2019.

Table 5.1   Employment in manufacturing in selected countries, 2005–19 (000s)

Country	2005	2010	2015	2019	% change, 2005-2019	% change, 2015-2019
France	4 015	3 373	3 221	3 194	-20.45	-0.84
Germany	8 017	7 580	7 759	8 013	-0.05	3.27
UK	3 780	2 865	2 993	2 990	-20.90	-0.10
USA	16 253	14 081	15 338	15 741	-3.15	2.63

Source: OECD (2020).

Key trends in employment and skills: insights from the UK

As indicated above, changing patterns of employment and skills in the UK are typical of many Western economies (with the exception of Germany), as they have deindustrialised. Over the long term, the number of jobs in manufacturing in the UK has more than halved in absolute terms over the last four decades. In 1981, there were 5.7 million jobs in manufacturing, comprising 23 per cent of total employment. By the early 2000s, there were around 3.5 million jobs in manufacturing, making up 11 per cent of total employment. A further shakeout of 1 million jobs in the following ten years brought the share total employment accounted for by manufacturing down to around 8 per cent. The number of jobs in manufacturing in the UK rose slightly over the period from the Great Recession to 2.7 million at the end of 2019.

In 2020, the COVID-19 crisis delivered a shock to the whole economy, with the manufacturing sector among the hardest hit. The UK Government announced the Coronavirus Job Retention Scheme (CJRS)[1] in March 2020 to support employers through the initial impact of the COVID-19 crisis, enabling employers to claim initially for furloughed employees with up to 80 per cent of their employees' salary, capped at £2500 per month per employee. Official statistics on the CJRS released in August 2020 covering the period from March to June 2020 indicate that out of 99 000 eligible employers in manufacturing in the UK, 74 800 furloughed staff, representing a scheme take-up rate of 76 per cent. This contrasts with a take-up rate of 61 per cent for eligible employers across all sectors in the UK. In all, 1.02 million employments in manufacturing were furloughed: a take-up rate of 42 per cent, compared with a take-up rate of 32 per cent across all sectors in the UK.

Although employment in manufacturing has declined over the medium and long term in the UK, there are significant job opportunities opening up. So called 'replacement demand' arises as a result of retirements, career moves, net geographical mobility and other reasons for leaving employment in a particular sector. A workforce with many people approaching statutory retirement age usually implies much higher replacement needs than a younger workforce (*ceteris paribus*). Working Futures projections for 2017 to 2027, although formulated while policies regarding Brexit remained uncertain and before the COVID-19 crisis, illustrate this general point. While a reduction of nearly 260 000 manufacturing jobs is projected to 2027, replacement demand projections suggest over 730 000 new job openings, with projected gross value added (GVA) growth of 0.9 per cent per annum for the manufacturing sector and productivity growth of 1.9 per cent per annum (Wilson et al., 2020).

One important factor driving replacement demand in manufacturing is the relatively older age profile of the workforce. Relative to the age and gender profile of the UK workforce on average, the manufacturing sector is characterised by an over-representation of males, especially in the 50 and over age groups (Boys, 2019). Females are under-represented in manufacturing in all age groups relative to the UK average.

Skills deficiencies

Survey evidence indicates that skills deficiencies are more prevalent in manufacturing than across the economy as a whole (Winterbotham et al., 2018). Such deficiencies on the external labour market are manifest as skills shortage vacancies. They are evident as skills gaps in the internal labour market when existing staff do not possess all of the skills required to do their job. Brexit may further exacerbate the extent of skills deficiencies, given uncertainty over future immigration policy. There is concern that employers may not yet understand the employment issues they will face as a result of post-Brexit mobility restrictions (De Ruyter et al., 2020). Small manufacturers in particular may struggle to cover the costs associated with foreign skilled labour (Make UK, 2019a).

Skill shortage vacancies (that is, vacancies which employers find hard to fill due to a lack of the required skills, qualifications or experience among applicants) accounted for 22 per cent of all vacancies in the UK in 2017 according to the Employer Skills Survey (Winterbotham et al., 2018), but for 29 per cent of all vacancies in manufacturing. This share of skill shortage vacancies in total vacancies has remained persistent in recent years at around three in every ten vacancies. Occupations where skill shortage vacancies have been most prevalent in manufacturing are skilled trades occupations and professional occupations, where skill shortage vacancies accounted for 40 per cent and 38 per cent of all vacancies in 2017, respectively. Relative to the occupational pattern of skill shortage vacancies across the economy as a whole, manufacturing records a particularly large share of skill shortage vacancies in professional occupations. The main impacts of skill shortage vacancies are increased workloads for other staff, difficulties in meeting customer services objectives, loss of business orders to competitors, an increase in operating costs, and delays in developing new products or services.

Turning to skills gaps, in 2017 employers in the manufacturing sector reported 5.8 per cent of the current workforce as being not fully proficient in their roles. This was the second-highest proportion in any sector. Occupations in manufacturing recording the highest prevalence of skills gaps were machine operatives and elementary roles requiring knowledge and experience to perform mostly routine tasks rather than formal qualifications. The single most important reason for skills gaps is that staff are new to their role and are not fully trained. Non-transient causes, such as staff lacking motivation, and either staff not improving sufficiently in their performance after receiving training or not receiving appropriate training, also contribute to skills gaps. The impact of skills gaps is felt in terms of increased workloads for other staff, increased operating costs, difficulties in meeting quality standards and difficulties in introducing new working practices.

Getting skills in place: key policies

Ensuring that the manufacturing sector has the skills that it needs is the subject of ongoing policy initiatives. Some of these focus on the supply side. Of central relevance here is making manufacturing an attractive sector, for young people moving from education to employment, for labour market re-entrants, and for workers moving between sectors. There is considerable policy emphasis on the role of apprenticeships in the UK and in other countries.

While the supply of skills is clearly important, how skills are utilised in practice is crucial for improving overall productivity. There is some evidence from the UK Employer Skills Survey that the proportion of employers reporting employees with underutilised skills is increasing over time (Winterbotham et al., 2018). So while skills policy focuses rightly on skills development (in order that workers are able to rise to the changing demands of employers), policy for improving overall productivity needs to consider the demand for, as well as the supply of, skills.

Linking both supply and demand, a key issue going forwards is (re)building the role of industrial commons. These are the research and development

(R&D) and manufacturing infrastructure, know-how, process development skills, and engineering and manufacturing capabilities resulting from the clustering of universities, suppliers and manufacturers in those manufacturing industries in which rapidly developing innovations in processes and process technologies are taking place (Pisano and Shih, 2012). This requires government, manufacturing (and related) companies, and education and training providers to develop and nurture an ecosystem for the common good where they work together to support the development and application of skills in manufacturing-related technologies, helping to ensure the symbiotic generation of basic, applied and commercial research that is key to innovation and commercialisation.

Changing skills needs

This section reviews changing skills requirements in manufacturing in the context of broader changes across the economy as a whole. It draws on projections of employment, the literature on the changing type and mix of skills required, and in-depth interviews with selected employers undertaken in 2019.

The type and mix of skills required by employers in manufacturing are changing, creating challenges and opportunities. Many of these trends are not unique to, but have special significance for manufacturing. Across most Western economies the average level of qualifications is rising in all occupations as people stay in education for longer and acquire more higher-level qualifications. The numbers in employment by qualification level represent both supply and demand.

The changing occupational structure of manufacturing in the UK illustrates some insights into the main features of changing skills needs, with a medium-term increase in professional and associate professional and technical occupations, and a decline in administrative and secretarial occupations, skilled trades occupations, and for plant and machine operatives. The occupational structure of employment varies regionally, illustrating a continuing spatial division of labour. In 2017, nearly 38 per cent of jobs in manufacturing in the UK were in managerial, professional and associate professional and technical occupations, associated with higher skills levels and longer periods of required training. In the West Midlands (one of the regions with the highest proportions of manufacturing employment in the UK) the share was 31 per cent, while in the South East the share was nearly 52 per cent. By contrast, skilled trades occupations accounted for 23 per cent of manufacturing jobs in the UK, but for 27 per cent in the West Midlands, and 19 per cent in the South East. These illustrative regional variations in occupational structure reflect the detailed industrial composition of manufacturing and occupational change (Wilson et al., 2020).

Changes in type of skills required

Technological change, globalisation and public policy are among the key external drivers of changing skills needs in manufacturing, while business strategies dictate skills requirements internally within the firm. Product quality and an emphasis on customer service are key factors here. Looking ahead, shifts will likely occur in formal qualifications (for example, degrees and technical certificates), knowledge (subject-matter expertise) and workplace skills (for example, management, critical thinking and digital skills). Knowledge may become less important as it becomes easier to access online and better embedded in automated systems (Bakhshi et al., 2017). Predicted accelerating growth in skills demand across sectors by 2030 (McKinsey, 2019) will increase the need for interpersonal and higher cognitive skills, including decision-making, creativity and complex problem-solving (Bakhshi et al., 2017). Employees will be required to spend less time on tasks requiring physical, manual and basic cognitive skills, and more time on tasks necessitating social and emotional skills (for example, leadership, teaching and training others) (McKinsey, 2019). In turn, demand for higher-level skills is expected to increase.

Within advanced manufacturing, 2.2 million jobs in the UK could remain unfilled due to a lack of adequately trained labour. Skills most needed are digital fluency; ability to write and understand code; ability to program manufacturing-specific machines and devices; experience in machining, fabricating and complex assembly; big data analytics; robotics soft skills; and industry-specific credentials. Science, technology, engineering and mathematics (STEM) skills core to manufacturing are likely to be among those in short supply, with underskilling expected in areas including mathematics, computer science and electronics (McKinsey, 2019).

A new wave of production models where digitalisation and digital services overlay manufacturing production is emerging, termed Industry 4.0. The manufacturing sector implements Industry 4.0 through smart manufacturing in fields including the Internet of Things, big data, cyber physical systems, machine learning, additive manufacturing and robotics (Ahuett-Garza and Kurfess, 2018). Ensuring employees can utilise technology fully to maximise return on investment will require employees to develop new competences in smart manufacturing techniques.

By 2030, severe shortages are predicted in basic digital, core management and STEM skills across the UK. By 2030, 5 million workers in the UK could be acutely underskilled across sectors in basic digital skills, and up to two-thirds of the workforce may be partially underskilled (McKinsey, 2019). For the advanced manufacturing sector, access to such skills will be crucial. Regions able to supply such skills will be at a significant advantage.

Leadership and management skills expected to be in short supply across sectors include leadership, communication, negotiation and critical thinking skills. Direct positive relationships exist in the manufacturing sector between the quality of leadership management and business outcomes (Homkes, 2014). The 2017 Management and Expectations Survey of 25 000 production and services enterprises identified a significant correlation between management practices and labour productivity. The UK stands out internationally for the low percentage of managers and non-managers with degrees. Management and leadership skills are particularly acute in the manufacturing sector (Homkes, 2014). MAKE, the UK Manufacturer's Association, contends that poor management practices are playing a part in underinvestment in capital equipment and, in turn, limiting productivity growth (Make UK, 2019b).

In-depth interviews in 2019 with manufacturing companies on skills system challenges, including access to skills and training at local level, revealed large companies as more likely than smaller companies to prioritise investing in management and leadership skills. Firms justified their long-term investment in such skills by stressing how the quality of managers is crucially important for skills development. A large digital technologies company stressed the importance of creativity skills (for example, creating a vision) as technology becomes powerful in developing solutions (Green and Taylor, 2020).

A key driver of changes in skills requirements is increased automation and the adoption of artificial intelligence (AI) (McKinsey, 2019). By 2021, approximately half of all global devices and connections are expected to be machine-to-machine (Cisco, 2019). Low- and middle-skilled roles in manufacturing are at increasing risk of automation (Bakhshi et al., 2017).

Longer working lives will increase the need for upskilling and retraining of employees, particularly in the context of rapidly changing technology. This may be exacerbated by the predicted acute shortage in teaching and training skills across sectors (McKinsey, 2019).

Change in mix of skills required

In addition to upskilling requirements, an arguably even greater demand is emerging for individuals and companies to develop a mix of skills. Changes are expected in the type of technical skills required, and other skills required alongside them. Most employers continue to prioritise recruiting employees with technical skills, and supporting employees to develop them. The increased speed with which technical skills are changing, together with greater pressure from clients to realise tasks 'cheaper, faster and smarter', is resulting in specific technical skills having to be developed at the point of need in order for new skills to be utilised immediately (Green and Taylor, 2020).

Looking ahead, a greater focus is expected on employees possessing social and emotional skills, analytical and interpretative skills, and digital skills to adapt to changing job requirements (Lyons et al., 2020). The exact mix of skills required will vary by location and subsector. For example, a large food manufacturer interviewed in 2019 prioritised developing rounded managers who have strong technical skills alongside strong softer skills (for example, negotiation skills for sales people, and wider team leadership skills including being able to hold difficult conversations). A large advanced engineering company looked for digital competence and awareness alongside other skills in most roles across the business.

Implications for training

Changing skills needs and mixes of skills required impact on training requirements. In-depth interviews with employers in different manufacturing subsectors in 2019 indicated how some companies are trying to develop these skills. Using business plans to design time-frames for skills planning appears to be critical. For example, as part of a restructuring process, a large food manufacturer realised the need to formalise skill development policy and implement short-, medium- and long-term skills planning to address skills deficiencies and drive company growth. Large firms appear to have greater capacity to switch from focusing solely on immediate skills needs to also developing longer-term approaches (Green and Taylor, 2020). Taking a longer-term approach to skills planning was motivated by fundamentally wanting to know 'the challenges that will affect us and the skills and capabilities that are going to be needed for the future', while an emphasis on tackling immediate skills needs reflected the pace of technological change and business developments. However, when introducing new training courses, even some large firms have encountered internal resistance among some managers to release staff for training. This resistance particularly occurs for softer skills, due to managers' primary focus on operational delivery, or concern over the costs involved in training and the primary need to generate revenue (Green and Taylor, 2020).

Disciplinary perspectives on skills in manufacturing

Different disciplinary perspectives further the understanding of how skills requirements in manufacturing have changed over recent decades in the context of broader changes across the UK economy.

Economics literature

Several theories discuss the shift from economies based on manufacturing to those based on service industries. They suggest that many services have limited potential for high productivity growth, and could be termed 'stagnant' in terms of productivity (Baumol, 1967; Baumol et al., 1985; Williamson, 1991). This implies that the observed slowdown in productivity growth is the consequence of the progressive shift to a 'post-industrial' service economy. Numerous service roles act as intermediary inputs to the manufacturing sector, contributing to increasing to productivity levels within the manufacturing sector and offering the scope to increase their own productivity (Oulton, 2001).

However, the main arguments focused upon here relate to human capital. The economics literature contributes to the understanding of decision-making regarding skills, through its focus on human capital and decision-making on training to enhance human capital. Blundell et al. (1999) distinguish three components of human capital: firstly, early ability (whether acquired or innate); secondly, qualifications and knowledge acquired through formal education; and thirdly, those skills, competences and expertise acquired on the job. However, the market value of human capital changes over time as jobs themselves and the broader work environment changes. Technical skills obsolescence occurs as workers' human capital deteriorates through lack of use and failure to reinvest (De Grip and Van Loo, 2002). Skills obsolescence is a particularly important issue for advanced manufacturing because of its intensive use of human capital, so highlighting the importance of lifelong learning.

From an economics perspective, decisions regarding investment in human capital are shaped by the rate of return expected from that investment. An individual might invest in non-compulsory education and training with a view to reaping higher earnings later, while a firm might invest in workforce training over and above minimal regulatory requirements to achieve productivity and broader performance gains for the business. An economically rational employer will seek to secure the skills it requires at the lowest price possible (Green and Hogarth, 2016). Such an employer will seek to invest in firm-specific skills (Becker, 1964), rather than generic transferable skills that other employers could acquire without such investment (for instance, via poaching). In simple terms, then, economic theory suggests that the state should invest in generic skills (through supply-side policies) and employers should invest in firm-specific ones.

Wilson and Hogarth (2003) argue that the equilibrium level of skills demand has settled at a lower level than policymakers consider desirable, especially in the UK. Hence policies are required to increase the demand for skills. In turn this means supporting employers to identify those skills that they would benefit from, and in turn communicate that demand to training providers in order to help overcome coordination failures in the skills system (Weaver and Osterman, 2017). The concept of a manufacturer's product market strategy is also relevant here. Some manufacturers have a product market strategy that does not require high-level skills. For example, in case studies from the food processing sector, Wilson and Hogarth (2003) distinguished between a low-value-added subsector where standard-quality foods are sold at a low margin driven by downward pressure from retailers to push down prices, and a premium-quality subsector where skills and knowledge are vitally important to maintain high standards. In the former subsector, issues faced by employers in accessing labour related more to low wages than to a lack of skills; whereas for the latter, investment in skills development was important. In the former subsector, improving skills without any change in product market strategy and work organisation would lead to overqualification and skill underutilisation.

It is possible to raise demand for skills by transitioning to a higher-value-added product market strategy. An example is the footwear sector in the Riviera del Brenta in northern Italy where a move into a high-quality, high-value-added market was supported by technical research at local educational institutions, and where trade unions played a supportive role in helping to improve working conditions (Froy et al., 2012). This example demonstrates a supportive local skills ecosystem in action.

Sociology literature

Studies examining work–life balance offer insights into key issues relating to the future of manufacturing. While most studies of work–life balance focus on how work impacts on non-work life, some evidence exists of positive and negative spillovers from work to non-work life within the manufacturing sector (Blyton and Jenkins, 2012; Guest, 2002). New forms of inequality are emerging because of the casualisation and recommodification of labour in the Global North as manufacturing firms relocate overseas (Blyton and Jenkins, 2012; Glucksmann, 2009). Blyton and Jenkins's study of the experiences of a largely female manufacturing workforce working full-time made redundant by factory relocation shows how most of the workforce subsequently found alternative employment, mainly in part-time service sector jobs.

Technology means work can be increasingly detached from place (Messenger and Gschwind, 2016). Studies suggest that supporting remote working and work-life balance among employees is beneficial for employers and employees. Across sectors, an association exists between remote working, higher organisational commitment, job satisfaction and job-related well-being. Increased work intensification and inability to stop thinking about work are, however, trade-offs (Felstead and Henseke, 2017). There is evidence that employee-friendly companies, including in the manufacturing sector, have better financial performance and lower risk compared to other companies (Blazovich et al., 2014). This literature helps to frame discussion about the consequences of COVID-19 on work-life balance, job satisfaction and productivity in the manufacturing sector (Wilson, 2020).

Existing literature also examines precarity (Standing, 2009, 2011) within the manufacturing sector. Hopkins (2012) examined how precarity plays out in terms of absence rates in the food manufacturing industry in the UK. The study found that variations in absence rates between directly employed temporary workers and agency workers are the consequence of varying levels of managerial absence control, with agency workers using absence as a way of escaping a low-skilled and monotonous work environment. Ensuring there is a reliable workforce in roles with lower requirements for training is more crucial and challenging in the context of the UK leaving the European Union and the recovery from the COVID-19 crisis. Bailey and De Ruyter's (2012) longitudinal study of former workers at the MG Rover car plant considers the experiences of UK autoworkers in the context of globalisation driving employment precariousness. The paper indicated a need for 'policy measures that go beyond reliance on a flexible labour market to address the inequities faced by workers in such situations' (ibid., p. 153).

Geography/regional development literature

The geography/regional development literature contributes to understanding of the manufacturing sector through analysis of the spatial division of labour. Historically, regional economic development in the UK economy has been uneven (Gardiner et al., 2013), with a North-South divide prominent in regional development debates.

A number of regional growth theories focus on industry structure and 'regional competitiveness' effects in spatially unbalanced growth. Kaldor's (1970, 1981) models of regional growth place the competitiveness of a region's export base at the heart of regional growth. They emphasise the role of spatial agglomeration in enhancing productivity and competitiveness, stressing how having a geographical concentration of skills was important alongside the ready communication of trade and managerial know-how, possibilities for joint production between specialised firms, and possibilities for monitoring other, competing firms' behaviour. Rowthorn's (2010) model of uneven and combined regional development suggests that the strength of a region's export base is the primary determiner of its long-term prosperity. He argues that migration flows affect regional stocks of human capital, with outflows of more skilled and educated workers creating negative multiplier effects on local business and employment. He suggests that this explains the creation and persistence of the North-South divide. Work associated with 'new economic geography' models implies that policies that aim to reduce regional economic inequality may be nationally inefficient (Martin, 2008).

Data indicates structural change in southern and northern British cities over the last few decades. The South East (apart from certain parts of London), the South West and East Anglia have been 'less vulnerable' to de-industrialisation and experienced more rapid growth in high technology and service industries (Martin, 1988). Despite faster falls in manufacturing employment in cities in the North than the South, manufacturing retains a larger share of total employment in the North. Growth in knowledge-intensive business services in northern cities has not matched that in southern cities (Keeble and Walker, 1994; Martin et al., 2018). The fortunes of industrial towns are 'sharply' differentiated from other places due to their continuing reliance on industrial employment (Beatty and Fothergill, 2020). The authors call for policy rebalancing national economic growth towards manufacturing, which remains the backbone of older industrial economies.

The literature provides further insight into skills issues in manufacturing. The low availability of skilled labour can be a barrier to reshoring (Vanchan et al., 2017). Reshoring in the UK is limited particularly by a lack of skilled labour, with some commentators calling for wider industrial policy to prioritise building manufacturing capacity (Bailey and De Propris, 2014). Several factors cited as being important for the development of a phoenix industry in old industrial areas relate to skills: the presence of relevant skills in the local labour force and in (potential) supplier firms; and technical skills and expertise in nearby colleges, universities and other training or research facilities. Retaining relevant skills even when larger firms in the region are lost is a key contributory factor in the development of a phoenix industry. There is a challenge in balancing traditional skills with new knowledge and skills necessary for the development and exploitation of new technologies (Amison and Bailey, 2014).

Education literature

The education literature is useful in understanding how training trends in manufacturing may change in future, including following a recession. Felstead and Jewson's (2014) conceptual framework for mapping and understanding training trends emphasises differences between different configurations of training, using the metonyms of 'floors' and 'ceilings'. The framework enables greater understanding of the factors that contribute to employers' decisions regarding whether to increase, decrease or maintain training activity during a recession. Examination of the impact of the 2008–09 recession on training activity in the UK found that the recession prompted many employers to find innovative ways of maintaining training coverage to meet these obligations, while reducing costs (for example, through group or block bookings for training) (Felstead et al., 2012). A key question is whether employers in the manufacturing sector will find similar ways to train smarter following the COVID-19 pandemic. Research also found that UK employers in some low-skill manufacturing sectors confined training to basic, mandatory training such as health and safety (Felstead et al., 2012).

One way in which employers in the manufacturing sector can become involved in training is through recruiting apprentices. Lewis (2013) discusses the concept of 'overtraining'. The paper analyses how the term 'overtraining' was traditionally used to refer to the way in which nationalised industries trained more apprentices than they needed, with apprentices who were not required at the end of their training period released to find another employer. It suggests that overtraining now typically involves large employers helping to train apprentices who are employed and paid by other firms.

Charting a future research agenda

There are several different directions that a future research agenda could take. The foregoing sections suggest there is a role for a skill-informed view of global value chains and global production networks. This needs to be broadly construed to cover demographic issues, lifelong learning and work-life balance issues.

In the UK, Europe and the USA there are similarities in key themes of relevance to skills in manufacturing that are identified as research priorities by research councils and other funding bodies. All point to interests in the impact of digitisation (including developments in artificial intelligence, automation and robotics) on product and technology development, on service delivery, and the implications for the future of work at the human-technology frontier, including on the ways workers collaborate with each other. There is widespread recognition of the role of advanced manufacturing as a key enabling technology, and the need to identify and address shortages in technical, non-technical and digital capabilities in the workforce in synergy with technological developments. This makes lifelong learning an important research priority, with demographic changes – including population ageing and more diverse populations – adding impetus to this. The social sustainability of manufacturing, focusing on how human skills are integrated with technology, is an important longer-term consideration. An additional ongoing priority in the UK is a concern with productivity, given the slowdown in productivity improvements in recent years. These research themes call for work across disciplinary boundaries, and engagement across academia, industry, trade unions, and education and training providers.

Here the focus is on three specific topics that remain of ongoing significance, given technological change, digitalisation, demographic change and other key priorities outlined above. They are also pertinent in the light of the shock of the COVID-19 crisis, its implications for global production networks and its differential impacts across manufacturing subsectors.

The first issue is making manufacturing an attractive sector, both to young people at the start of their labour market careers, and to workers considering moving between sectors. If manufacturing is to have in place the skills that it needs, it needs to be sufficiently attractive for current and potential workers that it does not put off those with the necessary skills from working in the sector. Research should take account of how capacity and resources to position manufacturing as a desirable career option are likely to vary considerably, between large firms with their internal labour markets and human resource development emphasis on talent attraction and retention, and small and medium-sized organisations where opportunities for progression may be more limited but job roles may be broader and human resource policies less developed. In policy debates in the UK and the USA there is an established view that manufacturing suffers a negative image, of being dirty, dangerous and dull.

This then may feed through to young people, especially in the light of parents' concerns that jobs in manufacturing are vulnerable to offshoring and that they are badly paid. There is limited evidence about the image of manufacturing, but existing evidence shows that secondary school students do appear to have a relatively negative image of manufacturing, with young women having a more negative view than young men. A substantial minority of the former describe manufacturing as 'male dominated' (Livesey, 2013). There is scope for further research to explore in more detail the image of manufacturing; how and whether this image is changing given trends in digitalisation, artificial intelligence and Industry 4.0; and the implications of manufacturing's image for attracting suitably qualified people to the sector. In the context of Industry 4.0, research could examine in detail the potential implications of utilising newer technology in terms of perceptions of manufacturing. For example, how do potential changes in technology impact on work patterns and perceptions regarding the attractiveness of the manufacturing sector? The Grand Challenges set out in the UK's Industrial Strategy emphasise the importance of manufacturing (for example, the use of low-carbon technologies) in addressing global trends to improve quality of life, and UK productivity. From a place-based perspective, a key question is whether and how the fortunes of local manufacturing, notably in terms of job losses, and regional variations in the adoption of modern smart technology, impinge on career choices of young people in different local areas.

A second issue worthy of further research is accessing and developing skills for manufacturing now and in the future, and new developments in types of training. Futures studies indicate that alongside core science, technology, engineering and mathematics (STEM) skills, the onus in engineering (and manufacturing more generally) will be on people skills (for working collaboratively in teams), creative thinking and enterprise skills. This emphasises a focus on human potential, rather than attainment to date, and a need to embrace technology for learning (Jackson et al., 2019). Rather than wholesale revision of the training system, the tendency to date has been to look internationally at how competitor economies have sought to ensure that they have skills in place to meet the requirements of manufacturing. For the UK and the USA, Germany is the country that is usually looked to for lessons in developing skills, in part because of its success in retaining a relatively large manufacturing sector. Political and cultural differences obviate direct policy transfer of the German dual system of education and work, in which young people develop workplace skills at employers' premises alongside theoretical training at a vocational school. The key learning points from the dual learning system are, firstly, that it provides a solid foundation of general skills for different clusters of industries, which in turn provide a platform for later development of specialised on-the-job skills. Secondly, it inculcates an active approach to learning. Thirdly, the German training system is based on close cooperation between companies, industrial chambers, regional research institutions and government agencies, which come together in a local ecosystem to address skills needs (Parilla et al., 2015).

There is scope for further research designed to glean lessons from international skills development initiatives and how they can be applied in local areas and regions elsewhere, and with what success. There are also opportunities for examining the implementation and contribution to current and future skills requirements of new skills initiatives, such as degree apprenticeships in the UK, developed by employers, universities and professional bodies, involving both work and study at university. A further example of an initiative seeking to support the development of advanced manufacturing skills among younger students and enhance the attractiveness of the sector to them is the PRIME (Partnership Response in Manufacturing Education) programme in the USA. Based on a network of industry, education and association partners, it connects schools to local manufacturers, and provides equipment, curriculum, professional development, scholarships and STEM-focused extracurricular activities to students and teachers. Research on skills development could also explore the suitability of current higher educational institutions in view of rapidly changing skills needs (McKinsey, 2019). Building on the concept of training smarter in response to economic recessions, and how the syllabus and modes of teaching are largely developed based on the days of conventional manufacturing, is there a need for structural reform of the higher education system? The Independent Commission on the College of the Future (2020) has emphasised the importance of greater college and university collaboration in achieving a skills-led recovery. How successful are the newly founded Institutes of Technology (IoTs)[2] in bridging skills needs in manufacturing? How do they support skills development in areas of manufacturing other than advanced manufacturing?

A third issue warranting further research attention is the utilisation of skills in manufacturing, with a particular focus on underutilisation of skills. As successive generations stay in education for longer and have more formal qualifications, so evidence for greater underutilisation of skills has emerged (as outlined above). In some instances such underutilisation may be due to worker choice, as they make trade-offs between work and non-work priorities (Lyons et al., 2020). Other possible reasons underlying skills underutilisation are mismatches due to imperfect information or labour market rigidities, and formal overqualification co-existing alongside skills levels appropriate for the job role undertaken (Green and McIntosh, 2007). There is scope for research on place-based aspects of skills underutilisation, mirroring research on regional skills shortages showing that agglomeration effects seem to moderate the impact of skills deficiencies through more efficient job matching at local level (Morris et al., 2020). Does the same hold true in terms of skills utilisation? What other measures, perhaps including job redesign, might help? And what potential is there to move to a higher-value-added product market strategy that better utilises available skills?

Conclusion

Despite a long-term decline in jobs in manufacturing, replacement demand requirements and new developments mean that exciting employment opportunities remain. While there is heterogeneity across the manufacturing sector in general, looking ahead manufacturing firms will need to pay much more attention to building multidisciplinary teams to develop increasingly complex products and innovative business models. This means that the mix of skills required in manufacturing is changing, with greater emphasis on people-focused team-working skills as well as on digital skills. Successive employer skills surveys in the UK reveal that around three in every ten vacancies were proving hard to fill due to difficulties in finding applicants with appropriate skills, qualifications or experience, and internal skills gaps among employees are greater than across the economy as a whole. This is an important deficit, because the quality and skills of the workforce is a critical factor in capturing competitive advantage in manufacturing. Yet, at the same time, skills underutilisation in manufacturing is increasing. Insights from the economics, sociology, regional development and education literature all provide perspectives on a research agenda for getting the right skills in place for current and future manufacturing.

Notes

1. The aim of the CJRS is to help businesses to get through the drop in demand experienced during the pandemic. It enables firms to retain skilled labour. Staff are furloughed at home, with the government part covering their wages until demand picks up.
2. Collaborations between further education providers, universities and employers across England, established following a government-led competition in 2019. A competition for a second wave of IoTs was launched in 2020.

References

Ahuett-Garza, H. and Kurfess, T. (2018). A brief discussion on the trends of habilitating technologies for Industry 4.0 and Smart manufacturing. *Manufacturing Letters*, 15(Part B), 60–63.

Amison, P. and Bailey, D. (2014). Phoenix industries and open innovation? The Midlands advanced automotive manufacturing and engineering industry. *Cambridge Journal of Regions, Economy and Society*, 7, 397–411.

Bailey, D. and De Propris, L. (2014). Manufacturing reshoring and its limits: the UK automotive case. *Cambridge Journal of Regions, Economy and Society*, 7, 379–395.

Bailey, D. and De Ruyter, A. (2012). Globalisation as a driver of employment precariousness? The labour market status of UK auto workers four years after plant closure. *Work Organisation, Labour and Globalisation*, 6(2), 153–167.

Bakhshi, H., Downing, J., Osborne, M. and Shneider, P. (2017). The future of skills employment in 2030. https://media.nesta.org.uk/documents/the_future_of_skills _employment_in_2030_0.pdf.

Baumol, W.J. (1967). Macroeconomics of unbalanced growth: the anatomy of urban crisis. *American Economic Review* 57, 415–426.

Baumol, W.J., Blackman, S.A.B. and Wolff, E.N. (1985). Unbalanced growth revisited: asymptotic stagnancy and new evidence. *American Economic Review*, 75, 806–817.

Beatty, C. and Fothergill, S. (2020). Recovery or stagnation? Britain's older industrial towns since the recession. *Regional Studies*, 4(9), 1238–1249.

Becker, G. (1964). *Human Capital*, New York: Columbia University Press.

Blazovich, J.L., Smith, K.T. and Smith, M. (2014). Employee-friendly companies and work–life balance: is there an impact on financial performance and risk level? *Journal of Organizational Culture, Communications and Conflict*, 18(2), 1–14.

Blundell, R., Dearden, L., Meghir, C. and Sianesi, B. (1999). Human capital investment: the returns from education and training to the individual, the firm and the economy. *Fiscal Studies*, 20(1), 1–23.

Blyton, P. and Jenkins, J. (2012). Life after Burberry: shifting experiences of work and non-work life following redundancy. *Work, Employment and Society*, 26(1), 26–41. https://doi.org/10.1177/0950017011426306.

Boys, J. (2019). Megatrends – Ageing gracefully: the opportunities of an older workforce. London: CIPD. https://www.cipd.co.uk/Images/megatrends-ageing-gracefully -the-opportunities-of-an-older-workforce-1_tcm18-64897.pdf.

Cisco (2019). *Cisco Visual Networking Index: Forecast and Trends, 2017-2022 White Paper*. Retrieved from: https://www.cisco.com/c/en/us/solutions/collateral/service -provider/visual-networkingindex-vni/white-paper-c11-741490.html.

De Grip, A. and Van Loo, J. (2002). The economics of skills obsolescence: a review. *Journal of Labor Economics*, 21, 1–26.

de Ruyter, A., Hearne, D., Bailey, D., Henry, I., Li, D. and Eade, R. (2020). Regional transport – a supply chain mapping exercise and Brexit exposure check of automotive, aerospace and rail value dependency in the WMCA region. Working Paper, Centre for Brexit Studies.

Duell, N. and Vetter, T. (2020). *The Employment and Social Situation in Germany*. European Parliament. europarl.europa.eu/RegData/etudes/STUD/2020/648803/ IPOL_STU(2020)648803_EN.pdf.

Felstead, A., Green, F. and Jewson, N. (2012). An analysis of the impact of the 2008–9 recession on the provision of training in the UK. *Work, Employment and Society*, 26(6), 968–986. https://doi.org/10.1177/0950017012458016.

Felstead, A. and Henseke, G. (2017). Assessing the growth of remote working and its consequences for effort, well-being and work-life balance. *New Technology, Work and Employment*, 32(3), 195–212.

Felstead, A. and Jewson, N. (2014). 'Training floors' and 'training ceilings': metonyms for understanding training trends. *Journal of Vocational Education and Training*, 66(3), 296–310.

Froy, F., Giguere, S. and Meghnani, M. (2012). *Skills for Competitiveness: A Synthesis Report*, Paris: OECD Publishing.

Gardiner, B., Martin, R., Sunley, P. and Tyler, P. (2013). Spatially unbalanced growth in the British economy. *Journal of Economic Geography*, 13, 889–928.

Glucksmann M (2009). Formations, connections and divisions of labour. *Sociology*, 43(5), 878–895.

Green, A. and Hogarth, T. (2016). *The UK Skills System: How Aligned are Public Policy and Employer Views of Training Provision*, UK Government Foresight Future of Skills and Lifelong Learning. https://assets.publishing.service.gov.uk/government/uploads/system/uploads/attachment_data/file/571695/ER8_The_UK_skills_system_how_aligned_are_public_policy_and_employer_views_of_training_provision.pdf.

Green, F. and McIntosh S. (2007). Is there a genuine under-utilization of skills amongst the over-qualified?, *Applied Economics*, 39(4), 427–439.

Green, A. and Taylor, A. (2020). *Workplace Perspectives on Skills*. University of Birmingham. https://www.birmingham.ac.uk/documents/college-social-sciences/business/research/city-redi/projects-docs/workplace-perspectives-report-final-version.pdf.

Guest, D. (2002). Perspectives on the study of work-life balance. *Social Science Information*, 41(2), 255–279.

Homkes, R. (2014). What role will leadership play in driving the future of UK manufacturing? Future of Manufacturing Project: Evidence Paper 15 Foresight, Government Office for Science. https://assets.publishing.service.gov.uk/government/uploads/system/uploads/attachment_data/file/302792/13-825-future-manufacturing-leadership.pdf.

Hopkins, B. (2012). Explaining variations in absence rates: temporary and agency workers in the food manufacturing sector. *Human Resource Management Journal*, 24(2), 227–240.

Independent Commission on the College of the Future (2020). *The UK-Wide Final Report from the Independent Commission on the College of the Future.* https://static1.squarespace.com/static/5c8847f58dfc8c45fa705366/t/5fa281933c71c92e01556060/1604485524723/CofT+October+report+-+English.pdf.

Jackson, P., Mellors-Bourne R. and Dahad, N. (2019). *Talent 2050: Skills and Education for the Future of Engineering, Final Report.* London: National Centre for Universities and Business.

Kaldor, N. (1970). The case for regional policies. *Scottish Journal of Political Economy*, 18, 337–348.

Kaldor, N. (1981). The role of increasing returns, technical progress and cumulative causation in the theory of international trade and economic growth. *Economie Appliquée*, 34, 593–617.

Keeble, D. and Walker, S. (1994). New firms, small firms and dead firms: spatial patterns and determinants in the United Kingdom. *Regional Studies*, 28(4), 411–427.

Lewis, P.A. (2013). The over-training of apprentices by large employers in advanced manufacturing in the UK. Available at https://ssrn.com/abstract=2895677.

Livesey, F. (2013). Public images of manufacturing in the UK: the current situation and future prospects. Future of Manufacturing Project: Evidence Paper 19, Foresight, Government Office for Science.

Lyons, H., Taylor, A. and Green, A. (2020) *Rising to the UK's Skills Challenges.* Industrial Strategy Council. https://industrialstrategycouncil.org/sites/default/files/attachments/Rising%20to%20the%20UK%27s%20skills%20challenges.pdf.

Make UK The Manufacturers' Association (2019a). *Preparing for Brexit: Deal or No Deal.* https://www.makeuk.org/-/media/eef/files/reports/industry-reports/make-uk-squire-patton-boggs-brexit-report.pdf.

Make UK The Manufacturers' Association (2019b). *Piecing Together the Puzzle, Getting UK Manufacturing Growth Back on Trend.* https://www.makeuk.org/-/media/eef/files/reports/industry-reports/make-uk-productivity-report-2018.pdf.

Martin, R. (1988). The political economy of Britain's north-south divide. *Transactions of the Institute of British Geographers*, 13(4), 389–418.

Martin, R. (2008). National growth versus spatial equality? A cautionary note on the new 'trade-off' thinking in regional policy discourse. *Regional Science Policy and Practice*, 1(1), 3–13.

Martin, R., Sunley, P., Gardiner, B., Evenhuis, E. and Tyler, P. (2018). The city dimension of the productivity growth puzzle: the relative role of structural change and within-sector slowdown. *Journal of Economic Geography*, 18(3), 539–570.

McKinsey (2019). UK skills mismatch in 2030. Industrial Strategy Council. https://industrialstrategycouncil.org/sites/default/files/UK%20Skills%20Mismatch%202030%20-%20Research%20Paper.pdf.

Messenger, J. and L. Gschwind (2016). Three generations of telework: new ICT and the (r)evolution from home office to virtual office. *New Technology, Work and Employment*, 31(3), 195–208.

Morris, D., Vanino. E. and Corradini, C. (2020). Effect of regional skill gaps and skill shortages on firm productivity. *Environment and Planning A*, 52(5), 933–952.

OECD (2020). Employment by activity, manufacturing. https://data.oecd.org/emp/employment-by-activity.htm.

Oulton, N. (2001). Must the growth rate decline? Baumol's unbalanced growth revisited. *Oxford Economic Papers*, 53, 605–627.

Parilla, J., Trujillo, J.L. and Berube, A. (2015). *Skills and Innovation Strategies to Strengthen U.S. Manufacturing: Lessons from Germany,* Washington, DC: Brookings Institution.

Pisano, G.P. and Shih, W. (2012). *Producing Prosperity: Why America Needs a Manufacturing Renaissance*, Boston, MA: Harvard Business Review Press.

Rhodes, C. (2020). Manufacturing: statistics and policy. House of Commons Briefing Paper Number 01942.

Rowthorn, R.E. (2010). Combined and uneven development: reflections on the north-south divide. *Spatial Economic Analysis*, 5, 355–362.

Standing, G. (2009). *Work After Globalization: Building Occupational Citizenship*, Cheltenham, UK and Northampton, MA, USA: Edward Elgar Publishing.

Standing, G. (2011). *The Precariat: The New Dangerous Class*, London: Bloomsbury Academic.

Vanchan, V., Mulholland, R. and Bryson, J. (2017). Repatriation or reshoring of manufacturing to the US and UK: dynamics and global production networks or from here to there and back again. *Growth and Change*, 49(1), 97–121.

Weaver, A. and Osterman, P. (2017). Skill demands and mismatches in US manufacturing. *International Labour Review*, 70(2), 275–307.

Williamson, J.G. (1991). Productivity and American leadership: a review article. *Journal of Economic Literature*, 29, 51–68.

Wilson, G. (2020). COVID-19: is manufacturing prepared for home working. Manufacturing Global, 18 March. https://www.manufacturingglobal.com/smart -manufacturing/covid-19-manufacturing-prepared-home-working.

Wilson, R. and Hogarth, T. (2003). *Tackling the Low Skills Equilibrium: A Review of Issues and Some New Evidence*, London: DTI.

Wilson, R., Owen, D., Barnes, S.-A., May-Gillings, M., Patel, S. and Bui, H. (2020). Working Futures 2017–2027: long-run labour market and skills projections for the UK: Annexes. https://assets.publishing.service.gov.uk/government/uploads/ system/uploads/attachment_data/file/863979/200204_Working_Futures_Annexes_ -_For_Publication.pdf.

Winterbotham, M., Vivian, D., Kik, G., Huntley Hewitt, J., Tweddle, M., et al. (2018). *Employer Skills Survey 2017*, Department for Education. https://assets.publishing .service.gov.uk/government/uploads/system/uploads/attachment_data/file/746493/ ESS_2017_UK_Report_Controlled_v06.00.pdf.

6 Addressing the evolution of clustering strategies in manufacturing: a policy research agenda

William Graves and Harrison S. Campbell, Jr

[E]conomic development policy cannot be premised simply on the notion that spatial industry clusters observed in a given point in time are likely to be the sites of substantial subsequent employment growth ... [C]lusters may represent useful targets for economic development but not because they are assured to produce strong job gains. The appropriate economic development strategies for an identified cluster ... may actually be job retention or workforce development programs aimed at helping redundant workers in the cluster obtain the necessary training and skills to assume employment in newer, emerging industries.

(Feser et al., 2008: 343)

Since the early twentieth century one of the most consistent paradigms in economic development policy is the expectation that manufacturing will generate substantial local spillovers (Marshall, 1919). These spillovers are produced both by the industry's relatively high wages and by local linkages that manufacturers cultivate to maximize efficiency. Such expectations have become paradigmatic, so scholars of economic development have been reluctant to probe the definitional aspects of clusters, their evolution, and how the form of clusters varies by industry, place and function (Grashof, 2020; Fang, 2019; Taylor, 2010). The absence of an evolutionary approach to the conceptualization of clusters exists despite significant change in the manufacturing and distribution processes and in geographic organization of production. Concomitant with the stasis of cluster theory is a reluctance to evaluate the effectiveness of cluster policy; an omission that reduces the efficiency of industrial development in the developed and developing world (Nathan, 2019; Puig and Urzelai, 2019; Smith et al., 2020).

This chapter presents a brief case study of the development of the auto assembly industry in the Southern United States (US) to illustrate the evolution of the clustering process in manufacturing. We view this particular context of cluster development as useful since auto manufacturing is considered a mature industry but is nonetheless seen as an archetype for production activities. The US South is also a growing region that had no prior specialization in vehicle production. Much of the Southern auto industry developed between 1983 and 2011, therefore this cluster emerged as contemporary logistics strategies, such as kitting, were forming. Further, the Southern auto industry operates free of interference from sunk costs, path dependence or the influence of a legacy corporate culture, making it a good candidate to illustrate the development of the centripetal and centrifugal forces involved in the creation of a *de novo* industrial cluster in a global industry. We believe our findings are generalizable to other geographic and industrial contexts, particularly in districts that are in the early stages of industrial development, such as Northern Mexico or portions of Southeast China.

Using observations from our case study, we found that the benefits of clustering may be overstated in some industrial settings; the nature of clusters is dependent on their spatial contexts; and forces external to a cluster, such as local economic development policy, can artificially disperse activity that would otherwise be co-located. From this we identify several critical questions that underpin our discussion of the contemporary clustering process and form the foundation of a research agenda for future studies of clustering. We categorize these questions into four broad thematic areas: increased dispersion of the workforce; industry maturity requiring cost reductions; regional economic development policy that discourages co-location; and the emergence of new logistical strategies such as kitting to utilize global supplier networks more efficiently. This analysis reveals that the traditional approach to clusters that assumes intensive co-location is not appropriate in every industrial context. Finally, we suggest some research strategies to inform discussion regarding the development of a new research agenda for understanding contemporary industrial clusters and their propensity to spatially cluster.

The roots of anti-cluster policy in the Southern United States

The Southern US remains the most impoverished region of the country. As such, the process of its industrial evolution tells us something about how manufacturing has adapted to non-traditional production locations in the world economy. In the Southern US, human and financial capital stocks are low, natural resource supplies scarce and transportation infrastructure sparse. These conditions created an active economic development community which was tasked with stimulating development, particularly in lagging portions of the South. The region's economic development process was largely centered on two characteristics of place: first, the region's low production costs (due largely to wages, energy and land costs); and second, the local willingness to provide direct incentive payments to firms in order to encourage their (re)location to the region. The focus on these two comparative advantages led to additional policies that were intended to preserve the regional advantage of low wages. The explicit policies used to limit wage growth include right-to-work laws that limit union membership (Maunula, 2009); rural highway and utility development intended to disperse economic activity into rural areas (Walker and Calzonetti, 1990); and limited funding for higher education (Cobb, 1993). This cost-minimization strategy has led some observers to refer to the Southern US as a region with a limited ability to encourage clustering and realize its associated productivity advantages (Glasmeier and Leichenko, 1996: 613). One contemporary example can be found in North Carolina, where development policy continues to favor rural locations over urban ones via a geographically selective financial incentives policy.

The lack of a sophisticated regional workforce limited the region's ability to recruit and nurture high-tech and advanced manufacturing industries. Similarly, the region's lack of investment in human capital or cluster development reinforced this deficit. Instead, industrial recruitment to the South has always focused on mature, low-skill and labor-intensive industries. The region's first, and arguably most substantial, economic development successes came from the attraction of the textile industry from New England in the late 1800s (Lemert, 1933), and the rise of the wood furniture industry in the late nineteenth century (Tewari, 2005). While these industries created jobs, their factories were, for the most part, isolated; a geography that was selected as a tool to limit competition for labor (Cobb, 1993). This rural-industrial strategy was enabled by the maturity of the textile and furniture industries which limited the need for local suppliers. Further, their non-perishable, low-value products made slow shipping viable. Consequently, industry clusters of any kind were rare, as the strategy created a dispersed urban system with centrally placed logistics centers scattered roughly every 60 miles across the region (Stuart, 1972). Such a dispersed industrial development pattern, coupled with the scattering of many small and mid-sized towns, prevented the establishment of threshold populations needed to support the emergence of a diverse array of specialized and complementary goods and service providers, typically found in larger urban areas. In short, the region's pattern of dispersed industrial development discouraged the development of an urban core, and the absence of a center to encourage clustering limited the diversification of the region's economy.

When these core industries began to offshore in search of lower costs in the late 1980s, economic developers were encouraged to attract more sophisticated forms of manufacturing to the region. The deindustrialization of the South began just as the auto industry began its transformation. Given the struggles of the US auto industry at the time, combined with import restrictions, foreign auto assembly was an attractive target for economic development in the South (Karan and Bladen, 2001). The region's right-to-work laws, port access, and intermediate location between suppliers in Mexico and the Midwestern US, combined to make the region attractive to the manufacturers; and the incentives packages offered by economic developers served to further increase the region's geographic advantages.

Clusters without co-location and the modern auto industry in the Southern United States

The first foreign auto maker to build a new assembly plant the US South was Nissan, which opened its plant in Smyrna, Tennessee (470 miles South of Detroit) in 1983. Toyota followed shortly after in Georgetown, Kentucky (300 miles South of Detroit) in 1988. These plant locations were chosen by the manufacturers largely for their low-cost and non-union labor, significant state financial incentives, and for their proximity to the core of the US auto industry just to the north (Karan and Bladen, 2001). These locational attributes allowed the two plants to use the existing supply chain for the US auto industry, if necessary, but were distant enough to justify the development of new suppliers in the new production region. Relatively quickly, these two plants triggered an extension of the Midwestern auto parts cluster to Tennessee and Kentucky (OSAT, 1995), effectively shifting the US auto production region south (Rubenstein, 2002).

The assembly-only model of production was relatively new to North America. Historically, auto production in the Midwest (exemplified by Detroit) was vertically integrated, with most parts produced on-site. Factory owners, like Henry Ford, firmly believed that no external firm could produce parts more efficiently. While Detroit producers began to adapt to a more flexible mode of production during the 1980s, the cultural preference for in-house parts production remained. Conversely, in Europe, where there was a tradition of vertical disintegration of parts production and assembly, outsourcing was common and most auto plants were simply assemblers. Foreign auto plants moving to the Southern US used the European model of assembly only, which increased their reliance on external parts providers and required a new geography of auto production (Hsieh et al., 1997).

Following the success of the new plants in Tennessee and Kentucky, eight additional foreign-owned manufacturing facilities were built in the South (in Alabama, South Carolina, Georgia, Tennessee and Mississippi) between 1994 and 2011. Economic development professionals were impressed by the substantial cluster development around the first two plants, which led to the provision of massive incentives packages (averaging more than $100 000 per initial worker) to the foreign firms to encourage site selection (OSAT, 1995; Karan and Bladen, 2001; Jacobs, 2015). The apparent success of the Nissan and Toyota plants provided a kind of demonstration effect for economic developers: the plants provided evidence that the needed promise of spillover development could indeed materialize, and the expectation that if it happened once, it would happen again.

Incentives packages from states to the foreign producers totaled more than $4.7 billion by 2011. These financial packages were justified largely by the promise of spillovers from an emergent supply chain surrounding the new assembly plants (Connaughton and Madsen, 2001). Economic impact reports projected total economic growth of as much as $7 billion per year for an individual plant, approximately $1.5 million in output per worker per year. This level of productivity was substantially above the region's average annual manufacturing productivity of $125 000 per worker (US Bureau of Economic Analysis, 2020).

Measuring the impact of a dispersed supply chain

Between 1983 and 2011, ten foreign-owned auto assembly plants were built in six Southern states. An examination of the local economic impacts of these plants, using counterfactual comparisons, was conducted by Graves in 2019. The study examined employment and income change in the counties (administrative areas that are roughly a 25 miles, or 40 km, radius in this portion of the US) where assembly plants are located (core counties) as well as the counties that are adjacent to those core counties. The intent of the analysis was to assess the degree of employment and income change occurring in five-year and ten-year periods following each plant opening. Changes in the counties of impact were compared to a set of control counties (16 counties that unsuccessfully vied for the auto plants) to assess the *de novo* manufacturing cluster in those rural areas receiving an auto plant. This counterfactual, or quasi-experimental, technique borrows from Isserman and Merrifield's (1987) study of regional growth poles, and controls for differences in history, demographics, governance and local behavior in policy evaluation and assessment.

The quasi-experimental approach has been used to evaluate economic impacts of universities and highways (Goldstein and Renault, 2004; Rephann and Isserman, 1994) as well as economic incentives programs (Rogers and Tao, 2004), but until recently the method was not commonly used in spatial analysis due to difficulties with the consistent selection of comparison sites. More recently, difference-in-difference (DiD) regression models have been used in quasi-experimental designs to account for local context and unexplained factors affecting control groups during the period under study. This advance in quasi-experimental studies has been widely employed in place-based investigations in a variety of settings, to address, for example, the impact of opportunity zones on employment growth (Arefeva et al., 2020), sports facilities on urban development (Agha and Rascher, 2020), housing development and neighborhood stability (Delmelle et al., 2017), and even the impact of craft breweries on surrounding property values (Nilsson and Reid, 2019). Despite early obstacles in control group identification, the quasi-experimental approach has gained wider acceptance as a research design that is especially useful for assessing the effectiveness of public policy initiatives.

While quasi-experiments have enjoyed a renewed interest in regional studies, there remain both theoretical and conceptual issues surrounding the choice and spatial extent of the control group "neighborhood" and the geographic size of observational units. Rather than take up these thorny issues here, we opted for a more direct comparison of employment and income impacts attributable to the auto plant. Changes in total employment and manufacturing-specific employment were examined in the counties where each plant was located, as well as the adjacent counties (Table 6.1). It was posited that, if the auto plants were seeding the development of a production cluster, employment growth in locations of direct impact should outperform the control location (as well as the surrounding state). These changes in employment and income were compared to the set of 16 control sites.

In terms of total employment change (Table 6.1), the data reveal that the areas around the ten assembly plants significantly outperformed the group of control counties. Tellingly, this outperformance loses its statistical significance if the first two arrivals to the region (Nissan in Tennessee and Toyota in Kentucky) are removed from the analysis: a suggestion of a first-mover advantage in cluster development. Keep in mind that the breadth of the total employment

Table 6.1   Change in economic characteristics of counties following
arrival of foreign owned auto assembly plant

	Plant counties		Adjacent counties (mean)	
Change in:	5 years after open	10 years after open	5 years after open	10 years after open
Total employment	37.0%*	73.3%*	16.4%*	23.9%*
Manufacturing employment	60.9%*	114.3%	0.2%	-18.7%
Per capita income	0.2%	-0.9%	-0.1%	-0.3%

Notes: *Significantly different than the control group at P < 0.10. Change figures are relative to state change. Only five of 12 observations are significantly different from the control group.

includes low-wage employment such as retail clerks and restaurant workers, most of which does not contribute to specialized cluster development.

Manufacturing employment shows a somewhat different trend (Table 6.1). For the first five years after plant opening, manufacturing employment change in core counties significantly outperforms the control set. However, the other three observations (core counties ten years after opening, and adjacent counties in both time periods) show that plant counties fail to outperform the control set. We would expect to see growth in manufacturing employment if a network of suppliers were attracted to the new auto assembly facilities. Our data fail to provide evidence for that trend: the change in manufacturing workers in the area surrounding auto plants did not consistently outperform our control set. It does not appear that cluster development occurred around these plants. As with the total employment change data, manufacturing employment did see strong growth in plant counties relative to their states; however, much of this change was again driven by the first two arrivals to the region, Nissan and Toyota. Control counties saw similar levels of growth without auto plants, so the auto plants had little additional impact. Finally, the absence of manufacturing employment growth in the adjacent counties is strongly suggestive that new manufacturing plants may be avoiding locations near assembly facilities, due to the relatively high wages being paid in the auto plants.

The same analysis was run for income change, a measure of aggregate economic development, surrounding the auto plants (Table 6.1). In theory, the productivity advantages of a manufacturing production cluster should drive wage growth. These data revealed that income growth was uneven surrounding the assembly facilities: seven plants experienced some income decline in the surrounding counties, while the remaining three experienced stagnation. There was no significant difference in income change between the plant location, adjacent counties and the control sites. Given that income declined in the majority of the areas around the ten plants, a situation that is antithetical to the intention of cluster strategies, it becomes difficult to justify the incentives used to attract these plants (Graves, 2019). In the language of growth pole theory, backwash effects (such as firms seeking to avoid wage competition) appear to dominate spread (cluster) effects. These results are consistent with those of Kim (2020), who contends that Hyundai's choice of Alabama, like other foreign direct investment (FDI) auto producers, was not only motivated by the availability of low-cost, non-unionized labor, but resulted in minimal employment rate gains and negative impacts on average weekly wages when compared with counties not receiving auto-related FDI over the 2005-01 period. Interestingly, these results, derived from a DiD framework applied at the labor market level (PUMA, or Public Use Microdata Area) seem to suggest that not only do local contextual effects matter, but that overall impacts also vary by source and timing of FDI ("early-mover" versus "late-mover"). Late-movers, seeking cost-efficiencies and cost reductions in both product lines and assembler–supplier relationships, now comprise much of the manufacturing branch plant investment, but likely will generate fewer economic impacts than their early-mover counterparts. With fewer interfirm linkages being established, the likelihood of spatially clustered supplier networks is also diminished.

Our findings cast doubt on the economic impact projections that assume suppliers will co-locate or that new arrivals will necessarily utilize local suppliers. Specifically, if spillover job and income impacts reported in impact studies materialize, they apparently were not realized in jurisdictions adjacent to the impact site. While the economic impact analyses are explicit about spillovers, none of them focus on local impacts, instead providing only statewide estimates (Connaughton and Madsen, 2001; Alabama Department of Commerce, 2013; University of South Carolina, 2014). This casualness with scale is contrary to the academic emphasis on clusters as co-location. One recent study of cluster micro-geographies used employment data to determine that the auto industry has an optimal cluster radius of 2 miles in the US (Fang, 2019); Bergman and Feser (2020: 52) report that in 1994 "spatial clustering is most significant at scales of two-to-six-kilometer radius" in the North Carolina vehicle manufacturing cluster. The academic emphasis on co-location is largely driven by the needs of either just-in-time (JIT) inventory management or requirements for information exchange in design, quality control or innovation. The maturity of auto production, along with the relatively uncongested highways in the rural South, largely eliminate these motivations for proximity in this case.

Further, there is some evidence that even as early as 1989, JIT delivery was not matched by JIT production in the US auto industry, such that "48 percent of suppliers ended up stockpiling inventory" (Helper and Sako, 1995: 77). That the geographies of cluster-based co-location have changed over time should come as no surprise, but the extent to which changing supply chain geographies are reflected in most economic impact studies in unclear. We found the mean distance between suppliers and the three assembly facilities in Alabama (Mercedes, Honda and Hyundai) to be 61 miles (98 km) (Alabama Department of Commerce, 2013; EDPA, 2017). The location of the Mercedes plant is typical in that there are few land constraints around these plants despite the plant being in operation for more than 25 years.

In summary, the evolution of the Southern auto industry illustrates three contemporary trends in the industrial clustering process. First, suppliers that built new factories in the region largely avoided co-location. This strategy of dispersion occurs not because of land or labor constraints, but in an environment where economic development policy encourages dispersion. Incentives policy in the region steers new manufacturing arrivals into the least-developed counties by providing larger per job incentives payments, thus providing a financial incentive to avoid clustering. For their part, firms are more than willing to oblige, because separation of the labor force reduces the likelihood of intra-industry labor disputes. While this policy has the explicit intent of developing impoverished regions, it has the consequence of limiting wage competition and dampening wage growth (Cobb, 1993; Luger, 2003; Kim, 2020). The absence of co-location eliminates the information sharing, transportation economies and worker access benefits of an industry cluster: the very efficiencies for workers and firms that cluster development is intended to produce. As a result, opportunities for industrial succession, local wealth accumulation and community development are limited.

The second trend is that workers appear to shun co-location as well. We traced worker residential locations using cellphone data for plant workers between April 2017 and April 2018 (Figure 6.1). The data revealed an average, one-way commute distance of 45 miles (72 km) for the ten Southern assembly plants; a significantly larger radius than the nationwide mean of 10 miles (16 km). While it is impossible to determine the causes of this worker dispersion, these data suggest that workers in the region have little motivation to live near their workplace. This distribution of workers effectively limits any face-to-face information exchange between workers outside of the workplace, and limits the ability of localities to leverage their supply of skilled labor in industrial recruiting. Indeed, none of the benefits of agglomeration (labor pooling, material linkages, information spillover) are apparent, largely because agglomeration itself, the *raison d'être* of cluster-based strategies, is absent.

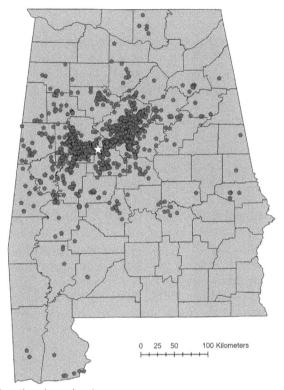

Note: Factory location shown by star.

Figure 6.1   Distribution of residence location of Mercedes-Benz, Vance
Alabama assembly workers, 2017–18

Finally, and consequently, the benefits of relatively high manufacturing wages (to the extent that they exist) are scattered, reducing the economic benefits of the facilities. Communities appear to be reaping few benefits from their efforts to recruit these facilities.

Clusters without clustering? A research agenda

Industry clusters are thought to be most productive when accompanied by the co-location of related industries, linked firms, specialized suppliers and service providers, logistical networks and supporting institutions. Clustering fosters relationships between linked firms and local institutions that help promote innovation and productivity, especially when establishments operate in flexible, unstable or vertically disintegrated environments. This would seem to suggest a set of environmental characteristics that promote the development of clusters, including a wide array of small and medium-sized goods and service producers, many of which operate flexibly over a range of product types and markets that achieve efficiencies through economies of scope rather than scale (much of which is absent in the Southern auto cluster).

While location is seen as a central ingredient at the firm level and cluster members benefit from agglomeration, co-location is not a necessary condition for cluster development (Gordon and Kourtit, 2020), although a sense of membership is critical (Shen and Puig, 2018). In this sense, the theory behind industry clusters shares several similarities with growth pole theory. When defining growth poles and growth centers, Perroux distinguished between propulsive and linked industries that operate in transactional "economic" space (growth poles) from those that operate in "banal" geographic space (growth centers). Similarly, industry clusters are not geographically constrained: they are first and foremost defined by interfirm linkages irrespective of location, such that the "geographic scope of a cluster can range from a single city or state to a country or even a group of neighboring countries" (Porter, 2000: 254). Simply put, industry clusters are largely analogous to growth poles, while growth centers are the geographic manifestation of clustering. Thus, as a practical matter of policy and practice, and consistent with our empirical results, "local economic development professionals should understand that clusters are not necessarily growth centers" (Feser et al., 2008: 344).

Contemporary discussions of the concept, however, continue to lean heavily on the expectation of co-location when discussing clusters as an economic development strategy (see Feser, 1998; Bergman and Feser, 2020, for extended discussions). The common assumption that co-location is a required element of clustering has caused some academics and practitioners to overlook the role of industry maturity, product life cycles, labor market dynamics, and changes in communications and transportation technology in firm location. In addition to our findings that the Southern US auto cluster lacks co-location of any kind, Kim (2020) found that one of the region's key tenants, Hyundai, actively avoided sites offering the potential for clustering. This leads us to question the paradigmatic assumption that all clusters require co-location. Indeed, it has been suggested that the quality of relationships between firms, as well as the nature of the connective transactions, may be more critical than co-location (Salder and Bryson, 2019). We must ask: is our current conceptualization well suited to all geographic contexts, industry types and technological eras? Can we expect to see this same lack of co-location in other geographic and industrial contexts? And, more specifically, what are the benefits of co-location, particularly in mature industries? Do co-located firms have greater resilience, longevity, productivity and employment? Our exploratory case study highlights some of these issues as particularly deserving of additional investigation.

Wage sensitivity and labor competition

As we witnessed in the Southern US auto industry, supplier firms may be reluctant to co-locate due to a desire to avoid labor competition. This firm location behavior may be confined to firms in rural areas and mature industries where worker skills can be commoditized easily. However, this type of firm location strategy may become more common as factory floor automation increases and design, research and development are increasingly offshored. This lack of co-location calls into question the specific elements of firm decision-making with regard to co-location, and a need to understand how this decision-making process varies with industry type, maturity and corporate structure. Other questions include: to what extent do assemblers and suppliers compete with one another for labor? What evidence would need to be marshalled to demonstrate that such a labor avoidance strategy is economically rational or beneficial to all firms involved, compared to the presumed benefits of labor pooling? What role does state and local policy play in preventing firms from creating co-located clusters?

Worker behavior and dispersed economic impact

The rural location of large assembly facilities requires an extensive labor shed to fill jobs. At the same time, relatively high wages paid by manufacturers who might benefit from clustering encourages and supports unusually long worker commutes. This dispersed pattern of workers raises several important questions for academics and policymakers alike. What is the effective size of the labor market for auto assemblers and suppliers? If labor market dispersion is common in other contexts, will suppliers rethink the need for co-location? Given the commuting patterns that have been revealed in this case study, are the geographic constraints of labor markets being overstated in manufacturing clusters? Finally, does a dispersed set of workers have opportunities to reskill to the degree that they may gain employment in emerging industries?

While such questions have been historically difficult to answer due to limited data availability, modern data sources such as cellphone tracking data offer new means for assessing worker behavior and its role in production in a variety of settings. As these data sets become more refined it will be possible to monitor specific interactions between suppliers and assemblers, as well as the behavior of corporate executives monitoring remote production sites.

Maturity of auto industry

While economic developers in the region view auto assembly as an advanced manufacturing activity, it is, in fact, a mature industry that is more than 125 years old. Electric auto manufacturing has not yet begun in the region's factories, and investment in the region's auto industry has been almost entirely led by foreign direct investment. The product life cycle position of autos has reduced industry emphasis on certain aspects of design and innovation, reducing the need for close coordination between assembly and supplier. Product life cycle issues exacerbate the isolation of these branch plant facilities: nearly all research, development and design work occurs at the Asian or European headquarters sites. In some ways, the basis for just-in-time (JIT) parts management has been reduced by both product maturity and a reduced demand for hardware variety in autos; most customization now being driven by software modifications rather than hardware configuration changes (Shimokawa et al., 2012). The need for supplier proximity has been reduced. With it, so too have some of the benefits from clustering as a locational strategy.

Given these changes, our case study suggests that it is time to question the current benefits to firms, as well as economic development officials, from clustering. If traditional reasons for agglomeration do not exist, what benefits do exist? Are there organizational or contractual arrangements associated with clustering that still make sense? Do these arrangements produce efficiencies or innovations that firms would not realize otherwise? Does cluster membership bestow other benefits to firms and workers? Do members of the cluster realize benefits that non-members do not? If so, cluster-based theory and practice remain relevant (though we suggest that the theory and its translation to practice need a facelift). If not, then other theory, perhaps akin to theories of product life cycles, may be a better depiction of today's US auto industry.

Such a paradigm shift, no doubt, would meet with some resistance. Policymakers and practitioners longed for a framework beyond economic base theory to guide their policies, processes and actions (Glasmeier, 2000), and industrial cluster theory provided the needed guidance. It is not far-fetched to note that policymakers and practitioners have embraced and internalized cluster-based approaches with such conviction that, for some, little else is conceivable. But if a paradigm shift is in order, how will economic development professionals respond? What does it imply in terms of what they do and how they do it? Can a new paradigm emerge that is as intuitive, instructive and action-oriented, that enhances the economic health and well-being of the region's residents while balancing efficiency and equity considerations (Tietz, 1994)?

Regional economic development policy

Our data suggest that this intentional policy design has the effect of discouraging traditional, co-located clustering. If correct, our observation has important implications for the practice of economic development and pursuit of economic spillovers through a variety of potential multiplier effects. One foundational premise of agglomeration and cluster-based theory is that firms are more competitive, more successful, and thus create more jobs when they interact with other firms in the region via buyer–supplier relationships. These other firms can be new or relocating firms to the region; they can also be existing firms seeking to establish regional supply linkages. Establishing material and service linkages with existing firms in the region is a low-cost and efficient way to build and/or strengthen clusters. In fact, it has been shown that many local firms have sufficient excess capacity to accommodate product demand from new regional employers, and connecting them to existing firms is a more efficient path to job creation than traditional targeting and recruitment (Campbell et al., 2012).

The steering of plant location, and thus economic development, away from potential growth centers in an effort to maintain supplies of low-cost labor begs the question: development for whom? Is the fundamental purpose of economic development activities as practiced by economic development professionals to help regions expand and enhance employment, income, quality of life and economic well-being of residents in their area? Does industrial recruitment success hinge on a region's "ability" to remain a low-cost, low-wage region? If so, how exactly does this benefit the region we seek to serve, especially if co-location of related firms is discouraged? Much of this suggests that there might be more to the practice of economic development than economic development, per se. Indeed, the currency of the economic developer is directly related to the size of the last project landed (Rubin, 1988). Might, then, the incentive structure facing state and local economic developers be fruitfully cast in terms of an institutional or managerial model, rather than a presumed economic model?

Global supplier networks and contemporary logistics strategies

As the auto industry has globalized aggressively over the past 40 years, relations between supplier firms have broadened and more dispersed supply chains have emerged. Relationships between global firms have reduced the tendency of auto producers to rely solely on nearby suppliers (Frigant and Zumpe, 2017). Shipping networks have also combined reliability with tracking mechanisms to allow for just-in-time inventory management to occur without proximity. While the Southern US auto cluster is relatively distant from the core of the US auto industry, based on the continued movement of assemblers to the region, it appears that this distance has not impeded productivity. Domestic supply chains now compete with international supply, and sourcing can change rapidly in response to fluctuations in product demand, short-term bottlenecks, exchange rates, tariffs and quotas, and a host of hard-to-measure organizational characteristics. While place and space continue to shape and mediate all forms of exchange, changes in global supplier networks are redefining place and space in varied and contingent ways that continue to deserve our theoretical and empirical attention.

A new set of logistical strategies have emerged in auto manufacturing to connect global supplier networks. The rise of kitting or parallelized assembly systems as a supply chain strategy for auto production has dramatically changed the logistics surrounding assembly. A global network of suppliers is utilized to assemble parts kits for individual vehicles. These kits are bundled and containerized for long-distance shipment to the assembly facility. Take, from our study area, the example of BMW in Greer, South Carolina. Parts kits land in the port of Charleston (200 miles/320 km to the south) and are then shipped by rail to a state-provided inland port facility adjacent to the plant. Kitting has the virtue of reducing the skill requirements of assembly workers, eliminating the need for local design expertise, and facilitates a wider range of customization of products. While beneficial for firms, these changes clearly limit economic impacts to host communities and their larger regional economies.

Extended parts networks such as these would not be possible without new infrastructure such as the state-provided inland port, shipment tracking technology, and a new set of international interfirm relationships. Kitting also requires a large amount of storage space for the deliveries, making it more space-intensive than just-in-time delivery (Boudella et al., 2018). The combination of infrastructure, inexpensive land and low labor costs combine to make the Southern auto cluster well suited to the use of kitting. The rise of kitting as a supplier strategy is consistent with our findings of a lack of supplier clustering in the Southern auto industry. The two assembly facilities that successfully created clustering were built before kitting was common practice, while eight remaining facilities (which were built after 1994) appear to rely heavily on kits for large portions of their supplier network. It appears that the Southern auto production cluster has become oriented towards global, rather than spatially constrained, Fordism (Feldman and MacIntyre, 1994), which raises the question of the continued relevance of cluster theory in late life cycle products such as autos.

Looking ahead

Addressing these questions will certainly require survey work of firms and case study approaches. Questions of geography, capacity and network development are critical to our understanding of contemporary clusters, as are more specific issues tied to production such as the mix of kits versus domestically sourced supplies. Addressing these questions in a way that is sensitive to the specific setting and age of producing firms is vital to developing this knowledge. In short, future research on the dynamics of clustering will need to be sensitive to the culture of the place, the maturity of the industry, and the influence of policy on industry location and relationship building. Clusters are as much a product of their immediate surroundings as they are industrial strategy.

Discussion: a growing disconnect between clusters and place?

Our case study yields several critical questions surrounding the theory and practice of industrial clusters and clustering. We categorized those questions into four broad areas: increased dispersion of the workforce; industry maturity requiring cost reductions; regional economic development policy that discourages co-location; and the emergence of new logistical strategies such as kitting to utilize global supplier networks more efficiently. Our findings indicate that our traditional understanding of clusters and economic development is divorced from the modern reality: co-location is not appropriate (or required) in every industrial context.

Cluster theory is appealing to economic development practitioners thanks to its intuitiveness and the substantial economic development potential that it

offers. However, our exploratory case study shows that the benefits of clustering may be overstated in some contexts. In addition, the co-located cluster
model may no longer be an efficient structure for some industries and some
spatial contexts. In the case of auto assembly in the South, economic impact
reports indicate that substantial benefits were anticipated in states where they
are located. However, little co-location is evident. This post-cluster geography
means that relatively few economic benefits have accrued to the communities
where the plants are located. Further, we found little evidence that the areas
with assembly plants outperformed a control group in terms of longer-run job
creation or income increase.

The economics of cluster development from the perspective of firms also comes
into question. Is there a point at which clusters lose their efficiency advantages
for their residents? Will the dispersed clusters found in the Southern auto
industry ever stimulate sufficient investment in innovation, human capital
and productivity growth that will allow the region to adapt to an increasingly
competitive global economy (Figlio and Blonigen, 2000)? Addressing these
questions is complicated by inconsistent, and sometimes ad hoc, definitions
of cluster composition across different industry cluster studies. Save a few
rigorous definitional studies, the academic concept of clusters has always relied
on fuzzy boundaries. Perhaps just as important is the tendency for cluster
studies to either ignore firm-specific attributes or assume manufacturing to be
a homogenous group of activities with respect to firm size, age, ownership and
stage in product life cycle (De Marchi et al., 2017). In fact, mature industries
have very different spatial needs than emerging ones. Industry clusters remain
an imprecisely defined concept even when their composition is clearly articulated, making it difficult to account for (and predict) the evolutionary effects of
technological and economic change in economic development studies.

The Southern auto industry shows us that some successful clusters may take
a very different form than is commonly predicted. Sweeney and Feser (1998)
provide us with some instructive examples from North Carolina, where the
tendency to spatially cluster depends on the organizational status of firms –
single-establishment versus branch plant – and firm size: branch plants tend to
be larger and are less likely to cluster, while the effects of firm size on clustering
assumes an inverted U-shape (firms with 10–50 employees were more likely to
cluster than very small or very large firms). Similarly, results can vary by industry, with printing and publishing along with vehicle manufacturing showing
a distinct tendency to cluster in North Carolina, while firms in the regional
wood products cluster displayed a significant tendency toward dispersion. All
this reminds us that regional industry clusters can take different forms: some
tend toward agglomeration while others do not; and in the process, we should

not expect all regional clusters to produce highly localized impacts or engage in other activities whereby industry-specific information, practices and technological know-how are readily shared.

Finally, it is important to realize that clusters do not always evolve organically. The most examined industry clusters are produced by imperfect markets operating in urban regions that have been nurtured by public policy and proactive institutions where capital availability, thick labor markets, production knowhow and a culture of innovation and entrepreneurialism have been cultivated across small and medium-sized firms operating in vertically disintegrated environments; most of which is missing from the auto industry in the US South. Instead, the South offered a blank slate of inexpensive land and worker training programs to foreign auto producers. Despite the geographic setting, the Southern auto cluster did not take the hoped-for shape. In this case policy, firm strategy, as well as competition between states to attract plants, skewed the firm location process away from co-location.

These findings suggest that a traditional, co-located industrial cluster strategy may not emerge from intentional rural development strategies such as those associated with the Southern auto industry. Changes in modes of production and supply chain geographies have allowed suppliers to be considerably more distant than traditional cluster theory would suggest, and regional policy seems to encourage this separation. In the case of the Southern auto production cluster, the long-term impacts of this dispersion are unknown, but it appears likely that the lack of concentration reduces economic benefits to governments, communities and their local workforce.

We hope the details of our regional case study do not obscure the larger conceptual issue that our case study illustrates. Geographers tend to explore production from either a local perspective (for example, relationships within the boundaries of a cluster), or a global perspective (for example, global production networks). Both these approaches force production processes into pre-existing conceptions of their spatial structure. This a priori application of geography might cause us to misread the nature and purpose of the interfirm relationships that comprise a cluster. Similarly, studies of the regional economic impacts of clusters tend to impose arbitrary (or political) geographic boundaries in their analysis. This can result in the misallocation of the benefits of job creation and supplier relationships in impact analysis. Finally, the tendency of academics to consider clusters to be organic creations causes them to overlook the role of the local and regional policy which also shapes these production systems. Policymakers in the Southern US feel that the economic benefits of co-located clustering may impose high costs on their (perhaps narrowly defined) communities by increasing wages and straining infrastructure. In short, future scholars of manufacturing should be aware of the wide, and constantly evolving, nature of production systems, and how the spaces which house them are not simply containers of this activity but are embedded in, and the products of, a socially and institutionally constructed policy environment.

References

Agha, N., and Rascher, D. (2020). Economic development of major and minor league teams and stadiums. *Journal of Sports Economics*, *20*(10): 1–21. DOI: 10.1177/1527002520975847.

Alabama Department of Commerce (2013). Alabama's Hyundai suppliers and vendors. Available at: http://www.madeinalabama.com/assets/2013/01/Hyundaimaplist3-15 -13.pdf.

Arefeva, A., Davis, M., Ghent, A., and Park, M. (2020). Who benefits from place-based policies? Job growth from opportunity zones. Available at SSRN: https://ssrn.com/ abstract=3645507.

Bergman, E.M., and Feser, E.J. (2020). *Industrial and Regional Clusters: Concepts and Comparative Applications*. Web Book of Regional Science. Edited by S. Loveridge and R. Jackson. Regional Research Institute, West Virginia University.

Boudella, M.E.A., Sahin, E., and Dallery, Y. (2018). Kitting optimisation in just-in-time mixed-model assembly lines: assigning parts to pickers in a hybrid robot–operator kitting system. *International Journal of Production Research*, *56*(16), 5475–5494.

Campbell Jr, H.S., Watkins, E., and Kunkle, G. (2012). Targeting vs. connecting in biotechnology. *Papers and Proceedings of the Applied Geography Conference*, *35*: 300–308.

Cobb, J.C. (1993). *The Selling of the South: The Southern Crusade for Industrial Development 1936–1990*. Champaign, IL: University of Illinois Press.

Connaughton, J.E., and Madsen, R.A. (2001). Assessment of economic impact studies: the cases of BMW and Mercedes-Benz. *Review of Regional Studies*, *31*(3), 293–303.

De Marchi, V., Di Maria, E., and Gereffi, G. (eds) (2017). *Local Clusters in Global Value Chains: Linking Actors and Territories through Manufacturing and Innovation*. New York: Routledge.

Delmelle, E.C., Morrell, E., Bengle, T., Howart, J., and Sorensen, J. (2017). The effectiveness of Habitat for Humanity as a neighborhood stabilization program: the case of Charlotte, North Carolina. *Community Development*. http://dx.doi.org/10.1080/ 15575330.2017.1344717.

EDPA (2017). Mercedes-Benz suppliers in Alabama. Available at: https://www.edpa .org/wp-content/uploads/Mercedes-Suppliers-in-Alabama-2017.pdf.

Fang, L. (2019). Manufacturing clusters and firm innovation. *Economic Development Quarterly*, *33*(1), 6–18.

Feldman, M., and MacIntyre, J. (1994). Flexible production: its incidence and implications for labor markets and economic development strategy. Final report to the Economic Development Administration, US Department of Commerce.

Feser, E.J. (1998). Enterprises, external economies, and economic development. *Journal of Planning Lierature*, *12*(3), 283–302.

Feser, E., Renski, H., and Goldstein, H. (2008). Clusters and economic development outcomes: an analysis of the link between clustering and industry growth. *Economic Development Quarterly*, 22(4), 324–344.

Figlio, D.N., and Blonigen, B.A. (2000). The effects of foreign direct investment on local communities. *Journal of Urban Economics*, 48(2), 338–363.

Frigant, V., and Zumpe, M. (2017). Regionalisation or globalisation of automotive production networks? Lessons from import patterns of four European countries. *Growth and Change*, 48(4), 661–681.

Glasmeier, A. (2000). Economic geography in practice: local economic development policy. In G. Clark, M. Feldman and M. Gertler (eds), *The Oxford Handbook of Economic Geography*, Oxford: Oxford University Press, pp. 559–579.

Glasmeier, A.K., and Leichenko, R.M. (1996). From free market rhetoric to free market reality: the future of the US South in an era of globalization. *International Journal of Urban and Regional Research*, 20(4), 601–615.

Goldstein H.A., and Renault C.S. (2004). Contributions of universities to regional economic development: a quasi-experimental approach. *Regional Studies*, 38, 733–746.

Gordon, P., and Kourtit, K. (2020). Agglomeration and clusters near and far for regional development: a critical assessment. *Regional Science Policy and Practice*, 12(3), 387–396.

Grashof, N. (2020). Firm-specific cluster effects: a meta-analysis. *Papers in Regional Science*, 99(5), 1237–1260.

Graves, W. (2019). Upgrading industrial capacity in the peripheral US: the failure of incentives policy to create a southern auto production network. Paper presented at the Association of American Geographers Annual Meeting, Washington, April 4.

Helper, S., and Sako, S. (1995). Supplier relations in Japan and the United States: are they converging? *Sloan Management Review*, 36(3), 77–84.

Hsieh, L.H., Schmahls, T., and Seliger, G. (1997). Assembly automation in Europe – past experience and future trends. In *Transforming Automobile Assembly*. Berlin and Heidelberg: Springer, pp. 19–37.

Isserman, A.M., and Merrifield, J.D. (1987). Quasi-experimental control group methods for regional analysis: an application to an energy boomtown and growth pole theory. *Economic Geography*, 63(1), 3–19.

Jacobs, A.J. (2015). *The New Domestic Automakers in the United States and Canada: History, Impacts, and Prospects.* New York: Lexington Books.

Karan, P., and Bladen, W. (2001). Japanese investment in Kentucky. In P. Karan (ed.), *Japan in the Bluegrass.* Lexington, KY: University Press of Kentucky.

Kim, E. (2020). The local labor effects of Korean automotive investments in the United States. *International Regional Science Review*, 20(10), 1–28. DOI: 10.1177/0160017620964849.

Lemert, B.F. (1933). *Cotton Textile Industry of the Southern Appalachian Piedmont.* Chapel Hill, NC: University of North Carolina Press.

Luger, M. (2003). *2003 Assessment of the William S. Lee Tax Act.* Office of Economic Development, Kenan Institute of Private Enterprise, UNC Chapel Hill.

Marshall, A. (1919). *Industry and Trade.* London: Macmillan.

Maunula, M. (2009). *Guten Tag, Y'all: Globalization and the South Carolina Piedmont, 1950–2000.* Athens, GA: University of Georgia Press.

Merrifield, D.B. (1987). New business incubators. *Journal of Business Venturing*, 2(4), 277–284.

Nathan, M. (2019). Does light touch cluster policy work? Evaluating the tech city program. https://papers.ssrn.com/sol3/papers.cfm?abstract_id=3457675.

Nilsson, I., and Reid, N. (2019). The value of a draft brewery: on the relationship between craft breweries and property values. *Growth and Change, 50*, 689–704.

Office for the Study of Automotive Transportation (OSAT) (1995). *Japanese and German Automotive Supplier Investment Directory*, 6th edition. Ann Arbor, MI: University of Michigan Transportation Research Institute.

Perroux, F. (1950). Economic space: theory and applications. *Quarterly Journal of Economics, 64*, 89–104.

Porter, M. (2000). Locations, clusters and company strategy. In G. Clark, M. Feldman and M. Gertler (eds), *The Oxford Handbook of Economic Geography*. Oxford: Oxford University Press, pp. 253–274.

Puig, F., and Urzelai, B. (eds) (2019). *Economic Clusters and Globalization: Diversity and Resilience*. New York: Routledge.

Rephann, T., and Isserman, A. (1994). New highways as economic development tools: an evaluation using quasi-experimental matching methods. *Regional Science and Urban Economics, 24*(6), 723–751.

Rogers, C.L., and Tao, J.L. (2004). Quasi-experimental analysis of targeted economic development programs: lessons from Florida. *Economic Development Quarterly, 18*(3), 269–285.

Rubenstein, J.M. (2002). *The Changing US Auto Industry: A Geographical Analysis*. New York: Routledge.

Rubin, H. (1988). Shoot anything that flies, claim anything that falls: conversations with economic development practitioners. *Economic Development Quarterly, 2*(3), 236–251.

Salder, J., and Bryson, J.R. (2019). Placing entrepreneurship and firming small town economies: manufacturing firms, adaptive embeddedness, survival, and linked enterprise structures. *Entrepreneurship and Regional Development, 31*(9–10), 806–825.

Shen, Z., and Puig, F. (2018). Spatial dependence of the FDI entry mode decision: empirical evidence from emerging market enterprises. *Management International Review, 58*(1), 171–193.

Shimokawa, K., Jürgens, U., and Fujimoto, T. (eds) (2012). *Transforming Automobile Assembly: Experience in Automation and Work Organization*. New York: Springer Science & Business Media.

Smith, M., Wilson, J.R., and Wise, E. (2020). Evaluating clusters: where theory collides with practice. *Regional Science Policy and Practice, 12*(3), 413–430.

Stuart, A.W. (1972). Metrolina: a Southern dispersed urban region. *Southeastern Geographer*, 101–111.

Sweeney, S.H., and Feser, E.J. (1998). Plant size and clustering of manufacturing activity. *Geographical Analysis, 30*(1), 45–64.

Taylor, M. (2010). Clusters: a mesmerizing mantra. *Tijdschrift voor economische en sociale geografie, 101*(3), 276–286.

Tewari, M. (2005). Nonlocal forces in the historical evolution and current transformation of North Carolina's furniture industry. In J. Peacock, H. Watson and C. Matthews (eds), *The American South in a Global World*. Chapel Hill: UNC Press, pp. 113–137.

Tietz, M. (1994). Changes in economic development theory and practice. *International Regional Science Review, 16*(1–2), 101–106.

University of South Carolina (2014). BMW's Impact in South Carolina: two decades of economic development. https://sc.edu/study/colleges_schools/moore/documents/division_of_research/bmw.pdf.

US Bureau of Economic Analysis (2020). Table 1. GDP in current dollars. Available at: https://www.bea.gov/data/gdp/gdp-county-metro-and-other-areas.

Walker, R., and Calzonetti, F. (1990). Searching for new manufacturing plant locations: a study of location decisions in Central Appalachia. *Regional Studies, 24*(1), 15–30.

7 Going global in one location: exploring SME manufacturer internationalization motives at a trade fair

Ronald V. Kalafsky and Douglas R. Gress

Introduction

Small and medium-sized enterprises (SMEs) are often found to be at a disadvantage against larger competitors in international markets. This is due to myriad factors, but among the most critical are an overall lack of international experience, comparatively limited capital, and diminished access to export intelligence (see Majocchi et al., 2005; Kalafsky and Gress, 2014a, 2020). Involvement in a trade fair can be a means for SMEs to overcome some of these barriers. These events can serve many functions depending on the participants and their aims; at the firm level, these motivations are a source of much research in recent years (Lee and Kim, 2008; Kirchgeorg et al., 2009; Lee et al., 2010; Bathelt and Gibson, 2015). Contemporary work from within economic geography circles has also expanded how researchers examine and interpret the trade fair environment, including how firms and other associated actors interact within these venues and why (e.g., Bathelt and Schuldt, 2008, 2010; Rinallo et al., 2017). This research has illustrated how trade fairs can serve as temporary, spatially confined venues of learning and information exchange (Maskell et al., 2006; Bathelt and Schuldt, 2010). Such works have further demonstrated how trade fairs can be an effective venue where researchers can explore firm-level strategies within one location (Bathelt and Schuldt, 2008), which include those related to firm-level export performance (Bello and Barskdale, 1986; Kalafsky and Gress, 2013).

When taken within an internationalization context, trade fairs can form a central element of firm-level export marketing activities (Bello and Barskdale, 1986; Wilkinson and Brouthers, 2006; Kalafsky and Gress, 2013, 2014a). Firms may be able to enhance their export performance and overall amounts of international 'experience' by participating in important trade fairs (see Oura et al., 2016). It stands to reason, then, that productive information exchanges, relationship building, and the reduction of transaction costs made possible by trade fair participation can be of particular benefit and interest to SME manufacturers attempting to move into international space, especially those with limited budgets. Thus, these events can be seen as a means by which smaller manufacturers are able to compete on a more level ground with their larger-firm counterparts (Tanner, 2002), and to expand their internationalization horizons. For the above reasons, then, trade fairs (especially those with a global orientation) can therefore provide a forum where such dynamics can be explored by researchers: essentially, wide-ranging, internationally-oriented studies can take place in one location. Taking the above into account, this chapter shows how SMEs from the Korean advanced machine tool sector utilized a major international trade fair to extend their geographical reach in terms of engaging with current and prospective, globally-located business partners. Connected to this, the chapter builds upon these analyses to add further insights into how effective trade fairs can be for developing research on the geographical aspects of the firm-level, but globally focused, strategies of manufacturers.

Related to the themes of this book, it is particularly critical to study SME internationalization activities with the aim of adding to the wider bodies of research on manufacturing. Global supply chains most often involve different types of inputs from different sizes of firms in different locations, while much of the literature tends to focus on larger firms and their roles within these networks. This gap in the literature therefore necessitates additional research on SMEs, especially those that manufacture finished products (that is, not just serving as component suppliers) for global markets. As a result of this, there is a need to rebalance the research agenda on manufacturers and their geographies by offering new or reframed research; in this case, on SME manufacturers specifically. Set within these contexts, this chapter provides value-added in two ways. First, these analyses explore the internationalization-related motives of manufacturers within the realm of trade fair participation, and how these relate to other export-related measures. In an exhaustive review of the trade fair literature, Tafesse and Skallerud (2017) found that firm internationalization is one key area of research that has been largely ignored. It is important to note that these motives and any associated structural outcomes are explicitly explored vis-à-vis SMEs. This is a critical environment in which to examine the activity of these Korean manufacturers, as standing research has demonstrated that smaller firms face critical export-related impediments in terms of access to market intelligence (Williams, 2003), trade-related expenditures (Kalafsky and Duggan, 2016) and overall performance in global markets (Verwaal and Donkers, 2002; Majocchi et al., 2005). The second contribution (one closely connected to the first) entails a description of the synergies between trade fair geographies and export geographies, and how these can be explored by researchers to better understand the internationalization strategies of SME manufacturers within a relational context. Tied to this, the chapter then proposes future avenues for research on these topics. The next section provides a brief description of the trade fair literature and a research context for the forthcoming analyses.

Trade fairs, clusters and export marketing

Trade fair geographies and temporary clusters

Over the past two decades, researchers from geography, management and other disciplines have explored how trade fairs can be considered as temporary clusters of sorts, given that business partners and various components of supply chains (including buyers) can congregate in proximity for a short time, yet still benefit from the same externalities seen in larger, more permanent agglomerations (see Bathelt and Schudlt, 2008, 2010; Maskell, 2014; Rinallo et al., 2017). In essence, trade fairs can provide a transitory forum for more information exchange and competitor analysis than would otherwise be available to many firms (Maskell et al., 2006; Bathelt and Schuldt, 2010). 'Buzz', or critical, product and market-oriented information that is 'out there', is also widely available at trade fairs (Bathelt and Schuldt, 2010), perhaps one reason that the study of non-selling activity at trade fairs concerns information gathering (e.g., Lee and Kim, 2008). These are also important venues that provide a location in which relationships can be developed (Rinallo et al., 2017; Sarmento and Simões, 2018), something that can be of particular importance to exporters at these events (Bello and Barksdale, 1986; Tanner, 2002).

Trade fairs themselves have widely varying objectives (Golfetto and Rinallo, 2015), so at the outset one cannot automatically assume that all firms at all trade fairs are pursuing the same goals, or are even capable of doing so; experience, in short, matters. Rosson and Seringhaus (1991: 882), for example, found that performance at trade fairs was affected by the amount of export experience firms had, 'probably reflecting firms' internal capacities and the pursuit of contrasting ITF [international trade fair] objectives'. Seringhaus and Rosson (2001) also showed that increased trade fair experience in and of itself positively impacted upon firm planning and performance. Likewise, firms must change strategies and adapt to different environments as a result of imperfect information at trade fairs (Bathelt and Gibson, 2015).

In this way, trade fairs may be able to act as the 'neutral ground' described by Skov (2006: 781) in which firms can stake out a position concerning potential and existing customers (as well as suppliers or other business partners). Firms can, for example, benchmark competitors, process customer feedback and acquire international market information at trade fairs (Maskell et al., 2006). Trade fairs in many ways therefore serve to advance internationalization-based functions of firms, as global business partners are brought together not only to facilitate sales, but also to forge and continue useful relationships (e.g., Lee and Kim, 2008; Bathelt et al., 2017). Essentially, the global is made local, which is especially beneficial for firms with comparatively less global experience (Ramírez-Pasillas, 2010). The present contribution takes into consideration the preceding, touching upon some activity in which Korean SME manufacturers of varying experience with exporting engage at trade fairs, to include relationships formed or continued, and foreign markets explored. So to researchers as well, these venues again serve as the above-mentioned 'neutral ground' where the global is made local (Ramírez-Pasillas, 2010) in terms of being a forum for studying these firm-level internationalization dynamics.

Trade fairs as market-makers

A particularly useful foundation for the ensuing analyses is offered by Bathelt et al. (2017), and the four types of trade fair 'market configurations' that they unearthed. Central to this discussion is that rather than being a microcosm of neoclassical, economistic 'markets' perpetuated by anonymous, price-based mechanisms, trade fairs represent more realistic environments for market formation, in part because there is a relational context to sales, and in part because participants actively seek to diminish, if not obliterate, conditions of anonymity. Some research, for example, has even pointed to new technological interfaces being deployed at trade fairs, whereby virtual searches and meetings can set the stage for on-site, face-to-face interaction (Kalafsky and Gress, 2013).

The first configuration concerns 'classic deal-making', which is a motivation inherent in most, if not all, trade fairs. As described, sales may be between the firm and existing customers or new customers, and trust impacts upon the terms of the sales, specifically with regard to downpayments. In the present chapter, these potentialities are explored regarding their impacts on relationships formed or continued at a trade fair. The second configuration is to establish 'long-term customer relations'. While this is critical in business relationships globally, it is especially important in much of East Asia, where establishing long-term, trust-based business relationships is crucial (Trompenaars and Hampden-Turner, 2011). In the present research, firms are asked directly about their motivations for strengthening existing customer and supplier relationships. It is worth noting here that there is an accelerating trend in trade fair research away from mere sales-only performance metrics toward analyses of relationships formed or continued at these events (see Tafesse and Skallerud, 2017).

The third type concerns 'immediate synchronized customization', which encompasses preliminary contact and potential customization (for example, innovation). This again entails concerted efforts between seller and buyer, where face-to-face contact (afforded by a trade fair) is almost essential. Here, because of the differing technological contexts, we may witness some divergence between the trade fair motives and activity of the high-tech Korean advanced machine tool manufactures, and firms in the lower-value-added goods sectors described by Bathelt et al. (2017). In that study, for example, only 4 per cent of interviewed firms were engaging in direct cooperative innovative activity, though some also benefited from suggestions for improvement proffered by customer firms. It is also worth noting that Bathelt et al. (2017) also found physical product displays integral in the first three configurations. The ensuing analyses also take this into consideration. Economic geographers have been the most forward-thinking in terms of specifically integrating innovation into firm-level studies of trade fairs, a recommended avenue of research going forward (see Tafesse and Skallerud, 2017). We know from the extant literature that attendees are seeking innovative products (Sarmento et al., 2015), and that attendees often prefer to deal with technical personnel at trade fairs (Haon et al., 2020; Tanner and Chonko, 1995), but not as much is known about the exhibitor firm perspective on innovating their own products.

The fourth and final configuration concerns 'follow-up' negotiations, where buyers, sellers or other participants have preliminary exchanges of information at a trade fair, but with the goal of having further discussions and relationship-building after the trade fair. The present chapter does not delve into this specific aspect of 'post-show' trade fair participation per se, but does examine some categories that impact on deal-making, in large part because, as Bathelt et al. (2017: 1498) suggest, 'little is known about the processes of how market relations unfold during a trade fair'. Taken together, these configurations also encapsulate many of the motives for SMEs attempting to internationalize via trade fairs, and further illustrate how these events have become, and will continue to be, important forums for those examining the geographies of manufacturing and exporting.

SMEs and exporting

The literature is replete with research concerning SME export performance and the challenges that face these firms in global markets. In many ways, SMEs have particular challenges when set against their larger competitors. On balance, these firms tend to be much less export-intensive than their larger competitors (e.g., Majocchi et al., 2005; Bashiri-Behmiri et al., 2019). Germane to this chapter, smaller firms encounter difficulties engaging with international markets, with much of the challenge linked to somewhat limited resources as well as limited intelligence-gathering capabilities (Hilmersson and Jansson, 2012). The costs related to meeting with international customers can be a hindrance to SMEs looking to expand their global reach as well (Kalafsky and Duggan, 2016). SMEs also tend to sell to proximate or long-time, traditional export markets (Holmes and Stevens, 2012), indicating that many firms will not take the risks involved with international market expansion, or do not have the resources to do so. On the other hand, it is important to note that firms that do move into international space earlier tend to have higher long-term export performance (Love et al., 2016). Thus, it is critical for SMEs to move into global space quickly if they intend to grow their markets.

It is important to note that SMEs have less ability to adjust to any type of uncertainty (Ghosal and Loungani, 2000; Morikawa, 2016). This in turn may explain why SMEs have considerable difficulties in formulating export plans (see Armario et al., 2008). Still, SMEs can succeed if they overcome this uncertainty by taking innovative, aggressive approaches to global markets (Miocevic and Morgan, 2018). A trade fair can therefore be an effective way by which smaller firms can then successfully expand their international presence (Oura et al., 2016; Kalafsky and Gress, 2020), particularly those with a high degree of commitment to exporting (Bello and Barksdale, 1986). Keeping all of this in mind, trade fairs can then be viewed as a nexus within which SME manufacturers can reduce some of the uncertainties involved with international ventures such as exporting, especially in terms of costs, relationship-building, information-gathering and innovative activity, particularly if staffed with personnel well versed in export processes (Bello and Barksdale, 1986). In the end, as O'Hara et al. (1993: 237) suggest, the 'costs seem trivial in light of the valuable cultural, economic, and business/regulatory experience to be gained at these events'. While all of the findings in this section apply to firms, they could just as easily pertain to what can be accomplished at trade fairs by those who research these topics. In essence, these events are important to firms and their internationalization strategies, yet trade fairs can be just as useful for researchers exploring the firm-level dynamics discussed thus far.

Data and methodology

With the aim of exploring the internationalization-focused motives of Korean SME manufacturers, the following analyses present a study of firms participating in the Seoul International Manufacturing Technology Show (SIMTOS), which was held in April 2018 (and is normally held every two years). SIMTOS is considered to be among the most important trade fairs for the global machine tool sector, along with others in China, Germany, Japan, Taiwan and the United States. Trade fairs are already recognized as an environment conducive to firm-level research and data acquisition efforts, given their accessibility to normally spatially disparate groups of firms as well as various other supply chain and non-firm actors (e.g., Bathelt and Schuldt, 2008, 2010; Bathelt et al., 2017). The present study was limited to firms adhering to the Korean delineation of an SME: that is, a firm with fewer than 300 employees (see Kushnir, 2010). The selection of firms was also limited to Korea-based SMEs that manufactured complete machine tools (i.e., metal cutting or forming equipment), a grouping that includes machining centres, lathes, grinding machines, presses, and other related machinery. As mentioned in the previous section, firm-level SME internationalization is an important topic and one that merits further investigation, especially within a geographical context. The sample set was determined in advance through an analysis of the SIMTOS floor plan, which organized firms by both industrial function (for example, complete machine manufacturer, supplier, service provider) and country (or region) of origin. This early reconnaissance facilitated a successful study and is recommended for future research of this type.

A structured survey instrument was distributed to the firms selected to take part in the study. The survey contained questions on trade fair participation motives (for example, relationships, information-gathering and innovation), numerous export-related metrics related to performance, and factors influencing relationship-building and maintenance at trade fairs. It was available in Korean and English; the Korean version was translated and back-translated in order to assure accuracy. Language did not prove to be an impediment in this research; the dual-language survey helped with this. While one of the researchers is fluent in Korean, this did not appear to benefit or detract from data acquisition efforts. Perhaps because this was a large international trade fair, most booths had at least one employee proficient in English. Researchers should take note that language and translation issues may be an issue at smaller, domestically oriented trade fairs, where SMEs may not staff with such personnel. The survey questions were informed by the literature on trade fair motives (e.g., Hansen, 1996; Blythe, 2002, 2010; Kalafsky and Gress, 2013;

Table 7.1   Rating the trade fair motives

Reason	Rating	% of firms rating 6 or 7
Displaying new or improved products	6.14	78
Innovation-related purposes	5.88	72
Benchmarking competitors	5.86	68
Discover industry trends	5.74	66
Forming relationships with potential int'l customers	5.62	54
Meeting with int'l sales agents, distributors, etc.	5.58	60
Forming relationships with potential int'l suppliers	5.56	60
Strengthen relationships with existing int'l suppliers	5.36	52
Strengthen relationships with existing int'l customers	5.32	48
Reducing export-related costs	5.22	44
Learning about new export market environments	5.16	44

Note: Motives rated on a scale of 1 (not important) to 7 (very important).
Source: Authors' survey.

Bathelt et al., 2017). Surveys were then distributed to a total of 93 firms that adhered to the above definitions in terms of firm size and product offering (that is, SMEs and manufacturers of complete machines); 52 valid surveys were returned, resulting in a response rate of 56 percent. Cross-tabulation tests established that the sample set was representative with respect to firm size (number of employees), product lines and export activity.

Analysing internationalization at SIMTOS

As a start, Table 7.1 illustrates how the surveyed SMEs assessed the importance of salient trade fair motives. The top four reasons for trade fair participation are basically in line with standing research results of firms in other industries (see Blythe, 2002). Also, akin to results presented in Bathelt et al. (2017) (that is, market configurations 1–3), there was an emphasis on displaying new or improved products. Displaying products and disseminating information about product offerings has long been recognized as a prime motivator for trade fair attendance (Rinallo and Golfetto, 2011).

The next three reasons revolve around innovation and innovative activity. Here, however, we see that firms in this high-tech industry are prioritizing these functions more than the firms in the lower-value-added industries in the Bathelt et al. (2017) study (market configuration 3). In that study, only 4 per cent of firms reported engaging in innovative practice. Here, by way of contrast, over 60 per cent of respondent firms were involved in monitoring trends, benchmarking and direct innovation-related activity. Prior research discovered that 'buzz' about both trends and firms can be created and disseminated at these events (Bathelt and Schuldt, 2008), and that temporary and organized proximity can increase knowledge exchanges, thereby kicking off innovative activity and collaboration (Torre, 2008).

Connected to the present analyses, however, are the remaining participation motives that were listed on the survey. All of these refer to the internationalization-related goals of these firms. The literature suggests that firms could (and perhaps should) use trade fairs for global engagement, especially in terms of export marketing (Wilkinson and Brouthers, 2006; Kalafsky and Gress, 2013; Sarmento and Simões, 2018). Of such measures listed on the survey, note, for example, that over half of the surveyed firms assigned a rating of a 6 or 7 (with 7 being 'very important') to four of the motivations (meeting with potential or existing suppliers, meeting with potential customers, and meeting with agents or distributors). These motives, along with one concerning firms engaging with existing international customers, will be examined in further detail throughout the remainder of the chapter. It should be mentioned, however, that two export-related motives (reducing costs and learning about new export environments) garnered the lowest ratings. So at the outset, even though cost reduction and export environment scanning are considered important (over the average of 4 on the Likert scales), it would appear that for this group of firms, the motives related to internationalization activities seem to be more largely focused on relationship-building, whether in terms of buyers, suppliers or business partners such as agents. In this sense, because there are emphases on forming new relationships and on strengthening existing relationships, these findings conform to market configurations 1, 2 and 4 (Bathelt et al., 2017). Even these initial findings shed light on how interfirm, international relationships can be explored by researchers within the trade fair environment.

Naturally, and as previously mentioned, firms will have different and evolving motives with respect to trade fair participation; the SMEs at SIMTOS were no different in this regard. Further, in light of findings that firms use, or should use, trade fairs as export marketing platforms (Wilkinson and Brouthers, 2006; Kalafsky and Gress, 2014b; Oura et al., 2016), it was worth examining how trade fair motives changed for firms that viewed exporting as important to their operations. Accordingly, one of the Likert-scale questions on the survey instrument asked firms to rate the importance of exporting to their operations. Table 7.2 presents the results of difference of means tests with two groups: those that ranked exports as highly important (that is, a 6 or 7 on the Likert scale) set against those that rated exports as comparatively less important. When viewed from this perspective, differences emerged in connection with the two groups of firms. The SMEs that assigned the highest priority to exporting were also among those that accorded significantly more importance to the role of SIMTOS in forming relationships with potential overseas customers and suppliers. Additionally, the firms for which exporting was a high priority were also those that saw SIMTOS as a venue in which to strengthen existing relationships with customers and suppliers. On balance, then, export-oriented manufacturers were using this trade fair for globally focused relationship-building (Rinallo et al., 2017; Sarmento and Simões, 2018).

From industry and policy perspectives, these results should be welcome news. Korean firms in this industry will increasingly have to compete for new markets against Chinese, Vietnamese and Indian firms as they further develop their advanced machine tools, so the fact that they are looking for new markets now potentially bodes well for them. In terms of policy, the Korean government, facing steadily decreasing exports since 2012 (OECD, 2018), has been promoting trade fairs in order to assist SMEs with exporting (Park et al., 2010; Kalafsky and Gress, 2015). The government may be able to learn from any success taken away from this trade fair and apply it to trade fairs in other industries as well as to the development of targeted SME support. Further, in terms of ongoing and future research, such findings are particularly noteworthy in that the relationships discovered in Table 7.2 can provide yet new angles on the trade fair motives of manufacturers.

Last, these firms also placed a higher level of importance on participating in this trade fair for developing relationships with international market intermediaries such as sales agents and overseas distributors. This bolsters findings from recent research in terms of the importance placed on gaining access to markets via agents and wholesalers as well as to potential new buyer firms at a trade fair (see Locatelli et al., 2019). For many firms, especially SMEs, these intermediaries can ease the international market entry process and reduce costs and risks for exporting firms; especially for smaller, resource-challenged manufacturers. Within these temporary clusters, firms also prioritized their motives just as they would in normal business operations. More specifically, these were the sorts of SMEs taking aggressive steps to internationalize (Love et al., 2016) and employing trade fairs to this end (Sarmento and Simões, 2018).

Table 7.2 Comparing trade fair motives based on the importance of exporting: difference of means tests

Motive	Importance rated 6 or 7	Importance rated 1-5	p-value
Displaying new or improved products	6.32	5.84	0.103
Forming new relationships with potential int'l customers	6.16	4.74	0.000
Forming new relationships with potential int'l suppliers	6.13	4.63	0.000
Innovation-related purposes	6.06	5.58	0.226
Meeting with int'l sales agents, distributors, etc.	6.03	4.84	0.021
Benchmarking competitors	6.00	5.63	0.334
Strengthen relationships with existing int'l suppliers	5.90	4.47	0.001
Strengthen relationships with existing int'l customers	5.90	4.37	0.000
Discover industry trends	5.81	5.63	0.658
Learning about new export market environments	5.26	5.00	0.584
Reducing export-related costs	5.23	5.21	0.974

Note: Rated on a scale of 1 (exporting is not important) to 7 (exporting is very important).
Source: Authors' survey.

Narrowing the focus of these analyses to the main five internationalization-focused trade fair motives, Table 7.3 provides comparisons with regard to three export metrics: export intensity (that is, percentage of sales from exports), number of export markets and export growth. In some ways, these difference of means tests mirror results presented in Table 7.2, albeit with some notable differences. The first set of tests concerns export intensity, with firms either above or below the mean export intensity for the sample: 31.3 per cent of total sales. Four of the five measures show significant differences regarding their importance as a participation motive at SIMTOS: those forming or strengthening relationships with potential or existing international customers (market configurations 1, 2, and/or 4, per Bathelt et al., 2017), and forming relationships with suppliers.

Table 7.3   Differences of means tests: export motives and firm-level export characteristics

Motive	Export intensity above mean	Export intensity below mean	p-value	Export markets above mean	Exports markets below mean	p-value	Export growth >20%	Export growth ≤ 20 percent	p-value
Strengthen relationships with existing int'l customers	5.90	4.86	0.015	5.80	5.06	0.114	5.62	5.00	0.148
Forming new relationships with potential int'l customers	6.20	5.17	0.004	6.20	5.29	0.014	6.03	5.15	0.011
Strengthen relationships with existing int'l suppliers	6.00	4.86	0.008	5.87	5.10	0.102	5.86	4.90	0.045
Forming new relationships with potential int'l suppliers	6.25	5.03	0.003	6.33	5.13	0.001	5.93	5.15	0.053
Meeting with int'l sales agents, distributors, etc.	6.00	5.24	0.105	5.87	5.26	0.235	5.83	5.15	0.149

Note: Motives rated on a scale of 1 (not important) to 7 (very important).
Source: Authors' survey.

The comparisons continue, this time in terms of the number of export markets (that is, countries) that the firm currently serves; the mean for the sample is 5.7 countries currently served. In this case, the only significant differences are between those concerning the formation of new relationships with potential buyers or suppliers. These findings are noteworthy in that firms that were more internationally involved, at least in terms of the number of export markets, were also those that placed a significantly higher rating on the role of a trade fair for establishing new global connections. Again, this conforms to the literature in terms of trade fairs serving as venues where global connections can be established (Maskell et al., 2006; Skov, 2006), as well as intimating that these were committed SMEs more aggressively engaging export markets (Bello and Barksdale, 1986; Love et al., 2016).

The final series of tests in Table 7.3 group the surveyed firms based on export growth. Similar to the first two export-related tests, high-growth (that is, greater than 20 per cent) exporters place a significantly higher emphasis on SIMTOS as a venue for forming new relationships with potential buyers (market configurations 1 or 4). Another significant relationship is found regarding maintaining existing overseas supplier relationships, nearly significant at a 95 per cent level of confidence (market configuration 2). On whole, the findings shown in Table 7.3 suggest that a comparatively export-savvy group of firms were indeed using trade fair involvement to improve their international connectivity. In one way, this contradicts earlier findings that firms do not have clear goals regarding their trade participation (see Blythe, 2010). Instead, these comparatively high-performing exporting SMEs place an emphasis on many trade-related motives. Added to this, the evidence also supports the above-mentioned works intimating that trade fairs such as SIMTOS can serve as forums for information-gathering and exchange, in essence granting researchers access to global relationships building in one space. Germane to what is shown in Table 7.3, it indicates to researchers that international market research (in this case, referring to multiple global markets) can be accomplished within the confines of a trade fair.

The survey instrument also included a query about the factors that influenced export-related business relationships created or maintained at trade fairs, thus helping to shed more light on the mechanics involved in the market configurations set forth by Bathelt et al. (2017). The questions were also included due to the relatively scant attention placed on export-driven rationales at trade fairs (Wilkinson and Brouthers, 2006; Tafesse and Skallerud, 2017); surprising, as these are especially applicable within the export context (see Kalafsky and Gress, 2014a). As shown in Figure 7.1, five factors stand out, yet the highest and fifth-ranked factors showed very little difference, ranging between 5.23

and 5.12, respectively. Given the emphases on personal and firm networks, and reputation, these findings offer further support for the market configurations put forward by Bathelt et al. (2017), but add a subtle nuance. In that study, the emphasis was on how firms at trade fairs gauged the trustworthiness of customer firms and on how participating firms felt they could benefit from relations with buyers, mostly in terms of sales, but also in terms of value-added from customization. Here, Korean firms were demonstrating how their reputation, knowledge and capabilities could better help position them vis-à-vis current and potential customers and suppliers.

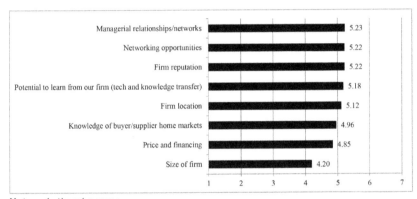

Note: Authors' survey.

Figure 7.1   Factors influencing export-related business at trade fairs

The interest in obtaining participating firm knowledge and technology transfer unearthed here should come as no surprise given the aforementioned results. Similarly, Bathelt and Zeng (2015) found that (at a Chinese trade fair) the second highest-rated motivation given by visitors for attendance was to find sources of innovation; backing up results from other work suggesting that many attendees seek out technical information and personnel, both for sources of innovation and as a prelude to making sales inquiries (Tanner and Chonko, 1995; Tafesse and Skallerud, 2017; Haon et al., 2020) This also backs up previous research (Babbar and Rai, 1993) concluding that concentrating analyses on sales activity at trade fairs alone may cloud other export-related goals such as innovating, and that buyer-tailored solutions improve prospects at these events (Sarmento et al., 2015; Bathelt et al., 2017).

It is also worth noting the attention paid to the benefits from firm location and knowledge of buyer/supplier home markets. Differences in culture, political systems, and in national and regional business practices may stymie internationalization efforts (Ghemawhat, 2001), and scholars have pointed out that this may be particularly the case for smaller Korean firms even if they happen to have competitive products (Seo and Choi, 2012). Here, Korean SMEs were cognizant of the value added achieved by knowing something about the markets they were targeting on the one hand, and the fact that potential client firms were interested in gaining similar information about Korea on the other. Relationships in that study, however, were important in the social context. Follow-up research on the firms that partook in SIMTOS would be required to delve into this potentiality, but it could be posited that given the Korean affinity for relationships as a bedrock for enduring business, it would not be surprising if this were the case.

Related to what has been discussed throughout this chapter, Table 7.4 examines the targeted markets at SIMTOS. Specifically, firms were asked what export markets (and potential customers) they were targeting at this trade fair. This measure was informed by previous findings suggesting that firms serving more distant markets were also better overall export performers (Kalafsky and Gress, 2014b; Ismail and Kuivalainen, 2015). The targeted market approach is comparatively novel and will be addressed further in the next section. Note that most of these manufacturers were aiming at meeting potential buyers from nearby or long-time markets such as China or Southeast Asia. Yet the data suggest an interesting relationship: firms that were targeting faraway and/ or unfamiliar markets such as Turkey or Brazil were also steering their efforts at more markets overall at this trade fair. This evidence again points to a select group of firms aggressively pursuing an export agenda at trade fairs, and fully taking advantage of this environment. Put more directly, these smaller manufacturers were capitalizing on the lower costs and increased networking opportunities inherent in trade fairs by exploring as many market opportunities as possible. Notably, the export market targeting aspect of trade fair strategies has received comparatively little attention, pointing to yet another avenue to be addressed in future research.

Looking ahead: further questions and future research avenues

The above findings lend support and add to the literature concerning the importance of these trade fairs as an export marketing platform, suggesting that SME manufacturers can increase their exports and market range via aggressive export strategies at trade fairs. In essence, SME manufacturers can

Table 7.4   Targeted markets at the trade fair

Market	% of firms targeting market at SIMTOS	Mean 'markets' targeted at SIMTOS
South Africa	10	8.8
Brazil	24	6.0
Turkey	26	5.8
North America	24	5.8
Western Europe	32	5.5
Eastern Europe	30	5.3
East Asia	31	4.8
India	52	4.5
China	44	4.1
Southeast Asia	64	4.0

Source: Authors' survey.

utilize trade fairs to engage with global supply chains and an international cus-tomer base. This shows how such events can be used by smaller manufacturers to establish relationships with existing customers and to develop relationships with potential buyers. The added benefit of the trade fair environment is that SME manufacturers can look at wider (that is, geographically distant) markets and business partners in a rather cost-effective manner. Trade fairs, then, provide a venue for this export activity by enabling SME manufacturers to overcome many commonly cited obstacles in their internationalization processes. Connected specifically to the mission of this book, these findings also demonstrate how trade fairs also can be utilized by researchers to explore the global connections of SME manufacturers, with the added benefit of being done in one location.

This chapter built upon the literature in two specific ways. The first concerns direct contributions to the trade fair literature. It demonstrated how export strategies at trade fairs are related to other firm-level export metrics, especially as it concerns networking opportunities for SME manufacturers and how specific markets (that is, buyers and other supply chain partners from specific countries) can be targeted at trade fairs, and how firms that target distant markets also tend to aim at wider markets overall. Second, these analyses addressed trade fair participation concerning innovation and knowledge flows; again, set within an SME manufacturer context. This was done both from the perspective of the participating firms' motivations, and from their understanding of how their knowledge, both place-based and technical, can lend itself to the creation and continuation of business relationships. Taken as a whole, the SME manufacturer-internationalization-trade fair dynamics described here build upon the larger bodies of literature on the geographies of manufacturing.

Admittedly, this chapter's analyses raise as many questions as they provide answers. For instance, a new, fifth market configuration (referencing Bathelt et al., 2017) may be suggested: 'targeted exploration'. This configuration, unlike the others, does not necessarily entail on-the-spot deal-making, or even establishing specific relationships that can be developed later. Rather, this configuration is a prelude to the four existing market configurations and, as analyses suggest, is a function of firm experience. It is in relation to this configuration that parallel assistance from export promotion agencies and professional associations may emerge as beneficial to firm-level efforts; this could be an important path for researchers to explore.

In light of this, there are three main ways in which research on SME manufacturers at trade fairs should move forward. First, additional attention should be paid to the export strategies of manufacturers at trade fairs. While this topic was indeed a theme of this chapter, more work needs to be done in terms of focusing on specific export-related motives for trade fair participation. Explicitly, do SMEs pair and deploy their capabilities to achieve successful export-centred execution at these events? As the previous literature showed, many of these firms do not have clear-cut motives for trade fairs. Future research on manufacturer-exporters should explore how (and indeed whether) motives are established before participating in trade fairs, and how exporting figures into these objectives. How to address this does pose a challenge. While a survey instrument provides a much easier and standardized approach, qualitative interviews might provide nuance in terms of goal-setting before trade fairs and the importance placed upon specific objectives.

The second potential research stream concerns the targeting of specific export markets at a trade fair. It is obvious that firms can meet with current and potential customers at these events (Ramírez-Pasillas, 2010; Bathelt et al., 2017). In addition to this, and as findings from this chapter suggest, it appears that SMEs can indeed look at specific geographical markets, in addition to their efforts aimed at specific buyers (Kalafsky and Gress, 2014a, 2020). Therefore, more efforts should be directed at understanding how SME manufacturers select these markets and what their motivations are for doing so. Given the reduced transaction costs involved with trade fairs, one could initially surmise that a wide range of markets (that is, potential export customers) would be engaged with at a trade fair. Yet, this is not the case, so what leads firms to engage with certain markets at the neglect of others? Moreover, how do firms go about engaging with these markets at trade fairs in terms of intelligence-gathering and pre-show preparation? Exploring questions such as these are critical to understanding SME internationalization trajectories and performance. As suggested above, this could be addressed in follow-up interviews with survey participants with a focus on the question: how and why does the firm choose which markets and buyers to target at a global trade fair?

The third and final possible opportunity for research concerns SME manufacturers specifically. It is well established that most of these firms face serious constraints concerning their export activities. Future studies should examine more about the SMEs themselves, or what in the trade fair vernacular are referred to as pre-show activities (Kim and Lee, 2008). What are their pre-existing levels of international experience, including firm management and ownership? There is now a fairly well-established literature on staffing and training in relation to trade fair attendance, but very little when it comes to the internationalizing efforts of firms. After all, many SMEs remain family-owned, so how does this play a role in export engagement? Also, how do comparatively limited resources play a role in: (1) the number and types of trade fairs in which SME manufacturers participate; and (2) the number of countries (export markets) that they target at these events? It is easy to assume that since customers are essentially in one place at a trade fair, SMEs should target as many as possible. However, it is worth exploring how smaller firms determine which international markets are even worth attempting, as the present analyses suggested that SMEs aim at specific export markets even with the reduced transaction costs inherent in trade fairs. Adding to this, does this market targeting stop at the trade fair level? Future research could examine whether or not post-show follow-ups add to a firm's ability to increase its geographical scope. From a policy perspective, the second and third avenues of inquiry could pay dividends, as research could help to guide policy regarding targeted funding, market information and export assistance, and the placement of necessary skilled personnel.

Given what has happened since late 2019, the ongoing restrictions and slow-downs in the global economy due to COVID-19 pose a number of challenges related to a central theme of this chapter: trade fairs as an export marketing platform for smaller manufacturers. It appears that well through 2021 and into 2022, international travel will be heavily restricted, along with most international trade fairs being cancelled or postponed. Where does this leave SME manufacturers in terms of their export marketing efforts? Moreover, once trade fairs are operating in earnest again (which is a hope), how will these events be transformed by the recent epidemic? Will these events emerge changed in terms of their benefits, namely as forums for face-to-face contact and as venues for information exchange, especially of the tacit variety? Indeed, many trade fairs that were to occur during the pandemic converted to various virtual iterations. While these forums could be useful in the interim, how do virtual trade fairs and their resultant iterations detract from the original benefits of these events? In turn, could these transformations place SME manufacturers at a decided disadvantage in terms of exploring international markets for sales opportunities, especially at a time when domestic or regional consumption might be curtailed? The very advantages of trade fairs for SMEs could thus be diminished, especially in terms of 'levelling the field' for smaller firms versus their larger competitors (Tanner, 2002). Trade fairs, overall, have provided a cost- and time-effective venue for firms to reach global audiences; these benefits have been especially important for SMEs. It will be critical for researchers who explore the dynamics of SME manufacturer internationalization to establish how these new environments might have transformed the rules of engagement for such firms in the global marketplace, as well as how it may transform their own research.

References

Armario, J.M., Ruiz, D.M., and Armario, E.M. (2008). Market orientation and internationalization in small and medium-sized enterprises. *Journal of Small Business Management* 46(4): 485–511.
Babbar, S., and Rai, R. (1993). Competitive intelligence for international business. *Long Range Planning* 26(3): 103–113.
Bashiri-Behmiri, N., Rebelo, J.F., Gouveia, S., and António, P. (2019). Firm characteristics and export performance in Portuguese wine firms. *International Journal of Wine Business Research* 31(3): 419–440.
Bathelt, H., and Gibson, R. (2015). Learning in 'organized anarchies': the nature of technological search processes at trade fairs. *Regional Studies* 49(6): 985–1002.
Bathelt, H., Li, P., and Zhu, Y-W. (2017). Geographies of temporary markets: an anatomy of the Canton Fair. *European Planning Studies* 25(9): 1497–1515.
Bathelt, H., and Schuldt, N. (2008). Between luminaires and meat grinders: international trade fairs as temporary clusters. *Regional Studies* 42(6): 853–868.
Bathelt, H., and Schuldt, N. (2010). International trade fairs and global buzz, part I: ecology of global buzz. *European Planning Studies* 18(12): 1956–1974.
Bathelt, H., and Zeng, G. (2015). Trade, knowledge circulation and diverse trade fair ecologies in China. In *Temporary Knowledge Ecologies: The Rise and Evolution of Trade Fairs in the Asia-Pacific Region*, edited by H. Bathelt and G. Zeng. Cheltenham, UK and Northampton, MA, USA: Edward Elgar Publishing, pp. 154–176.
Bello, D.C., and Barksdale, H.C. (1986). Exporting at industrial trade shows. *Industrial Marketing Management* 15(3): 197206.

Blythe, J. (2002). Using trade fairs in key account management. *Industrial Marketing Management* 31(7): 627–635.

Blythe, J. (2010). Trade fairs as communication: a new model. *Journal of Business and Industrial Marketing* 25(1): 57–62.

Ghemawat, P. (2001). Distance still matters: the hard reality of global expansion. *Harvard Business Review* 79(8): 137–147.

Ghosal, V., and Loungani, P. (2000). The differential impact of uncertainty on investment in small and large businesses. *Review of Economics and Statistics* 82(2): 338–343.

Golfetto, F., and Rinallo, D. (2015). The evolution of trade show systems: lessons from Europe. In *Temporary Knowledge Ecologies: The Rise and Evolution of Trade Fairs in the Asia-Pacific Region*, edited by H. Bathelt and G. Zeng. Cheltenham, UK and Northampton, MA, USA: Edward Elgar Publishing, pp. 42–66.

Hansen, K. (1996). The dual motives of participants at international trade shows: An empirical investigation of exhibitors and visitors with selling motives. *International Marketing Review* 13(2): 39–53.

Haon, C., Sego, T., Drapeau, N., and Sarin, S. (2020). Disconnect in trade show staffing: A comparison of exhibitor emphasis and attendee preferences. *Industrial Marketing Management*. https://doi.org/10.1016/j.indmarman.2020.03.016.

Hilmersson, M., and Jansson, H. (2012). International network extension processes to institutionally different markets: entry nodes and processes of exporting SMEs. *International Business Review* 21(4): 682–693.

Holmes, T.J., and Stevens, J.J. (2012). Exports, borders, distances, and plant size. *Journal of International Economics* 8(1): 91–103.

Ismail, N.A., and Kuivalainen, O. (2015). The effect of internal capabilities and external environment on small- and medium-sized enterprises' international performance and the role of the foreign market scope: the case of the Malaysian halal food industry. *Journal of International Entrepreneurship* 13(4): 418–451.

Kalafsky, R.V., and Duggan, D.T. (2016). Overcoming trade impediments: considering SME exporters from Nova Scotia. *Professional Geographer* 68(4): 613–623.

Kalafsky, R.V., and Gress, D.R. (2013). Trade fairs as an export marketing and research strategy: results from a study of Korean advanced machinery firms. *Geographical Research* 51(3): 304–317.

Kalafsky, R.V., and Gress, D.R. (2014a). Go big or stay home? Korean machinery firms, trade fair dynamics, and export performance. *Asia Pacific Business Review* 20(1): 136–152.

Kalafsky, R.V., and Gress, D.R. (2014b). Getting there: trade fair participation and its importance for Korean machinery exporters. *Professional Geographer* 66(4): 621–630.

Kalafsky, R.V., and Gress, D.R. (2015). How and where tigers roam: the role of Korean trade fairs in supporting firms' export activities. In *Temporary Knowledge Ecologies: The Rise and Evolution of Trade Fairs in the Asia-Pacific Region*, edited by H. Bathelt and G Zeng. Cheltenham, UK and Northampton, MA, USA: Edward Elgar Publishing, pp. 273–290.

Kalafsky, R.V., and Gress, D.R. (2020). Minimizing distance: international trade fairs and SME targeting of specific export markets. *GeoJournal* 85(4): 1025–1037.

Kim, Y.-Z., and Lee, K. (2008). Sectoral innovation system and technological catch-up: the case of the capital goods industry in Korea. *Global Economic Review* 37(2): 135–155.

Kirchgeorg, M., Springer, C., and Kästner, E. (2009). Objectives for successfully participating in trade shows. *Journal of Business and Industrial Marketing* 25(1): 63–72.

Kushnir, K. (2010). *How do Economies Define Micro, Small and Medium Enterprises (MSMEs)?* Washington, DC: International Financial Corporation and World Bank.

Lee, C.-H., and Kim, S.-Y. (2008). Differential effects of determinants on multi-dimensions of trade show performance: by three stages of pre-show, at-show, and post-show activities. *Industrial Marketing Management* 37(7): 784–796.

Lee, M.J., Yeung, S., and Dewald, B. (2010). An exploratory study examining the determinants of attendance motivations as perceived by attendees at Hong Kong exhibitions. *Journal of Convention and Event Tourism* 11(3): 195–208.

Locatelli, R.R.S., da Silveira, M.A.P., and Mourão, P. (2019). Speed dating or marriage? Brazilian business fairs according to a sample of metal/mechanic companies. *Journal of Business and Industrial Marketing* 34(1): 80–94.

Love, J.H., Roper, S., and Zhou, Y. (2016). Experience, age, and exporting performance in UK SMEs. *International Business Review* 25(4): 806–819.

Majocchi, A., Bacchiocchi, E., and Mayrhofer, E. (2005). Firm size, business experience and export intensity in SMEs: a longitudinal approach to complex relationships. *International Business Review* 14(6): 719–738.

Maskell, P. (2014) Accessing remote knowledge – the roles of trade fairs, pipelines, crowdsourcing and listening posts. *Journal of Economic Geography* 14(5): 883–902.

Maskell, P., Bathelt, H., and Malmberg, A. (2006). Building global knowledge pipelines: the role of temporary clusters. *European Planning Studies* 14(8): 997–1013.

Miocevic, D., and Morgan, R.E. (2018). Operational capabilities and entrepreneurial opportunities in emerging market firms: explaining exporting SME growth. *International Marketing Review* 35(2): 320–341.

Morikawa, M. (2016). Business uncertainty and investment: evidence from Japanese companies. *Journal of Macroeconomics* 49: 224–236.

OECD (2018). *OECD Economic Surveys. Korea 2018.* Paris: OECD Publishing.

O'Hara, B., Palumbo, F., and Herbig, P. (1993). Industrial trade shows abroad. *Industrial Marketing Management* 22(3): 233–237.

Oura, M.M., Zilber, S.N., and Lopes, E.L. (2016). Innovation capacity, international experience, and export capacity of SMEs in Brazil. *International Business Review* 25(4): 921–932.

Park, C-O., Lee, S.-H., and Kang L.-W. (2010). The influence of the pushing and pulling factor on exhibition quality evaluation. *Knowledge Management Research* 11: 67–77.

Ramírez-Pasillas, M. (2010). International trade fairs as amplifiers or permanent and temporary proximity in clusters. *Entrepreneurship and Regional Development* 22(2): 155–187.

Rinallo, D., Bathelt, H., and Golfetto, F. (2017). Economic geography and industrial marketing views on trade shows: collective marketing and knowledge circulation. *Industrial Marketing Management* 61(1): 97–103.

Rinallo, D., and Golfetto, F. (2011). Exploring the knowledge strategies of temporary cluster organizers: a longitudinal study of the EU fabric industry trade shows (1986–2006). *Economic Geography* 87(4): 453–476.

Rosson, P.J., and Seringhaus, F.H.R. (1991). International trade fairs: firms and government exhibits. In *Export Development and Promotion: The Role of Public Organizations*, edited by F.H.R. Seringhaus and P.J. Rosson. Boston, MA: Kluwer Academic Publishers, pp. 163–187.

Sarmento, M., and Simões, C. (2018). The evolving role of trade fairs in business: a systematic literature review and a research agenda. *Industrial Marketing Management* 73(1): 154–170.

Sarmento, M., Simões, C., and Farhangmehr, M. (2015). Applying a relationship marketing perspective to B2B trade fairs: the role of socialization episodes. *Industrial Marketing Management* 44: 131–141.

Seo, M.-S., and Choi, B.-H. (2012). The study on plan of practical application of marketing for securing global competitiveness of small-medium sized enterprises. *Journal of Trade Association* 37(1): 257–286 (in Korean).

Seringhaus, F.H.R., and Rosson, P.J. (2001). Firm experience and international trade Fairs. *Journal of Marketing Management* 17(7–8): 877–901.

Skov, L. (2006). The role of trade fairs in the global fashion business. *Current Sociology* 54(5): 764–783.

Tafesse, W., and Skallerud, K. (2017). A systematic review of the trade show marketing literature: 1980-2014. *Industrial Marketing Management* 63: 18–30.

Tanner, J.F. (2002). Leveling the playing field: factors influencing trade show success for small companies. *Industrial Marketing Management* 31(3): 229–239.

Tanner, J.F., and Chonko, L.B. (1995). Trade show objectives, management, and staffing practices. *Industrial Marketing Management* 24: 257–264.

Torre, A. (2008). On the role played by temporary geographical proximity in knowledge transmission. *Regional Studies* 42: 869–889.

Trompenaars, F., and Hampden-Turner, C. (2011). *Riding the Waves of Culture: Understanding Diversity in Global Business* (3rd edn). New York: McGraw-Hill.

Verwaal, E., and Donkers, B. (2002). Firm size and exporting: solving an empirical puzzle. *Journal of International Business Studies* 33(3): 603–613.

Wilkinson, T., and Brouthers, L.E. (2006). Trade promotion and SME export performance. *International Business Review* 15(3): 233–252.

Williams, J.E.M. (2003). Export information use in small and medium-sized industrial companies: an application of Diamantopoulos' and Souchon's scale. *International Marketing Review* 20(1): 44–66.

8 The transformation of Asian electronics production networks: evidence from the participation of Vietnam

David Yuen Tung Chan and Chun Yang

Introduction

The global value chains (GVCs) (Gereffi, 1994) and global production networks (GPNs) frameworks (Coe et al., 2004; Dicken et al., 2001; Henderson et al., 2002), particularly the newly developed GPN 2.0 analytical framework (Coe and Yeung, 2015), have been widely used to understand the geographical and structural configuration of the increasingly organizationally fragmented and spatially dispersed production networks since the 1990s. Coordinated by a small number of lead firms, GVCs and GPNs of various industries are formed via cross-border investment and trade engaged by variegated suppliers and customers worldwide. To stay competitive, lead firms from the advanced economies, such as the United States, European countries and Japan, as well as later the newly industrialized economies (NIEs), namely South Korea, Taiwan, Singapore and Hong Kong, have offshored and/or outsourced their relatively low-value-added production activities to the developing countries where the overall production costs are relatively lower. As a result, the developing countries, such as China, have been able to join the global and regional production networks coordinated by these lead firms (Borrus et al., 2000). Notably, in the electronics industry, a so-called 'triangular trade' pattern (Baldwin and Lopez-Gonzalez, 2015) has been witnessed among the countries in East Asia after they have participated in the production networks over the past decades. China has become the 'world factory', by assembling the components and parts imported mainly from the Asian NIEs and Japan into final goods and exporting them to the external markets mainly in the United States (US) and European countries.

Since the early 2000s, '(T)he centuries-old international trade geography, where the South served as hinterlands of resources and captive markets for finished goods of the North, is changing' (UNCTAD, 2004: 1). Although the 'triangular trade'-based paradigm of the Asian electronics production network is still valid, it could not fully capture the emergence of the changing dynamics in the global economy and subsequent effects on the reconfiguration of the Asian production networks, particularly since the late 2000s. On the one hand, the rise of Asia and particularly China have been reflected not only in productive capacity, but also in the rising demand from the increasing expansion of its middle-income population (Horner and Nadvi, 2018; Horner and Murphy, 2018). On the other hand, the increasing participation of the developing Southeast Asian countries in the regional production networks has been evident (Yeung, 2017). Since the 2000s, apart from the 'going west' initiatives to inland China, relocating to the neighbouring Southeast Asian countries engaged by electronics transnational corporations (TNCs) has been increasingly witnessed (Zhu and Pickles, 2014; Yang, 2016). However, the subsequent effects on the patterns of the Asian production networks remain under-researched in the academic literature. In response to the changing dynamics at national, regional and global levels, this chapter aims to offer an updated investigation on the configuration of the Asian production network since the late 2000s, through the case of the electronics industry. In doing so, it is hoped not only to understand the latest changing dynamics in the global economy and their implications for the restructuring of regional production networks in Asia, but also to provide some insights to outline the potential avenues for future research on manufacturing, particularly the electronics industry.

As illustrated by Sturgeon and Kawakami (2010), the electronics industry accounts for a growing share of the total manufactured intermediate goods trades and the highest share compared to other industries common in the studies of global production systems, such as automotive and apparel industry. Unlike other technology-intensive sectors that need the co-location of the engineers and other capital-intensive sectors where the intermediaries are cost-inefficient to transport, it is relatively common for electronics firms to engage in the twin strategies of offshoring and outsourcing, given the advanced technologies and the cheaper transportation costs nowadays. Given the fierce global competition, electronics firms are sensitive and would respond quickly to the changing global economy. Moreover, apart from the importance for the electronics manufacturing industry of forming production networks at the global level, the industry is particularly important for the formation of the Asian regional production network, as illustrated by Thorbecke (2016): not only was the intra-regional trade volume in Asia in electronics parts and component three times greater than the trade in the next leading category in 2014, but there has also been a tight relationship between the trade within the region and the exports of final electronics products from the region to the world, forming a spatially wider network. While recent research has demonstrated that the Asian electronics production networks have started to transform with the increasing participation of the Southeast Asian countries such as Vietnam (Sturgeon and Zylberberg, 2016), many pertinent questions are yet to be answered, including: how have these developing economies joined the regional production networks? What are their roles, and the changing roles of the members already in the networks? And how have the networks reconfigured?

Existing literature has mainly focused on the national-level analysis of the advantages and disadvantages for Vietnam of its global engagement in order to make policy recommendations (see, for example, Sturgeon and Zylberberg, 2016). Little effort has been made to understand the current changing dynamics at a transnational level, that is, at the Asian regional and global levels. Hence, this chapter offers an updated investigation on the transformation of the Asian electronics production networks, based on the participation of Vietnam, to fill in the gaps in the literature. Particular attention is paid to the investment into Vietnam by both established and emerging transnational corporations from the relatively developed and the developing economies, such as South Korea and China, respectively, since the late 2000s.

The remainder of the chapter is organized as follows. First, an overview on literature on the reorganization of the global production networks of the electronics industry is conducted to highlight the transformation of the regional production networks in Asia. The chapter then investigates the changing patterns of the Asian production networks based on the statistical trade data. This is followed by interpretation of the regional production networks by delineating the changing dynamics at global, regional and national levels. The chapter concludes with a summary of main findings and, more importantly, a discussion and suggestions for future research directions on the global and regional production systems in the volatile context of exogenous shocks.

Reorganization of the electronics production networks in Asia: an overview

The spatial reorganization of electronics production began in the 1960s, when the electronics manufacturers in the US, Western Europe and, later, Japan started to offshore their production activities to the Asian NIEs for relative lower production costs. While keeping the higher value-added activities at home, these TNCs managed to relocate their lower-value-added production activities to the relatively developing Asian NIEs, and to export the final products back to the advanced economies. At that time, East Asia simply acted as the assembly base for these TNCs as only a limited number of firms in the Asian NIEs were able to participate in the production network, serving as the lower-tier suppliers (Yeung, 2007).

Starting from the 1980s, the global electronics industry started to grow and become more competitive. Given that the production process of the electronics firms has become more standardized and modularized due to technological advancement on one hand, and the improved capabilities of the domestic suppliers in the Asian NIEs on the other hand, these leading manufacturers started to outsource parts of their production, mainly the manufacturing activities, to focus on developing their core technologies. As illustrated by Read (1997), the organizational shift of the electronics value chain from vertical integration (keeping all activities in-house) to specialization (outsourcing some of the activities, usually the lower-value-added ones) could not only increase the cost-efficiency of the production process, but also provide an important chance for the electronics firms in the Asian NIEs to participate in the global electronics production networks. The changing organizational structure of the electronics value chain also gave rise to a number of higher-tier suppliers, such as manufacturing service providers, modular manufacturers, specialized suppliers and, later, contract manufacturers, according to their divergent development paths, especially in the 1990s, when nearly all major product-level electronics firms decided to go 'factory-less' (Gereffi et al., 2005). Based on their corporate strategies and their home-based advantages, and through participating in the global production networks as well as receiving help from the national state, firms in the Asian NIEs have become not only the suppliers of different tiers, but also the lead firms in their own right, such as Samsung and LG based in South Korea (Lee et al., 2016; Yeung, 2007).

The production relocation of the electronics industry has extended further beyond the Asian NIEs since the 1980s. The export-oriented development model that prevailed in the Asian NIEs was followed by China, particularly starting from the 1980s when TNCs started to move into the Pearl River Delta (PRD) in China, mainly due to the price pressure and the growing competition from firms in other Asian countries (Yeung, 2001). Besides the PRD, the Yangtze River Delta (YRD) has become another hotspot for the inflows of foreign direct investment (FDI), particularly for Taiwanese investors, since the late 1990s. Taiwanese electronics and information technology manufacturers began to establish a new industrial cluster by expanding from Taiwan and the PRD region to the YRD region. A major share of investment from Taiwanese firms has been recorded in the cities in the YRD region, such as

Suzhou, Wujiang and Kunshan (Yang, 2009). Notably, this wave of production relocations of the Asian NIEs-based TNCs has, to a large extent, been pushed by the global lead firms from the advanced economies, mainly to lower their production costs (Yang and Hsia, 2007).

Since the 1960s and 1970s, 'Factory Asia' has been regarded as a manufacturing power. China, which implemented opening and reform at that time, replaced Japan and later the Asian NIEs to become the 'world factory'. Nowadays, China contributes more than half of the manufacturing output of 'Factory Asia'. Notably, as pointed out by Baldwin and Lopez-Gonzalez (2015), a so-called 'triangular trade' pattern has emerged and dominated the countries in East Asia over the past decades. While the components and parts have been imported from Asian NIEs and Japan, China has acted as the assembly hub, by manufacturing and exporting the final products for the external markets in the US and European countries.

Although the 'triangular trade' pattern among the East Asian countries has still dominated, a transformation of the 'world factory' has started since the 2000s, especially in the aftermath of the 2008 global financial crisis. The export-led regions in coastal China have faced unprecedented challenges, such as the rising cost of labour and land, policy changes, and shrinking market demand from Western advanced economies, which have engendered spatial relocation of labour-intensive manufacturing firms from China to lower-cost locations, for example inland China and neighbouring Southeast Asia (Yang, 2016). While achieving a lower cost–capability ratio is not the only reason for the recent spatial relocations, increasing numbers of studies have pointed out that these relocations could also serve as a way for the TNCs as well as the domestic firms in China to engage with emerging markets: the vast domestic market in China, as well as other developing economies in Southeast Asia (see, for example, Horner and Nadvi, 2018; Fu et al., 2020; Yang, 2017). As pointed out by Yang (2016), the existing literature has primarily focused on the internal production relocation within the 'world factory', while little academic attention has been paid to the restructuring of Asian production networks with the increasing participation of the Southeast Asian countries, particularly the cross-border production expansion of established and emerging TNCS from China to these countries, such as Vietnam. This chapter thus aims to address the literature gap by contributing to understanding the restructuring of regional production networks in Asia, so as to provide an up-to-date discussion of the relatively isolated debates on manufacturing in Asia and to outline the potential research agenda.

Vietnam's participation in the global and Asian electronics production networks

Before the start of the *doi moi* reform in the late 1980s, Vietnam was a backward agricultural country. Since the late 1980s, Vietnam started to reform its economy, and followed the path of China to open up and leverage trade, inflows of FDI and TNCs in order to achieve economic growth and reduce poverty. Through integrating into the global production systems via international trade, Vietnam has grown its competitive advantage in terms of industrial performance. According to the United Nations (UN) Industrial Development Report 2018, the competitive industrial performance ranking of Vietnam increased from 59th place to 41st place within a short span of five years from 2010 to 2015. It has been proved that the export-led development model adopted by Vietnam over the past decades has had a positive impact on its ability to maintain economic growth in the long run (Hai and Hung, 2018). Notably, the inflows of FDIs and TNCs have been critical in the process. In Figure 8.1, one can see that, since the 1990s, the FDI inflow to Vietnam has been increasing significantly. After participating in the World Trade Organization (WTO) in 2007, the FDI inflow multiplied fourfold from US$2400 million in 2006 to US$9579 million in 2008. Despite the global financial crisis in 2008–09, the FDI inflow rebounded after 2010. This indeed indicates that the rapid participation of Vietnam in the global and regional economies has been driven by the inflows of FDI since the mid-2000s.

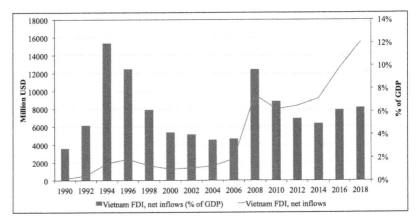

Figure 8.1   Net inflows of foreign direct investment to Vietnam, 1990–2018

Table 8.1   Major export goods and shares of total exports in Vietnam (USD million)

Item	2010	Share (%)	2012	Share (%)	2014	Share (%)	2016	Share (%)
Phone and accessories	2.3	3.2	12.8	11.2	24.0	16.0	34.3	19.4
Textiles	11.2	15.5	14.4	12.6	20.7	13.8	23.8	13.5
Computers, electronics products	3.6	5.0	7.8	6.8	11.6	7.7	19.0	10.7
Footwear	5.1	7.1	7.3	6.4	10.2	6.8	13.0	7.4
Seafood	5.0	6.9	6.1	5.3	7.9	5.2	7.1	4.0
Wood and wood products	3.4	4.7	4.7	4.1	6.1	4.1	7.0	4.0
Crude oil	5.0	6.9	8.2	7.2	7.2	4.8	2.4	1.4

Source: Based on data from the Statistical Yearbooks of the General Statistics Office of Vietnam (2010–2016).

During the period from 2010 to 2016, the export values of phone sets and accessories, as well as computers and electronics products, increased from US$2.3 million and US$3.6 million to US$34.3 and US$19 million, respectively (Table 8.1). The contribution of electronics products to Vietnam's total export value increased from less than 10 per cent in 2010 to nearly 30 per cent in 2016 (Table 8.1). In consequence, in 2018, Vietnam ranked 12th in the world in terms of electronics export values (VietNamNet Bridge, 2018). After 2010, although the export value of the primary products, such as wood and seafood, has been increasing, their shares of national total export value have been decreasing. This implies that the FDI-induced development model adopted by Vietnam after the *doi moi* reform has brought about the structural transformation of exports in Vietnam. In association with the transformation of the 'world factory' and the consequential production relocations out of coastal China, there has been witnessed an increasing participation of the Southeast Asian countries, such as Vietnam, in the Asian electronics production network.

According to data from the General Statistics Office of Vietnam, by the end of 2018, 57 per cent of the registered capital of the FDI inflow to Vietnam was invested in the manufacturing sector, rising from 53 per cent in 2006. Since the early 2010s, Vietnam has gradually emerged as an attractive destination for manufacturing investments by TNCs. A more in-depth analysis regarding the production relocations and shifting investment destinations between China and Vietnam is clearly demonstrated by Table 8.2. China's share of Japan's outward FDI dropped from 5.4 per cent in 2009 to 2 per cent in 2017, while Vietnam's share increased from 1 per cent to 3.7 per cent during the same period. Among the destinations for South Korea's outward FDI, China's share fell from 15.7 per cent to 7.8 per cent during the period of 2009–2017, while Vietnam's share increased from 9.7 per cent to 25.6 per cent. Vietnam's share of Singapore's outward FDI surged from 2 per cent in 2007 to 21.9 per cent in 2017 (Table 8.2). Besides, the ratios of FDI invested by Japan, Korea and Singapore in Vietnam, compared to China, increased from 0.18, 0.62 and 0.1 in 2009, to 1.81, 3.26 and 1.93 in 2017, respectively. Particularly, the value of the investment from Korea to Vietnam was 3.26 times more than that to China. Obviously, Vietnam has taken China's place as one of the major destinations for the FDI outflows by the established TNCs from Japan, South Korea and Singapore. Clearly, increasing cross-border investments and expansion of manufacturing activities from China to Vietnam emerged.

Changing dynamics and transformation of the Asian electronics production networks

The production relocation and the reconfiguration of the electronics production networks have not been solely led by the established TNCs from Japan and the NIEs, as shown above. As Table 8.3 shows, Japan and the Asian NIEs have contributed the most to Vietnam's FDI inflow since the 2010s. In 2018, they contributed more than 70 per cent of the total inflows of FDI to Vietnam. Yet, China-based emerging TNCs have made an increasing contribution to Vietnam's FDI inflow, from only 2 per cent in 2010 to 7 per cent in 2018. China has turned into the fifth-largest investor in Vietnam, just behind Japan, Korea, Singapore and Hong Kong. As it is common for the Chinese investors to venture abroad through Hong Kong, if the investments from Hong Kong are also included then China would become the third-largest investor in Vietnam, sharing 16 per cent of the FDI inflow to Vietnam in 2018. Notably, apart from the relatively large state-owned enterprises (SOEs), an increasing number of Chinese privately owned firms, most of which are small and mediumsized enterprises (SMEs), have started to internationalize since the early 2000s (Huang and Chi, 2014). According to China's Ministry of Commerce, the outward FDI stock of China shared by these private firms increased from 19 per cent in 2006 to 51 per cent in 2017. While existing literature postulates that the Asian electronics production networks primarily driven by the established TNCs originated mainly from Japan and the Asian NIEs, this chapter

Table 8.2 Comparison of FDI inflows from Japan, South Korea and Singapore to China and Vietnam, 2009–17

Sources	Destinations	2009	2011	2013	2015	2017
		FDI amount (million USD)				
Japan	China	4015	6330	7058	3195	3261
Korea	China	2700	2551	3054	4034	2673
Singapore	China	3605	6097	7229	6905	4763
Japan	Vietnam	719	2306	4769	2083	5895
Korea	Vietnam	1661	1540	4466	6983	8720
Singapore	Vietnam	373	2622	5876	1803	9205
		Share of respective total outflows of FDI (%)				
Japan	China	5.4	5.9	5.2	2.5	2.0
Korea	China	15.7	8.6	10.8	17.0	7.8
Singapore	China	19.5	19.4	16.6	22.0	10.9
Japan	Vietnam	1.0	2.1	3.5	1.6	3.7
Korea	Vietnam	9.7	5.2	15.7	29.4	25.6
Singapore	Vietnam	2.0	8.4	13.5	5.7	21.1
Ratios						
Japan to Vietnam/Japan to China		0.18	0.36	0.68	0.65	1.81
Korea to Vietnam/Korea to China		0.62	0.60	1.46	1.73	3.26
Singapore to Vietnam/ Singapore to China		0.10	0.43	0.81	0.26	1.93

Source: Based on the World Investment Report 2018 from UNCTAD (2018).

argues that the emerging TNCs from emerging economies, such as China, have contributed to the current transformation of the Asian electronics production networks.

With the increasing participation of the Southeast Asian countries, the 'triangular trade' pattern and the roles of different economies in the Asian production network warrant an updated understanding. Besides the 'world factory', the developing Southeast Asian countries, such as Vietnam, have emerged to become a manufacturing base for electronics products in Asia; in particular

Table 8.3   Share of the sources of FDI inflows to Vietnam, 2010–18 (%)

Sources of FDI	2010	2011	2012	2013	2014	2015	2016	2017	2018
Hong Kong	1	22	4	3	14	5	6	4	9
China	2	5	2	10	2	3	8	6	7
Singapore	24	15	12	21	13	9	9	16	14
South Korea	13	10	8	20	35	29	30	24	20
Japan	12	17	34	26	10	7	11	25	25
Taiwan	5	4	16	3	6	6	8	4	3
ROW	43	27	24	17	20	41	28	21	22

Note: ROW = Rest of the World.
Source: Based on data from the Statistical Yearbooks of the General Statistics Office of Vietnam (2009–18).

phones sets, computers and other electronics products have been the main export items from Vietnam in recent years (Table 8.1). According to Table 8.4, despite the fact that China was still the largest exporter in the region and accounted for 43 per cent of the world's total transmission apparatus export value in 2018, Vietnam has emerged rapidly from exporting only 1.2 per cent in 2010 (ranked in 14th place) to 8.2 per cent in 2018, and was ranked the third-largest manufacturer and exporter in the world just behind China and Hong Kong.

According to the data from the UN Comtrade database, the US was the biggest destination of the electronics products exported by Vietnam. For example, 21.8 per cent of the automatic data processing machines, 23.5 per cent of the office machines, and 11.8 per cent of the transmission apparatus exported by Vietnam in 2017 went to the US. Besides the US, most of the top electronics exports from Vietnam are destined for the advanced developed economies, that is, Germany, the United Kingdom and France.

Moreover, the ongoing transformation of the Asian electronics production networks has been characterized by the changing role of China as the main exporter of electronics parts and components. Unlike what has been described as the 'triangular trade' pattern in which China has been solely an intermediary importer, importing the parts and components largely from Japan and the NIEs, China has now become a major intermediaries exporter. In this connection, Vietnam has imported a large amount of electronics parts and components from China. According to Figure 8.2, although Japan and the NIEs

Table 8.4   Top exporters of transmission apparatus and respective shares of the world total export value (%), 2010–18

Ranking	2010		2012		2014		2016		2018	
1	China	34.5	China	42.3	China	48.4	China	50.3	China	43.1
2	South Korea	11.2	United Arab Emirates	7.3	Hong Kong	9.2	**Vietnam**	**11.8**	Hong Kong	10.8
3	Mexico	7.3	South Korea	6.3	Vietnam	8.9	Hong Kong	10.3	**Vietnam**	**8.2**
4	Hungary	7.2	Hong Kong	5.9	USA	5.6	USA	5.1	USA	7.1
5	Taiwan	5.6	**Vietnam**	**5.3**	South Korea	5.2	South Korea	3.5	United Arab Emirates	4.1
6	USA	5.6	USA	4.9	Germany	2.4	Germany	2.8	Netherlands	4.0
7	Hong Kong	5.1	Taiwan	3.2	Singapore	2.0	Singapore	2.3	Germany	2.9
8	Germany	2.6	Hungary	2.7	United Arab Emirates	1.7	Slovakia	1.5	Czech	2.0
9	Singapore	2.5	Germany	2.6	Slovakia	1.7	United Arab Emirates	1.5	Singapore	2.0
10	ROW	18.3	ROW	19.5	ROW	14.8	ROW	10.8	ROW	15.6

Note: ROW = Rest of the World.
Source: Based on data from the UN Comtrade Database of the United Nations (n.d.).

in total contributed more than 50 per cent of the parts and components for the automatic data processing machines and other electronics products, such as office machines imported by Vietnam in 2010, their shares were reduced in 2017 (in total, to around 40 per cent). Whereas China alone accounted for more than half of Vietnam's total import value in 2017, rising from 34 per cent in 2010. Apart from emerging as Vietnam's main investor, China has also become Vietnam's dominant electronics intermediaries importer, replacing Japan and the NIEs, since the 2010s. This shows that, apart from the developed economies in the region, such as Japan and the Asian NIEs, China has become more influential in the organization of the electronics regional production network in Asia nowadays, instead of its relatively passive role of simply acting as the 'world factory' in the past decades. Notably, the emergence of a market imperative in the vast domestic market in China has further increased China's role in the restructuring of production networks at both regional and global levels (Fu et al., 2020).

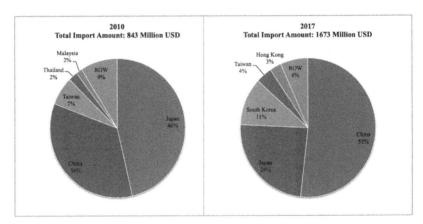

Figure 8.2   Top importers of Vietnam's electronics parts, accessories for automatic data, processing machines and office machines, 2010 and 2017

This section delineates the participation of Vietnam in the global and regional production networks, based on the changing dynamics at global, regional and national levels. On the one hand, the push factors in relation to the current wave of production relocation of labour-intensive industry away from China are mostly due to the increasingly upsurge of production costs in China. According to a report from the Economist Intelligence Unit (2014), manufacturing labour costs per hour in China were 177 per cent of those in Vietnam in 2019, rising from 147 per cent in 2012. Apart from the rising production costs, which has been the focus of majority of the previous research, the changing institutional environment could be another driver (Yang and He, 2017). On the other hand, the pull factors in Vietnam could be reflected by its efforts in regional and global economic integration. Since the *doi moi* reform and after joining the WTO in 2007, the FDI inflow to Vietnam started to boom (see Figure 8.1). In order to promote its integration with the global economy, Vietnam has also become a member of different trade associations at different spatial levels. For instance, Vietnam joined the Association of Southeast Asian Nations (ASEAN) as well as the ASEAN Free Trade Area (AFTA) in 1995, and in 2016, Vietnam signed the Trans-Pacific Partnership (TPP) and the updated Comprehensive and Progressive Agreement for Trans-Pacific Partnership (CPTPP) in 2018.

The transformation of the Asian production network has been driven by the changing dynamics at the national, regional and global levels. Hence, besides the endogenous factors at the national level as mentioned above, the exogenous factors at a broader spatial scale also led to the reconfiguration of the regional and global production networks, particularly the changing international political economy. One of the factors is China's 'Belt and Road Initiative', launched in 2015 with the main objective to promote economic cooperation among countries in Asia, Europe and Africa by different means, such as increasing the trade and investment, as well as strengthening the transport infrastructure among the countries involved. Although it is not written as an official objective, different updated studies have found that the Belt and Road Initiative has indeed encouraged the production relocations of labour-intensive industries out from China (see, for example, Chan et al., 2019; Lian, 2018), particularly to the nearby countries in association with the Belt and Road Initiative, such as Vietnam and India (Lee and Zhou, 2019). Besides, it is worth noting that the outbreak of the US–China trade war since 2018 also accelerated the production relocation from China to the nearby countries, in order to avoid the extra tariffs imposed. According to the 'winners' list of the trade war calculated by the Economist Intelligent Unit (2018), Vietnam and other developing Southeast Asian countries have clearly been big winners in the information and communications technology sector, while Malaysia and Vietnam are nominated as the winners with strong benefits. More recently, the outbreak and widespread of the COVID-19 pandemic has exerted unprecedented challenges on the global supply chains of various sectors, which may accelerate the transformation of the regional electronics production networks in Asia. The changing dynamics in the exogenous shocks and subsequent effects on the Asian production networks have entered the agenda for future research on manufacturing.

Discussion and conclusions

Through an updated investigation of the configuration of the Asian electronics production network after the late 2000s, particularly the increasing participation of Southeast Asian developing countries such as Vietnam, this chapter showcases the changing organizational and spatial configurations of the electronics production networks. Moreover, the findings of this study could advance the GPN literature by highlighting the evident relocation of production activities engaged in by established and emerging TNCs from China to Southeast Asian countries, and the subsequent restructuring of the Asian regional electronics production networks.

Based on the case study of Vietnam, we argue that Asian electronics production networks have been transforming, led not only by the TNCs from Japan and the NIEs, but also by the emerging TNCs from China. The changing and growing roles of the developing economies - that is, China and, more recently, Vietnam - are reflected in the current reconfiguration of the production networks. Following China, Vietnam has gradually become the electronics assembly hub since the early 2010s, not only driven by the established TNCs from Korea, Japan and other Asian NIEs as in previous rounds of production relocation, but also driven by the emerging TNCs, including the SMEs, from the emerging economies in the region, such as China. By importing electronics intermediaries mainly from China, as well as Japan and the Asian NIEs, and exporting the final goods mainly to the advanced economies such as the US and the European countries, Vietnam is now actively participating in the global and regional electronics production networks. In the meanwhile, apart from its role as a 'world factory', China has emerged as a dominant investor driving the current production relocations to Southeast Asia, and the biggest electronics intermediary exporter in the region, outpacing Japan and the Asian NIEs. In addition to the endogenous push and pull drivers at the national level, the exogenous factors at a broader spatial scale - in particular the situation of the international political economy, such as the US-China trade war since 2018, and recent outbreak of the COVID-19 pandemic in 2020 - have accelerated the current reconfiguration of the global and Asian regional production networks, the dynamics and impacts of which warrant closer investigation and systemic exploration in future.

Although an overview of the changing Asian electronics production networks has been shown, more in-depth and empirical questions ought to be asked to better understand the ongoing reconfiguration of the electronics industry at various levels, ranging from global, regional and national to local contexts.

For example, how do the firms respond to the changing capitalist dynamics? How do the firms govern their production networks or participate in other networks? How did the firms decouple with the 'old' regions/markets and recouple with the new ones? Apart from offering an updated investigation on the restructuring of the global and regional production networks of the manufacturing industries in general, and electronics industry in particular, as indicated by this chapter, some inroads for further enriching the GPN literature have been discovered. The conventional conceptualization of the global production system has to be readjusted so that the research framework can be more attuned to pay attention to the increasingly influential actors and issues in the current changing global and regional contexts.

Both GPNs, including the GPN 2.0, and GVC frameworks have primarily conceptualized the globalization as a set of geographically dispersed production activities coordinated by the lead firms, mostly from the developed counties, to maintain control of the core nodes of value creation and retention in their home countries, and to offshore and outsource the peripheral and lower-value-added activities to the developing countries (Neilson et al., 2014). Compared to these lead firms, insufficient attention has been paid to the emerging transnational corporations (ETNCs) from the emerging economies, such as China. Yet, the changing dynamics of global production systems can be seen, as firms originating from the developing economies nowadays play a significant role in the spatial and organizational configurations of the global value chains and production networks (see, for example, Azmeh and Nadvi, 2014; Lee and Gereffi, 2015; Yeung, 2017); therefore, more research should be done to explore these ETNCs. For instance, how did they expand and govern their production networks, given their limited resources, experience, and even market power? More fundamentally, why and how did they internationalize? Notably, unlike the four competitive dynamics mentioned in the GPN 2.0 framework – that is, cost-capability ratio, market imperative, financial discipline and risk environment – some Chinese firms ventured abroad as part of the state's economic diplomacy (Yeung and Liu, 2008). That said, unlike the previous strategic coupling studies where the focus has been largely on the firms in the networks and the host institutions, there is a need to also concern the active role of the home governments of these ETNCs. Besides paying more attention to the home institutions, in order to better understand these ETNCs their cultural legacies should also be taken into account, as these are highly relevant to the strategies they used in orchestrating their production networks both spatial and organizationally.

Apart from the firms per se, in the 'Northern lead-firm centric' (Horner and Nadvi, 2018) definition of the global production systems, the final markets of the chain and the network are presumed to be the developed economies in the North. Despite the fact that this is not clearly reflected by the case study of Vietnam above, different studies have clearly shown that the tails of the networks/chains have shifted gradually to the developing economies (for example, Athukorala and Nasir, 2012). Although the domestic market/ emerging market-orientated reconfiguration of production networks is not uncommon, not much effort has been made to understand this restructuring and the related mechanisms. Notably, in looking into the question of how the lead firms and the domestic firms engage or re-engage with these emerging markets, ample research opportunities remain to be taken up regarding the governance dynamics in the networks. Not only the 'new' governance structure of the emerging leading firms, but also the new standards in these markets required by the consumers and the institutions, also deserve more attention as they affect the power balances and relationships among the actors involved, as well as the upgrading opportunities available in the networks (see, for example, Kaplinsky and Farooki, 2011).

This chapter has also illustrated the increasingly regionalized operation of the global electronics production networks in Asia since the 1960s. Nowadays, different production networks have gradually narrowed down spatially, from global to regional and even national, together with the emerging markets, for example the vast domestic market of China, as well as the rise in trade protectionism and reindustrialization, for example the 'Made in America' campaign. Echoing Horner and Nadvi (2018), we have to scale down and focus more on the regional and domestic aspects of the production networks. Be that as it may, another lesson learned from our case study of Vietnam is that the exogenous shocks could impact upon the operations of and interactions between multiple production networks and chains at different scales. For example, the trade friction between China and the US has accelerated production relocations from China to the Southeast Asian countries nearby, as well as the reconfiguration of the electronics production network in the region. In addition to the situations of international political economy, it would also be interesting to explore how the COVID-19 pandemic has influenced the production systems at multiple levels. Research has highlighted that because of the coronavirus pandemic, the decline in production and trade due to the factory closures in China caused by the restrictions on movements of labour could have a strong effect on countries further up and down the supply chain (Šerić et al.,2020). Yet, whether this disruption of the global and regional production systems would leave a long-term impact and lead to further pushback against the cross-border organization of production, deserves study. As shown above, exogenous shocks of different levels could influence the multiple production networks at various scales. Hence, we urge more awareness on the scalar dimension of the global production systems; a truly multi-scalar understanding is earnestly needed for studying the constantly changing operations of the production networks in the recent decade.

Acknowledgements

The financial support of Hong Kong Research Grant Council GRF grant (HKBU12600120) and National Natural Science Foundation of China grants (41571119 and 42071149) are gratefully acknowledged.

References

Athukorala, P.C., and Nasir, S. (2012). Global production sharing and South–South trade. *Indian Growth and Development Review, 5*(2), 173–202.
Azmeh, S., and Nadvi, K. (2014). Asian firms and the restructuring of global value chains. *International Business Review, 23*(4), 708–717.
Baldwin, R., and Lopez-Gonzalez, J. (2015). Supply-chain trade: a portrait of global patterns and several testable hypotheses. *World Economy, 38*(11), 1682–1721.
Borrus, M., Ernst, D., and Haggard, S. (eds) (2000). *International Production Networks in Asia: Rivalry or Riches?* London: Routledge.
Chan, E.M.H., Ho, C.K.D., Yip, T.L., Cheung, J., and Gunasekaran, A. (2019). The Belt and Road initiative's impact on textile and clothing supply chains in Asia: views from Hong Kong industrial stakeholders. *International Journal of Applied Business and International Management, 4*(2), 9–16.
Coe, N.M., Hess, M., Yeung, H.W.C., Dicken, P., and Henderson, J. (2004). 'Globalizing' regional development: a global production networks perspective. *Transactions of the Institute of British Geographers, 29*(4), 468–484.
Coe, N.M., and Yeung, H.W.C. (2015). *Global Production Networks: Theorizing Economic Development in an Interconnected World.* New York: Oxford University Press.
Dicken, P., Kelly, P.F., Olds, K., and Yeung, H.W.C. (2001). Chains and networks, territories and scales: towards a relational framework for analysing the global economy. *Global Networks, 1*(2), 89–112.
Economist Intelligence Unit (2014). Still making it: an analysis of manufacturing labour costs in China. Available at: http://www.truevaluemetrics.org/DBpdfs/Economics/Economist/EIU-China-manufacturing-labor-cost-report-2014.pdf (accessed 10 May 2020).
Economist Intelligence Unit (2018). Creative disruption: Asia's winners in the US–China Trade War. Available at: https://pages.eiu.com/Nov-18---Creative-disruption-Asias-winners-in-the-US-China-trade-war-MKT_registration-page.html (accessed 6 May 2020).
Fu, T., Yang, C., and Li, L. (2020). Market imperative and cluster evolution in China: evidence from Shunde. *Regional Studies, 54*(2), 244–255.

General Statistics Office of Vietnam (2009–2018). *Statistical Yearbook of Vietnam 2009–2018*. General Statistics Office of Vietnam: Vietnam. Available at: https://www.gso.gov.vn/default_en.aspx?tabid=515&idmid=5&ItemID=10439, 11974, 12576, 13762, 14079, 15197, 16052,18533, 18941,19299.

Gereffi, G. (1994). The organization of buyer-driven global commodity chains: how US retailers shape overseas production networks. In: Gereffi, G., and Korzeniewicz, M. (eds), *Commodity Chains and Global Capitalism*. Westport, CT: Greenwood Press, pp. 95–122.

Gereffi, G., Humphrey, J., and Sturgeon, T. (2005). The governance of global value chains. *Review of International Political Economy, 12*(1), 78–104.

Hai, N.M., and Hung, N.M. (2018). Analysing the effects of the exporting on economic growth in Vietnam. In: *International Econometric Conference of Vietnam*. Cham: Springer, pp. 597–610.

Henderson, J., Dicken, P., Hess, M., Coe, N., and Yeung, H.W.C. (2002). Global production networks and the analysis of economic development. *Review of International Political Economy, 9*(3), 436–464.

Horner, R., and Murphy, J.T. (2018). South–North and South–South production networks: diverging socio-spatial practices of Indian pharmaceutical firms. *Global Networks, 18*(2), 326–351.

Horner, R., and Nadvi, K. (2018). Global value chains and the rise of the Global South: unpacking twenty-first century polycentric trade. *Global Networks, 18*(2), 207–237.

Huang, X., and Chi, R. (2014). Chinese private firms' outward foreign direct investment: does firm ownership and size matter? *Thunderbird International Business Review, 56*(5), 393–406.

Kaplinsky, R., and Farooki, M. (2011). What are the implications for global value chains when the market shifts from the North to the South? *International Journal of Technological Learning, Innovation and Development, 4*(1-3), 13–38.

Lee, J., and Gereffi, G. (2015). Global value chains, rising power firms and economic and social upgrading. *Critical Perspectives on International Business, 11*(3/4), 319–339.

Lee, J., Kim, J.C., and Lim, J. (2016). Globalization and divergent paths of industrial development: mobile phone manufacturing in China, Japan, South Korea and Taiwan. *Journal of Contemporary Asia, 46*(2), 222–246.

Lee, A., and Zhou, C. (2019). China's belt and road may accelerate exit of manufacturing. *South China Morning Post*, 23 April. Available at: https://www.scmp.com/economy/china-economy/article/3007183/chinas-belt-and-road-may-accelerate-exit-manufacturing (accessed 25 October 2019).

Lian, C. (2018). Relocating China's manufacturing capacity and industrialization to Africa. In: Simelane, T. and Managa, L. (eds), *Belt and Road Initiative: Alternative Development Path for Africa*. Pretoria: Africa Institute of South Africa, pp. 89–100.

Neilson, J., Pritchard, B., and Yeung, H.W.C. (2014). Global value chains and global production networks in the changing international political economy: an introduction. *Review of International Political Economy, 21*(1), 1–8.

Read, R. (1997). Innovation in East Asia: the challenge to Japan. *Business History, 39*(2), 148–150.

Šerić, A., Görg, H., Mösle, S., and Windisch, M. (2020). Managing COVID-19: how the pandemic disrupts global value chains. United Nations Industrial Development Organization (UNIDO), April. Available at: https://iap.unido.org/articles/managing-covid-19-how-pandemic-disrupts-global-value-chains (accessed 29 May 2020).

Sturgeon, T., and Kawakami, M. (2010). Global value chains in the electronics industry: was the crisis a window of opportunity for developing countries? In: Olivier

Cattaneo, O., Gereffi, G., and Staritz, C. (eds), *Global Value Chains in a Postcrisis World*. Washington, DC: World Bank, pp. 245–301.

Sturgeon, T., and Zylberberg, E. (2016). *The Global Information and Communications Technology Industry: Where Vietnam Fits in Global Value Chains*. Washington, DC: World Bank.

Thorbecke, W. (2016). *Understanding the Flow of Electronic Parts and Components in East Asia*. Research Institute of Economy, Trade and Industry (RIETI), Japan.

UNCTAD (2004). *The New Geography of International Economic Relations*. New York: Office of the Chairman of the Group of 77.

UNCTAD (2018). *World Investment Report 2018*. Geneva: United Nations Publications.

United Nations (n.d.). UN Comtrade Database. Available at: https://comtrade.un.org/data/ (accessed 15 April 2020).

VietNamNet Bridge (2018, 26 April). Vietnam ranks 12th globally in electronic exports. Available at: https://english.vietnamnet.vn/fms/business/199406/vietnam-ranks -12th-globally-in-electronic-exports.html (accessed 9 November 2019).

World Bank (n.d.). World Bank Open Data. Available at: https://data.worldbank.org/ (accessed 15April 2020).

Yang, C. (2009). Strategic coupling of regional development in global production networks: redistribution of Taiwanese personal computer investment from the Pearl River Delta to the Yangtze River Delta, China. *Regional Studies*, 43(3), 385–407.

Yang, C. (2016). Relocating labour-intensive manufacturing firms from China to Southeast Asia: a preliminary investigation. *Bandung*, 3(1), 1–13.

Yang, C. (2017). The rise of strategic partner firms and reconfiguration of personal computer production networks in China: insights from the emerging laptop cluster in Chongqing. *Geoforum*, 84, 21–31.

Yang, C., and He, C. (2017). Transformation of China's 'World Factory': production relocation and export evolution of the electronics firms. *Tijdschrift voor economische en sociale geografie*, 108(5), 571–591.

Yang, Y.R., and Hsia, C.J. (2007). Spatial clustering and organizational dynamics of transborder production networks: a case study of Taiwanese information-technology companies in the Greater Suzhou Area, China. *Environment and Planning A*, 39(6), 1346–1363.

Yeung, G. (2001). *Foreign Investment and Socio-economic Development in China: The Case of Dongguan*. Basingstoke: Palgrave.

Yeung, H.W.C. (2007). From followers to market leaders: Asian electronics firms in the global economy. *Asia Pacific Viewpoint*, 48(1), 1–25.

Yeung, H.W.C. (2017). Global production networks and foreign direct investment by small and medium enterprises in ASEAN. *Transnational Corporations*, 24(2), 1–42.

Yeung, H.W.C., and Liu, W. (2008). Globalizing China: the rise of mainland firms in the global economy. *Eurasian Geography and Economics*, 49(1), 57–86.

Zhu, S., and Pickles, J. (2014). Bring in, go up, go west, go out: upgrading, regionalisation and delocalisation in China's apparel production networks. *Journal of Contemporary Asia*, 44(1), 36–63.

9 How to increase the usefulness and relevance of operations and supply chain management research?

Donato Masi and Jan Godsell

Relevance of management research: an old problem

Operations and supply chain management (O&SCM) is a key element for the improvement of productivity in businesses around the world from both manufacturing and service industries. It includes a broad set of activities, embedded in the functions of sourcing, materials management, operations planning, distribution, logistics, retail, demand forecasting, sales and operations planning, and more. Scientific research in the field of O&SCM inherits the complexity and breadth of the described activities, and it is traditionally divided into two separate streams: operations management and operations research. At the conceptual level, operations management focuses on the design, operation, control and updating of production resources critical for the development of a product or a service; it is therefore managerially and activity-oriented. Operations research focuses on developing analytic models for a problem and on finding an optimal solution for it; it is therefore mainly technique and mathematically oriented (Fuller and Mansour, 2003).

There is increasing recognition that academic excellence requires both rigour and relevance, a balanced set of outcomes long recognized in O&SCM. Business schools strive to produce knowledge that is relevant for practice and policymakers. They strive to conduct impactful research that stimulates economic growth and improves the competitiveness and sustainability of companies. The funding schemes for higher education are more and more aligned with this objective. The formal assessment of the research outcome of an institution that is regularly conducted by funding agencies (such as the Research Excellence Framework in the United Kingdom) includes research among the target criteria that academics should follow. Research grants increasingly target applied problems, and require a clear explanation of the pathways to impact that the researchers intend to follow.

Despite this vision, relevance is frequently overlooked. Even within the highly applied field of O&SCM, the production of knowledge can lack practical application. Wickham Skinner is a founding father of modern operations management (OM). At the 2010 Decision Sciences conference, in his keynote address, Skinner wondered whether OM was losing its industrial relevance as a result of academics prioritizing publications over the solution of the 'big' problems that are relevant for Industry (Skinner, 2010). At the same conference, Narasinham (2010; cited in Coughlan et al., 2016) suggested that addressing these challenges requires focusing on the cycle of conceptual theory building. The concerns of Skinner and Narasinham demonstrate that the debate is not new. In the light of this debate, a young scholar should answer a set of questions (initially proposed by Narasinham, 2010 and Coughlan et al., 2016) through their research journey:

- What are the big societal and industrial problems that O&SCM scholars can inform?
- What methods could O&SCM scholars use to tackle these problems?
- How can I ensure that my research design is rigorous enough to satisfy the scrutiny of high-quality journals?
- How could realist logics and abduction support my research agenda?
- What strategies can I use to increase my knowledge of the problems that society and industry are facing first-hand?

This chapter provides some food for thought to answer these questions, being aware that there is no 'right' or single approach, but that each young scholar will provide the answer aligned with their career choices. The chapter is structured as follows. The section on 'Research and practice: two schools of thought' provides an overview of the ongoing academic debate on the relationship between research and practice. The section on 'Implications for research design' explores the role of different research design approaches in ensuring the usefulness and relevance of research work. This is the core section of the chapter, since research design approaches are at the core of the rigour versus relevance debate. The section on 'The role of a publication strategy' discusses how some specific publication strategies might be in tension with the achievement of both rigour and relevance. The final section brings the chapter to a close with some concluding thoughts.

Research and practice: two schools of thought

The relationship between research and practice has been discussed over recent decades for many scientific disciplines, but it has produced the liveliest debates in the area of management research. Several empirical and conceptual studies have investigated the reasons for the fracture between research and practice, and proposed solutions to overcome this fracture. From this debate, Van de ven and Johnson (2006) identify two different schools of thought.

The first school of thought (Rogers, 1995; Tranfield et al., 2003, cited in Van de ven and Johnson, 2006) holds that the cause of the fracture between research and practice is the way in which academics transfer the knowledge that they produce. According to this school of thought, academic research could be relevant for practice, but it is not put into a form that makes it applicable by practitioners. A primary reason for this failure is the limited focus on translating research outcomes into formats that are easy to understand and adopt by practitioners. This may be a result of disinterest, or alternatively a lack of time, as dissemination activities are frequently not funded. The academic hamster wheel dictates that focus moves on to the next grant application or academic paper (Coughlan et al., 2016).

The second school of thought (see, e.g., Kondrat, 1992; Aram and Salipante, 2003, cited in Van de ven and Johnson, 2006) adopts a more radical view, stating that research and practice are intrinsically different types of knowledge. According to this school of thought, academics study generalizable problems that are independent from a specific context, while practitioners use knowledge that is customized for a specific context and dealing with specific situations. Therefore, scientific knowledge and practical knowledge follow fundamentally different rules.

In the light of this debate, a question arising for young scholars is: What are the big societal and industrial problems that O&SCM scholars can inform?

There have been different attempts at answering this question. The most well-known approach is the idea of 'engaged scholarship', introduced by Boyer (1990) and Pettigrew (2001), and further developed by Van de Ven (2007). According to Van de Ven and Johnson (2006: 809), engaged scholarship includes a 'set of reforms to break down the insular behaviours of academic departments and disciplines'. The 'dialectical form of engaged scholarship' consists of five 'dimensions' (Van de Ven and Johnson, 2006: 809-815):

1. A focus on big questions grounded in reality.

2. A collaborative learning community.
3. An extended time over which to build relationships.
4. Multiple models and methods.
5. A re-examination of researchers' assumptions and self-reflection.

It is not without critics: McKelvey (2006) described engaged scholarship as overly optimistic, and far from the conflicting interests and biases that define the real context in which academics operate.

Implications for research design

Having understood the importance of ensuring both rigour and relevance, as well as the difficulty of achieving both in O&SCM, young scholars should answer the following question: What methods could O&SCM scholars use to tackle these problems?

Skinner (2010; cited in Coughlan et al., 2016) and Narasinham (2010; cited in Coughlan et al., 2016) suggested increasing the usefulness and relevance of O&SCM research by focusing on the conceptual theory-building process and by improving research methodologies. The improvements should start from acknowledging the nature of O&SCM scholarship as a form of management research. Management research has distinctive characteristics compared to other forms of research. In a seminal paper, Tranfield and Starkey (1998) analyse the nature of management research, using a conceptual framework originally developed by Becher (1989; cited in Tranfield and Starkey, 1998) for the characterization of any discipline, summarized in Table 9.1. They define management research as a soft, applied, divergent and rural field of study. Soft, because both its contents and its methods are heterogeneous, fragmented, and often borrowed from other disciplines in the social sciences and in engineering. Applied, because of its focus on the optimal organization of resources, similarly to engineering. Divergent, because it comprises a broad range of ontological and epistemological views. Rural, because it covers a wide area that includes, among others, management, social and behavioural sciences (Tranfield and Starkey, 1998).

The 'new production of knowledge'

In 1994, Gibbons et al. (1994) introduced the terms Mode 1 and Mode 2, referring to Mode 2 as the 'new production of knowledge'. Their main proposition was the emergence of a new and 'socially distributed' knowledge production

Table 9.1   Conceptual framework for the characterization of any discipline

Extent to which a body of theory is subscribed to by all members of the field	Hard disciplines – natural sciences and engineering	Soft disciplines – humanities and education
Concern of the area with application to practical problems	Pure disciplines – humanities, social sciences, branches of mathematics and physics	Applied disciplines – education and engineering
Degree of togetherness and shared purpose	Convergent disciplines exhibit shared ideologies, values, and quality judgements	Divergent disciplines do not exhibit shared ideologies, values, and quality judgements
Narrowness of area of study	Urban disciplines focus on narrow areas with a limited range of commonly agreed discrete and separable research problems	Rural disciplines focus on wide areas of study, with no clear discrete and separable research problems

Source: Originally developed by Becher (1989) and adapted from Tranfield and Starkey (1998).

system. Until the early 1990s, knowledge production was largely located at scientific institutions and organized in a set of clearly distinguished disciplines. Gibbons et al. argue that a new knowledge production model was becoming dominant. Hessels and Van Lente (2008) summarize the novelty of this knowledge production model in five main attributes, shown in Table 9.2.

The first distinctive characteristic of Mode 2 knowledge is its generation in the context of application. While the traditional knowledge assumed a clear distinction between theory and practice, and it required a knowledge transfer

Table 9.2   Attributes of Mode 1 and Mode 2 knowledge production

Mode 1	Mode 2
Academic context	Context of application
Disciplinary	Transdisciplinary
Homogeneity	Heterogeneity
Autonomy	Reflexivity/social accountability
Traditional quality control (peer review)	Novel quality control

Source: Adapted from Hessels and Van Lente (2008).

process to move from theory to practice, in Mode 2 knowledge theory and practice operate in synergy and progress is a synchronous and joint act.

The second distinctive characteristic of Mode 2 knowledge is its transdisciplinarity. While traditional knowledge was producing clearly recognizable disciplinary parts, Mode 2 knowledge promotes the dynamic interaction of different scientific disciplines and the creation of a holistic approach, focused on the solution of problems.

The third distinctive characteristic of Mode 2 knowledge is its production in a range of diverse organizations. While traditional knowledge was produced in universities, institutes and research centres, the new knowledge can be also created in consulting firms, companies, government agencies and think tanks. These new actors naturally interact and collaborate through networks.

The fourth attribute is reflexivity. Compared to Mode 1, Mode 2 knowledge is the result of a dialogic process able to incorporate multiple views, including the views of the stakeholder directly affected by the results of the research. Thanks to this approach, researchers are aware of the impacts of their work, and impact is clearly and explicitly considered from the early stages of the research process.

Novel forms of quality control constitute the fifth characteristic of the new production of knowledge. While traditional knowledge progressed through peer review systems, Mode 2 knowledge progresses while assessing the broader economic, political and social implications of a new theory, in addition to the traditional criteria of novelty and rigour. Assessing what is 'good science' is thus more difficult, since the quality standards of science must not be lowered.

The concept of productivity offers the opportunity of understanding the difference between Mode 1 and Mode 2 research. There is a difference between the way in which productivity has been studied by different academic communities, such as economists and management researchers. Both economists and management researchers tend to produce definitions of productivity for the purposes of their own field of study: economists tend to produce aggregate definitions, while management researchers tend to produce definitions at a firm level. The difference between the definitions developed by the two academic communities creates a barrier for common understanding and knowledge-sharing, and as a consequence for the development of aligned interventions at a macroeconomic and firm level.

Mode 2 research offers the possibility of overcoming these limitations. New knowledge can be generated in the context of application, meaning that academics, practitioners and policymakers can collaborate in the development of a definition, gaining immediate feedback on the usefulness of the definitions and the metrics by their practical users. Moreover, Mode 2 approaches such as the involvement of diverse organizations and a dialogic process enable the involvement of other stakeholders with valuable ideas on productivity, such as unions, government agencies and think tanks. A transdisciplinary approach to productivity means that management researchers and economists can work on shared definitions and metrics, effective both at the aggregate level of the economists and at the firm level of managers. These definitions will thus be able to influence policy.

Design science

Van Aken (2004) distinguishes three categories of scientific discipline: the formal sciences, the explanatory sciences and the design sciences. The formal sciences aim at building theories and propositions tested by their internal logical consistency. Therefore, they are not necessarily interested in grounding their propositions on empirical data. Examples of formal sciences are philosophy and mathematics. The explanatory sciences aim at building causal models that are capable of describing, explaining and possibly predicting observable phenomena within their field. The causal models are generally tested with empirical data, and both the causal models and the empirical data can be expressed in quantitative terms. Examples of explanatory sciences are the natural sciences and many social sciences. The design sciences aim at creating knowledge for the solution of practical problems or for the improvement of the performance of a system. Examples of design sciences are engineering and medical science. There is a clear difference between the creation and the use of design knowledge. The users of design knowledge are individuals with formal education in that field. Each time they face a unique and specific problem for a client, they will solve it by planning, implementing and evaluating a specific intervention. The creators of design knowledge are not necessarily involved with action, but they rather focus on the knowledge used to support the design of interventions. While design knowledge is general and valid for classes of cases, the problems of the professional are always unique and specific, and their job consists of adapting general knowledge to the specific case at hand.

Van Aken (2004) acknowledges that in the last decade the approach to management research as an explanatory science has produced impressive results and enhanced the academic prestige of the field. However, he suggests that the explanatory and description-driven side of management research could be complemented by an approach to management research as a design science. In order to describe the difference between the two approaches, he uses Miner's distinction between organization theory and management theory. According to this distinction, organization theory is related to the exploratory sciences, while management theory is related to design sciences. Organization theory can still provide contents that will be subsequently tested and further developed by management theory.

Van Aken (2004) argues that a common approach for building management theory is based on multiple case studies. This approach can either extract rules from best practices, or develop and test rules from a close collaboration between the researcher and the people in the field. Examples of management theory developed from the extraction of rules from best practices include the study of Womack et al. (1990) of Japanese practices in the automotive industry, which has produced theories such as the Kanban system and just-in-time (JIT) delivery. To quote Van Aken (2004, p. 241):

> Research in management theory is aimed at developing sound technological rules and at uncovering the generative mechanisms that link (immaterial) intervention with (material) outcomes ... such generative mechanisms can be of a material nature, but are mostly of an immaterial, sense-making nature. The question that follows is: Which epistemological perspective could accommodate this approach?

Critical realism

The field of management research has long been dominated by the distinction between positivist and constructivist paradigms. The adoption of one of the two paradigms implies specific choices in terms of ontology, epistemology and methodology. On the one hand, the adoption of a positivist paradigm implies a realist ontological approach and an objectivist epistemological approach, implying that there is an objective reality and an objective truth, independently of whether and how we may decide to study it. The methodologies that are aligned with this positivist paradigm are typically quantitative, such as experiments or statistical tests of hypotheses. On the other hand, the adoption of a constructivist paradigm implies a relativist ontological approach and a subjectivist epistemological approach, implying that there is no objective reality and objective truth, but rather local and specific co-constructed realities that are dependent on whether and how we decide to study them. Knowledge is thus a social product. The methodologies that are aligned with this constructivist paradigm are typically qualitative, such as case studies or ethnographic studies. Recently, several researchers (see, e.g., Wiltshire, 2018) highlighted that the strict distinction between the positivist and constructivist paradigms can inhibit the accomplishment of interdisciplinarity and impact, by limiting methodological plurality. Therefore, they suggest the adoption of critical realism (Bhaskar, 1978), a paradigm that combines elements of the positivist and constructivist paradigms and that encourages impact by focusing on the social relations that produce real-world problems.

In the light of the theme of this chapter, a young scholar might ask: How could the realist logic support my research agenda?

Critical realism aims at overcoming the limitations of both the positivistic paradigm focused on regularities and laws, and the constructivist approach focused on description and interpretation at the cost of causation (Archer et al., 2016). According to the realist paradigm, knowledge is still a social product, but there is a reality, which is what it is independently of whether and how we decide to study it. This separation between the observer-independent reality and the observer-dependent theories on reality is summarized by the Bhaskar's stratified ontology with its domains of the empirical, the actual and the real.

The empirical consists of the observer-dependent experience and events; the actual describes the observer-independent reality; and the real indicates the processes or mechanisms – the generative mechanisms – that cause events. Generative mechanisms are a key element of the critical realist approach, and their study is the purpose of the scientific enquiry. Thanks to the assumption that the empirical and the actual operate on different levels, critical realism overcomes the strict distinction between positivist and constructivist paradigms, with their related epistemological and methodological assumptions.

From an epistemological perspective, critical realism creates models of underlying mechanisms of reality that can explain the examined phenomenon. In the O&SCM context, critical realism allows the identification and the explanation of the underlying rules or mechanisms of a specific managerial phenomenon. The knowledge of these mechanisms enables decision-makers to intervene on the real causes of an observed problem, thus solving problems or making improvements. Therefore, researchers in the field of O&SCM can use the critical realist paradigm to conduct research that is both relevant and rigorous, because they can solve the actual problems that managers face while using a consolidated and recognized theory-building cycle (Coughlan et al., 2016).

Abduction

In parallel with the distinction between the positivist and the constructivist paradigms, the field of management research has discussed for a long time the difference between induction and deduction. Deductive reasoning works from the general to the specific, beginning with a theory or a set of hypotheses and collecting observations to test and confirm (or not) the theory or the hypotheses. Inductive reasoning works the other way round, beginning with specific observations to create broader generalizations and theories. These two approaches have several limitations: the deductive approach does not clarify how to select the theories to test, while the inductive approach does not provide guidance to decide the amount of empirical data enabling theory-building (Saunders et al., 2012). The realist paradigm rejects both pure induction and pure deduction in favour of the logic of abduction, able to overcome the limitations of the pure deductive and inductive approaches.

Again, in the light of the theme of this chapter, a young scholar might ask: How could abduction support my research agenda?

Abductive reasoning starts with surprising facts or inexplicable events, and devotes the research process to their explanation (Bryman and Bell, 2015). Surprising facts or inexplicable events emerge when a researcher observes a phenomenon that cannot be explained with the existing theories, and the researcher will seek to identify the best theory among many alternatives to explain an empirical observation, by combining different types of data and cognitive reasoning. In other words, the researcher will reconcile theories and empirical observations through 'theory matching' (Dubois and Gadde, 2002). This approach is iterative in nature, because theory is progressively refined through several cycles of comparison and matching with empirical observations, until a convincing explanation for the empirical observations is achieved (Andreewsky and Bourcier, 2000). The abductive approach overcomes the traditional inductive and deductive approaches in terms of creativity and innovation potential (van Hoek et al., 2005).

The abductive cycle enables the production of relevant and impactful O&SCM research, because of the intertwined nature of the different activities that characterize research focused on real-life problems. An inductive or deductive research process includes several planned and subsequent steps. This approach does not match the solution of real-life managerial problems, since these problems can rarely be solved through a set of clearly planned and subsequent steps.

An abductive researcher goes back and forth from empirical observations to theory, exploring a broad range of theories as well as a multitude of heterogeneous empirical observations. The preliminary theories will be progressively refined according to what is discovered through the empirical fieldwork, as well as through analysis and interpretation. The evolving theory directs the search for empirical data, and empirical data might suggest the need to redirect the current theory. This process mirrors the problem-solving cycle of real-life managerial problems, and again allows the solution of the actual problems that managers face while using a rigorous research philosophy.

The role of a publication strategy

Having discussed the different research design approaches for the achievement of rigorous but relevant research, it is necessary to discuss publication strategies. Indeed, each research-related choice is made in a specific academic context and as part of a specific career. Since publications drive careers in academia, and some specific publication strategies might be in tension with the achievement of both rigour and relevance, this section will briefly describe the context in which publication strategies are formulated and some frequent issues in the formulation of a strategy. The idea is that young scholars should be able to avoid errors made in the past, and to adopt a strategy that pays off both in terms of relevance and in terms of career.

The pressure to publish research papers is huge, both in academia and in the publishing industry. From the academic perspective, the motive behind this pressure is clear. Publishing papers implies more prestige and visibility for the university, with more financial support from the government and more students enrolling into the university's programmes. The promotion of researchers is also dependent on the number of published papers, thus giving researchers a strong motive for publishing more. From the perspective of the publishing industry, it is interesting to observe that academic publishing is among the most profitable businesses in the world, with profit margins in the region of 40 per cent (*New Scientist*, 2018).

The pressure to publish can have positive implications for academia. A researcher can find additional motivation in undertaking additional projects and generating significant new publications. Moreover, research can find a strong incentive in prioritizing research over the multiple commitments of academic life. However, at the same time, a researcher can adopt several strategies, not always ethical, to increase the number of papers published: republishing the same material, slicing up of results to produce as many separate publications as the editors will bear, or increasing the number of co-authors on each paper published. Another significant consequence is that the pressure encourages scientists to adjust their priorities, neglecting the work with high scientific potential and focusing on trivial research that can produce quick results. Practically relevant research is not quick. The formulation of a practically relevant research question requires academics to read the industrial press or establish a long-term relationship and a dialogue with practitioners.

So, a young scholar is faced with a difficult choice when deciding whether to pursue academic publications or do research that is relevant to practice. Moreover, the identification of problems that society and industry are facing first-hand is not immediate, and young scholars often ask the following question: What strategies can I use to increase my knowledge of the problems that society and industry are facing first-hand?

PhD programmes should also evolve to ensure that the students engage with practitioners. Credits could be awarded for the publication of magazine articles, and eventually, more credits could be awarded for the evidence of high engagement with these articles by practitioners. Doctoral students could participate in industrial conferences. Consulting could be promoted by universities at the stage of the doctoral programme. Training to become consultants could be provided in parallel with training to become good practitioners. The track to tenure could be less closely linked to academic publication, giving more credit to the impact of research with respect to its novelty and rigour. These innovations in the nature of PhD programmes are also aligned with the career that most of the students will pursue. Recent statistics show that only 30 per cent of all doctorate holders stay in academia, mostly as postdocs. Ten per cent of all postdocs stay in academia, and of these postdoctoral researchers only one in ten finally attains a long-term academic position as a professor, which means that 3 per cent of all doctorate holders become professors. In other words, if you are a PhD holder there is a 97 per cent chance that you are going to work in a non-academic environment (Hendrix, 2014).

An overview of management journals

Publishing in the higher-ranking journals is challenging. Young scholars with the ambition of building a career in academia, while producing impactful research, should answer the following question: How can I ensure that my research design is rigorous enough to satisfy the scrutiny of high-quality journals?

Table 9.3 summarizes the profile of research methods that the journals favour, showing how analytical methods account for most of the research in O&SCM. Therefore, a young scholar wanting to publish in a higher-ranking journal should use analytical mathematical methods to maximize the chances of acceptance of the paper. In this context, achieving both industrial relevance and rigour could be a tough challenge, since analytical mathematical methods

Table 9.3   Profile of research methods favoured by O&SCM journals

Journal	profile of research methods
International Journal of Operations and Production Management (IJOPM)	statistical nature (38.9 per cent) case-based nature (24.8 per cent) analytical mathematical (21.5 per cent)
Journal of Operations Management (JOM)	empirical statistical (34 per cent) analytical mathematical (28.1 per cent) conceptual papers (12.3 per cent)
International Journal of Production Research (IJPR)	analytical mathematical (61.6 per cent) analytical conceptual papers (22.3 per cent)

Source: Adapted from Coughlan et al. (2016).

are not necessarily the best approach to accommodate the realistic perspective and the abductive cycle that facilitates the production of industrially relevant O&SCM research.

There are some exceptions. The *International Journal of Operations and Production Management* (IJOPM) recently launched a new type of article called 'Impact Pathways' aiming at explaining a contemporary issue, problem or challenge directly relevant to the O&SCM domain that is being faced by business leaders and/or policymakers. POM recently launched an alternative approach by creating a 'POM Practice' area to encourage studies that highlight problems in a particular industry sector and develop improved OM solutions.

Concluding thoughts

Effective and efficient operations are critical to ensuring that we receive products and services, at the lowest potential cost, in a sustainable way that ensures equity to all those across the supply chain. They are critical to life, the economy and the planet. It is a critical area for research, that can address contemporary real-world challenges, and be done in a way that enables those brave scholars who address these challenges to flourish in their academic careers.

The messy reality of manufacturing and service operations is context-specific and requires a transdisciplinary approach to truly address today's big issues, such as net zero carbon emissions manufacturing by 2050 and responsible consumption and production. While there is no 'right' or single approach to increase the usefulness and relevance of O&SCM research, there are some indicators of pathways that might make it easier to achieve this balance.

Looking beyond the traditional positivist logics of deduction and induction to the more contemporary realist logic of abduction could be a solid first step. Adopting a research design that enables a researcher to go back and forth from empirical observations to theory, and explore a broad range of theories as well as a multitude of heterogeneous empirical observations, is a more accurate reflection of reality. Executed well, abductive research also has sufficient academic rigour to ensure publication in the highest-quality journals. Taking this one step further, academics may even consider careers that move seamlessly between roles in industry and academia, or even portfolio careers that create a balance between the two.

One size does not fit all. Be the scholar that you want to be.

References

Andreewsky, E., and Bourcier, D. (2000). Abduction in language interpretation and law making. *Kybernetes* 29(7/8): 836–845. https://doi.org/10.1108/03684920010341991.

Archer, M., Decoteau, C., Gorski, P., Little, D., Porpora, D., et al. (2016). What is critical realism? *Perspectives* 38(2): 4–9.

Becher, A. (1989). *Academic Tribes and Territories: Intellectual Enquiry and the Cultures of Disciplines*. Milton Keynes: Society for Research into Higher Education and Open University Press.

Bhaskar, R. (1978). *A Realist Theory of Science*. Hassocks: Harvester Press.

Boyer, Ernest L. (1990). *Scholarship Reconsidered: Priorities of the Professoriate*. Lawrenceville, NJ: Princeton University Press.

Bryman, A., and Bell, E. (2015) *Business Research Methods*, 4th edition. Oxford: Oxford University Press.

Coughlan, P., Draaijer, D., Godsell, J., and Boer, H. (2016). Operations and supply chain management: the role of academics and practitioners in the development of research and practice. *International Journal of Operations and Production Management* 36(12): 1673–1695. https://doi.org/10.1108/IJOPM-11-2015-0721.

Dubois, A., and Gadde, L.E. (2002). Systematic combining: an abductive approach to case research. *Journal of Business Research*, 55(7), 553–560.

Fuller, J.A., and Mansour, A.H. (2003). Operations management and operations research: a historical and relational perspective. *Management Decision* 41(4): 422–426. https://doi.org/10.1108/00251740310468117.

Gibbons, M., Limoges, C., Nowotny, H., Schwartzman, S., Scott, P., and Trow, M. (1994). *The New Production of Knowledge: The Dynamics of Science and Research in Contemporary Societies*. London: SAGE.

Hendrix, S. (2014). Should I become a professor? Success rate 3%! Accessed 29 March 2021 at https://smartsciencecareer.com/become-a-professor/.

Hessels, L.K., and van Lente, H. (2008). Re-thinking new knowledge production: a literature review and a research agenda. *Research Policy* 37: 740–760.

Kondrat, M.E. (1992). Reclaiming the practical: formal and substantive rationality in social work practice. *Social Service Review* 166: 237–225.

McKelvey, B. (2006). Van De Ven and Johnson's 'engaged scholarship': nice try, but … *Academy of Management Review* 31(4): 822–829.

Narasinham, R. (2010). Panel debate. Decision Sciences Institute Annual Meeting, San Diego, CA, 20–23 November.

New Scientist (2018). Time to break academic publishing's stranglehold on research. *New Scientist*. Accessed 29 March 2021 at https://www.newscientist.com/article/mg24032052-900-time-to-break-academic-publishings-stranglehold-on-research.

Pettigrew, A.M. (2001). Management research after modernism. *British Journal of Management* 12(Special Issue): S61–S70.

Rogers, E.M. (1995). *Diffusion of Innovations*, 4th edition. New York: Free Press.

Saunders, M., Lewis, P., and Thornhill, A. (2012). *Research Methods for Business Students*, 6th edition. Harlow: Pearson Education.

Skinner, W. (2010). Keynote speech. Decision Sciences Institute Annual Meeting, San Diego, CA, 20–23 November.

Tranfield, D., Denyer, D., and Smart, P. (2003). Towards a methodology for developing evidence-informed management knowledge by means of systematic review. *British Journal of Management* 14: 207–222.

Tranfield, D., and Starkey, K. (1998). The nature, social organization and promotion of management research: towards policy. *British Journal of Management* 9(4): 341–353.

Van Aken, J.E. (2004). Management research based on the paradigm of the design sciences: the quest for field-tested and grounded technological rules. *Journal of Management Studies* 41(2): 219–246.

Van de Ven, A.H. (2007). *Engaged Scholarship: A Guide for Organizational and Social Research*. Oxford University Press on Demand.

Van de Ven, A.H., and Johnson, P.E. (2006). Knowledge for theory and practice. *Academy of Management Review* 31(4): 802–821.

van Hoek, R., Aronsson, H., Kovács, G., and Spens, K.M. (2005). Abductive reasoning in logistics research. *International Journal of Physical Distribution and Logistics Management* 35: 132–144.

Wiltshire, G. (2018). A case for critical realism in the pursuit of interdisciplinarity and impact. *Qualitative Research in Sport, Exercise and Health* 10(5): 525–542.

Womack, J.P., Jones, D.T., and Roos, D. (1990). *The Machine that Changed the World*. New York: Macmillan.

10   Corporate interviewing and accessing elites in manufacturing companies: a framework to guide qualitative semi-structured interviews

John R. Bryson, Chloe Billing, Chantal Hales, Rachel Mulhall and Megan Ronayne

Introduction

Interviewing is one of the most widely used fieldwork methodologies (McGuirk and O'Neill, 2016; Teti et al., 2020). This process involves negotiating complex relationships and situations, which can create challenges for researchers. Minimising such challenges, and especially some of the risks associated with unequal power dynamics, accessing the right informants or the relevant information, requires careful planning and preparation. The literature on social surveys has tended to focus on the technical aspects of survey design and development (Holstein and Gubrium, 1995; Poon, 2005; McGuirk and O'Neill, 2016), including concerns with positionality (Herod, 1999). For the interviewer, the design, development and testing of a survey tool is a critical task, but implementation is dependent on accessing potential respondents. This chapter focuses on exploring approaches for negotiating access.

Whilst the role of the corporate interview has received much attention in academic research (Healey and Rawlinson, 1993; Hughes, 1999; Smith, 2006), much of this analysis has been based on accessing elites employed in businesses and professional services (McDowell, 1998) or the public sector (Desmond, 2004; Ward and Jones, 1999; Woods, 1998) rather than manufacturing, and critically much of this literature predates the emergence of social media. Management teams in firms vary and the term 'elite' is difficult to define. Elites may take the form of a global corporate executive or a 'one-man band' decision-maker who has just come off the shop floor. Within this setting it might be difficult to define a clear leadership role or image of the 'elite' prior to the interview. The term 'elites' is widely used amongst academics (Desmond, 2004; Harvey, 2010; Rice, 2010; Smith, 2006; Woods, 1998), despite its exact meaning being extensively debated (see Hughes and Cormode, 1998, 1999). Categorisations of elites are largely centred on the group's relative power (Cormode and Hughes, 1999), rather than hierarchical position (Woods, 1998).

Developments in social media are transforming how researchers access potential respondents. Social media needs to be considered as a core research tool. The restructuring of manufacturing towards core tasks in international production systems has transformed organisational structures and made research access difficult. In small and medium-sized enterprises (SMEs), for example, staff levels have been reduced and receptionists are rare. Physical entry to sites is often by locked doors with intercoms, which hinders impromptu and uninvited access. Registered addresses are likely to be part of a complicated ownership structure that might reflect a series of company administrations, management buy-outs and mergers and acquisitions, reducing the ability to correctly target participants. Accessing the sector is increasingly about the individual's connectivity and ability to bypass these obstacles. By exploring these challenges, in the context of the manufacturing sector, this chapter develops a framework to guide novice researchers and those new to the field by drawing upon the experiences of a series of interview-based research projects. No such framework currently exists to inform the design of research in organisational-based studies that provides contextually driven guidance. The framework embraces the entire research process including the role of access post-fieldwork. This is an important part of the design for research impact, and tools that can aid dissemination and engagement are identified and included in the concept of access. Social networks and social media platforms are highlighted as routes for access throughout this framework, providing tools for connectivity, impression management and the distribution of outputs across mass and tailored audiences.

The chapter is organised as follows. First, the literature on access, power, positionality and interviews is explored. The next section explores the methodology applied to construct the access framework. Following this, the core part of the chapter provides social scientists with a practical toolkit to inform the process of accessing and investigating firms. The final section provides concluding comments on the significance of such a tool and the role of social networking in accessing research participants.

Access, power and positionality

Semi-structured interviews have played an important role in enabling research-ers to get closer to actors in the corporate world (Hughes, 1999). These allow interviews to start with a broad idea of the topics that researchers wish to explore, and facilitate the course of the conversation to dictate both order and content (Crang, 2005). Within corporate interviews, researchers have to be critically aware of how power, positionality and gender relation dynamics between the researcher and the researched shape the research process (Herod, 1993). This is particularly the case when researchers are investigating elites (Aberbach and Rockman, 2002). Research on elite interviewing has explored four principal themes: power and positionality, researcher behaviour, inter-viewee openness and access.

Power relations between the interviewee and their informant are in a continual process of change and are dependent on time and space (Harvey, 2010; Smith, 2006; Ward and Jones, 1999). Elite interviewees may hold positions of power based on specialised knowledge. This transforms researchers into 'supplicants' who must be grateful for the elite's cooperation (Welch et al., 2002). The adoption of the right positionality strategy eases tensions between researcher and informant. In Rice's (2010) research on United Kingdom (UK) elites, he adopted the 'stretching of elasticity of positionality' strategy, which involves manipulating the gap between the researcher and interviewee to negotiate unequal power relations. Smith (2006) and her colleague's interviews with policymakers led her to argue that the perception of whom the power belongs to vis-à-vis the researcher is difficult to determine. She argues that power rela-tion dynamics are influenced by macro structures such as organisational and national contexts.

Social scientists have explored the impact of the place or setting, social inter-actions and power dynamics on knowledge construction and interpretation that occurs during interviews (McDowell, 1998). In this context, McDowell suggests that reflexivity, the distinction between the self and the interviewee, or assessment of a range of visual and verbal clues before the interview, will influence researcher's positionality, power dynamics and the outcome of the interview. Based on her interactions with elites in the City of London, she reported having to 'play dumb' with an older, charming and rather patriarchal interviewee, whilst acting 'sisterly' with another female informant of similar age, to influence the research outcome (McDowell, 1998). In these situations, the researcher controls the impression that the participant has on both the individual and the situation, by finding common ground which is suitable to both the participant and researcher and that clearly defines the nature of the interaction. Similarly, other researchers have suggested adopting multiple positionalities, such as 'betweenness', in which the researcher's positionality changes depending on the setting, context or positionality of the informant. Betweenness implies that the researcher is never an insider or outsider, but someone who is always able to negotiate various degrees and kinds of difference based on race, religion, gender, and so forth.

The methodological literature guides the techniques surrounding the process of preparing for and conducting interviews (Gubrium and Holstein, 2002). It emphasises the selection and mode of access to informants, and how to conduct interviews in different spaces (Sin, 2003). Much of the work in this area fails to provide a detailed consideration of accessing respondents and avoids advice on post-interview relationship management techniques. Access is a central consideration in qualitative interviewing because it frames the research process and ultimately the information acquired to inform the analysis (Ward and Jones, 1999). The availability of information in society mirrors the power structure of a society. Relatively uncontroversial data is freely available (census data and opinion polls), while highly confidential data is suppressed and is often impossible to access. This distinction between freely available and highly confidential data is also mirrored in issues over access to potential interviewees. In corporate interviews, smaller firms are often easier to access compared to larger firms, and in larger firms it is much harder to gain access to the managing director compared to someone involved in operations or marketing. The methods employed to access participants and their organisations influence the interaction between, and positionality of, interviewer and interviewee (Cochrane, 1998). The researcher needs to be aware of who they need to access, and ultimately what exactly they have accessed, and which of the multiple voices of the participants are being shared during the interview (Oinas, 1999).

Access to people does not necessarily mean access to knowledge (Desmond, 2004; Wrigley et al., 2003). There are several influences on access to knowledge. Ward and Jones (1999) highlight the impact of timing on the people and spaces accessible to the researcher. This temporal variation is of particular relevance during periods of political or economic instability, as it characterises what is viewed as potentially sensitive information and what is more open to discussion (Desmond, 2004). It may reflect difficulties experienced in organisations with high levels of staff turnover. Interviewing recently retired members of staff, or employees who have left an organisation, is a useful strategy to access a more open voice; but like all respondents, there will be problems with inclusion, exclusion, underemphasis and overemphasis. Schoenberger

(1991) highlights the importance of respondents' knowledge of the subject for generating accurate information, and the advantage of interviewing in enabling access to the most knowledgeable person on the subject. McDowell has highlighted the unrealistic nature of assuming that the researcher will have access to 'the particular industry, location, site and respondents [that are] the optimal or ideal for investigating the particular issue in which we are interested, we all know that the "reality" … is a lot messier' (McDowell, 1998: 2135). Hughes (1999) suggests that the researcher plays a central role in accessing information through the methods employed and must be flexible in terms of acquiring information in the interview context. The closeness of the researcher to the interviewer and their capability to engage in 'close dialogue' is central to accessing knowledge (Wrigley et al., 2003). If access to knowledgeable respondents is obtained, then distortion will occur during the interview due to communication difficulties, including issues related to language; two interviewers participating in the same interview will have very different experiences and will come away with often radically different understandings. Oinas (1999) also proposes that the multiple positionalities of elites can be an influencing factor. Individuals are constantly facing pressure to hide, obscure or present certain viewpoints influenced by their status, thus making it more difficult to construct a sound logic to the participants' input. In addition, the wider political and social context of the research setting can pose challenges for research design (Turner, 2013), and particularly in emerging market regions, such as the Asia Pacific, where research is increasingly focused. These difficulties highlight the need for incorporating methods of access into research design. To obtain useful data from organisations requires facilitating access to participants and information which informs understanding of corporate behaviour.

Methodology: creating the framework

This analysis is based on the experience of six researchers who conducted studies on British and international manufacturing firms between 2001 and 2016. These studies focused on different manufacturing sectors, including but not limited to the resilience of manufacturing firms under fluctuating economic conditions, and their response to megatrends including globalisation, resource scarcity and climate change. The businesses surveyed were SMEs and large companies operating in the areas of metal processing, carpet manufacturing, manufacturing locks, bricks, tiles and insulation products, technical textiles and satellites. Data was acquired through semi-structured interviews with managing directors and/or factory managers. Overall, 351 semi-structured interviews were conducted, and most were held on-site; site visits play an important role in manufacturing research.

The characteristics of the manufacturing sector pose specific challenges for access and interviewing, which have rarely been addressed in the literature. The manufacturing sector is characterised by varying organisational forms including old family businesses, micro enterprises and large multinational companies, with corporate elites holding different roles including owners and managers. In SMEs, the managing director might 'do everything' and needs to come 'off the line' to participate in the interview. The setting of the business, often in a threatening urban environment, lacking a clear entrance, often noisy, untidy, potentially dangerous and with the majority of employees being male, offers additional considerations for the fieldwork process and, particularly, accessibility. Many smaller manufacturers are located on streets of windowless buildings, often in semi-derelict buildings and frequently on streets empty of people. The shop floors of many manufacturing firms are masculine spaces. The walk through the male space of the factory to the office was a walk that often juxtaposed the researcher against a backdrop of oil-smudged Pirelli calendars and glamour photographs. In this context the female researcher must endure the male gaze that transforms, objectifies and sexualises the body.

The corporate interview access framework

Access is an ongoing process and challenge throughout the research process (Newton et al., 2012), and can be constrained by many factors including the type and nature of the organisation, the timing of access, the role that individuals or organisational gatekeepers play, and power dynamics in the researcher–researched relationship. Negotiating access to manufacturing firms can be a daunting task. The first questions that researchers should ask themselves about the manufacturing firms they are targeting are 'Why should the employees/owners give up their time to engage in an interview?' and 'What are the consequences for the firm taking part?' The answer(s) to these questions should allow researchers to plan their access strategy and increase their chances of securing an interview with the targeted individual(s).

Four key stages have been identified in the interview process that are critical for securing access to informants: identifying firms and respondents; negotiating access to organisations and participants; generating information; and maintaining the relationship (Figure 10.1). These stages provide a framework for planning a research project's fieldwork stage. Each stage is explored in the following sections.

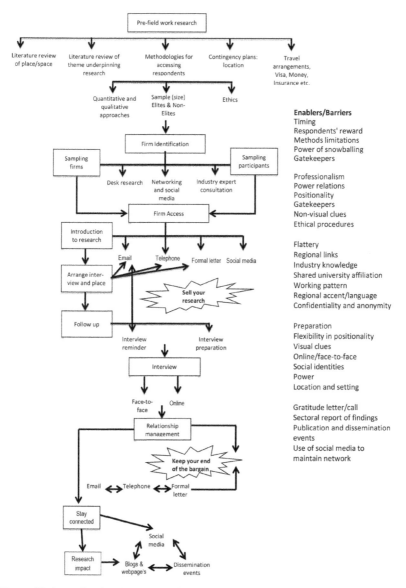

Figure 10.1   Qualitative research: a framework for accessing manufacturing firms

Identifying firms and informants

The initial stage of any research methodology is the development of a sampling procedure. This frames what the researcher has access to during the fieldwork, in terms of people and knowledge. At this stage, some factors should be considered when identifying firms and participants, especially the environmental context within which the target firms operate.

Finding the right firms and then identifying the right respondents employed by a firm is difficult (England, 1994). Information sources can be limited and inaccurate, particularly during times of economic difficulty when firms may be undergoing restructuring. To reduce a firm's exposure to headhunters, employees' identities are increasingly hidden, making it difficult for researchers to identify potential interviewees.

Manufacturing is in a constant process of restructuring as firms experience mergers, acquisitions and closures. Corporate databases provide a useful mechanism for identifying firms, but these under-represent smaller firms, recently established and closed firms. Multiple sources need to be identified and used to compile a list of potential firms active in a sector. For example, through the triangulation of current databases (Companies House (UK), FAME), telephone records and company websites the sample can be narrowed, but this still may not provide a comprehensive list of all surviving firms. For instance, the FAME[1] Database identifies the names of company directors, which may also be found on websites, in company accounts and trade literature. Individuals identified in these records may have died or left the company due to the time lag between events and record updates. Thus, whilst useful, the published records are often incorrect.

The onset of social networking provides an important mechanism for identifying individuals employed by a particular company or industry. Social networking platforms, such as LinkedIn and Facebook, are designed to connect individuals and develop networks. The architecture of the platform determines the content and type of connections available (Papacharissi, 2009). LinkedIn, for example, is designed to support the development of professional networks. The restricted formatting or style options on this platform generate a linear CV-type appearance, and content that promotes information about an individual's professional background and current status. LinkedIn can be used to identify potential interviewees and to construct career biographies. By contrast, the Facebook platform has more flexible content and style forms that include multimedia content, allowing others to generate content for an individual's page. Social networking sites are often used in human relations management, community engagement and to build business brands but they may also be used to successfully integrate researchers into the research environment they intend to explore.

LinkedIn is the most obvious social networking platform to support social science research, as it is the most professionally orientated social networking site. In China, Maimai has emerged as the most popular career and social networking platform, surpassing LinkedIn. The researcher must develop an active profile on LinkedIn that involves entering many online conversations. This is a time-consuming process, but a LinkedIn identity as 'industry expert' may be constructed relatively rapidly and does significantly enhance access. This means that the researcher must create a LinkedIn identity that may rapidly become that of industry expert. This may blur the boundaries between the researched and the researcher, as the researcher develops a presence on LinkedIn that may spread between individuals involved in the industry.

Social media is associated with distinct forms of inclusion and exclusion. Membership is based on self-selection and, as such, individuals act as a form of gatekeeper. Key groups of potential respondents may be under-represented, including older respondents, and it is perhaps more relevant for some sectors and occupations. Some employees are actively excluded from participation in social networks by employers, to maintain confidentiality and restrict the poaching of employees (Bryson, 2009). We have found that accessing an individual via e-mail and/or telephone is not nearly as successful as accessing an individual via LinkedIn. The benefits of a network such as LinkedIn are that it builds connections with individuals rather than businesses, and it overcomes many of the barriers to entry that have been developed by firms. The network also acts as a springboard for developing other contacts: as your network begins to extend so does your attractiveness to others in the field. The scale of an individual's network provides reputational and credibility benefits.

Attendance at industry events such as breakfast meetings, and developing a working relationship with trade and professional bodies, is another way of facilitating access to key players in an industry, especially at the start of a research project. Trade associations may be willing to 'sell' the project to some of their members. Such selling is only effective if representatives of the trade association have established working relationships with members of a company's management team. This method is useful in many cases, but does not guarantee access. Industry experts are often reluctant to become involved in academic research, as it is not part of their core business activity.

Snowball sampling has become an important technique for researching difficult-to-access populations (Atkinson and Flint, 2001), and has been found to be useful when conducting qualitative research on manufacturing. Firms can be identified initially through extensive desk research, and access negotiated. Interviewed respondents can be requested to recommend other individuals who fit the same selection criteria. This type of third-party referral can be useful in avoiding gatekeepers that control access to key informants. Here social networking is an important tool. By building connections to individuals online the researcher is instantly a step closer to accessing the individual's network. An initial and visual link to an individual developed on a social media platform can often prompt a connection attempt from their extended network, without the researcher's involvement.

Gaining access and the importance of the initial contact

The timing of data collection is important. Awareness of the temporal structure of the industry or firms under study can result in an agreement to participate, or might prompt a decline or a non-response. Manufacturing firms may experience sequences of inactivity or activity related to the seasonality of their products. Many SMEs close for two weeks during the summer. It is important to avoid contacting firms towards the end of the tax year and during the weeks immediately after a period of closure. Access to firms during an economic downturn can be difficult, but similar access problems may occur during times of boom. During the 2020 COVID-19 pandemic researchers found that some firms were more willing to take part in research as they had spare time on their hands. In this case, access to firms was optimised because the focus of the research was on understanding firm adaptation and competitiveness during periods of economic stress. In other cases, plants were closed, and staff were furloughed, which made it very difficult for researchers to continue their research. COVID-19 lockdowns, combined with social distancing, prevented face-to-face interviewing. Qualitative researchers had to rapidly adopt video-conferencing platforms, including Skype and Zoom (Dodds and Hess, 2020; Lobe et al., 2020; Teti et al., 2020). Switching to online interviewing comes with savings in time and travel, and other advantages including automated transcription. Nevertheless, face-to-face interviewing provides an opportunity for a site visit that provides important non-verbal information.

The initial contact with firms and individuals is a critical point in the research process. At this point first impressions are formed, and it provides the researcher with the opportunity to 'sell' their research and start to build a relationship with gatekeepers and informants.

Creating a positive impression, and being professional, is important and solidifies the researcher's position as a worthwhile recipient of the informant's time. The research encounter must be marketed to potential respondents as an opportunity to offer their opinions and insider knowledge, reinforced by the direct relevance of the research for the individual firm. Researcher identity and impression management is critical in developing credibility and positioning the researcher to suit the context and environment of the situation. Social networks are particularly useful and can be used to actively construct and control an impression of the researcher's identity that suits the context of the network (van Dijck, 2013). Ultimately this forms a type of social capital (Papacharissi, 2013) that can be used to circumvent barriers to uninvited access.

In all cases, the firms should be persuaded that they could benefit from participating in the project. Benefits include the discussion that occurs during the interview, the interview as a special moment for the respondent to reflect on the firm's activities, and the provision of a summary report to the firm on the conclusion of the project. Every researcher needs to have considered how the project is going to be 'marketed' to potential participants. This marketing must be based on an accurate reflection of the project's aims, but should position the project in the minds of potential respondents. Understanding the role gatekeepers play in controlling access can be critical. For instance, the researcher should sell the benefits of the project to personal assistants (PAs) as if they were in discussion with their manager. PAs have the power to facilitate or constrain access to informants, and should be treated sensitively. Often their role in empirical research is oversimplified (Campbell et al., 2006). A good rapport developed with them is especially useful in identifying names of potential respondents, obtaining e-mail addresses and information regarding the current state of the firm and industry. It is critical to be able to convince gatekeepers that the project has value for their employer. The size of a business and method of initial contact can influence the type of gatekeeper that researchers interact with. Many SMEs do not have PAs, and in our projects phone calls were answered directly by the plant manager or managing director. In addition, contacting individuals through social networking sites is one way of working around gatekeepers. In these cases, the ability of the researcher to engage directly with the respondent and to be ready to undertake the interview at that time is critical.

The authors have identified a series of enabling and inhibiting factors for this stage of the research process (Figure 10.1). Tools that have aided this stage include flattery of informants' usefulness in the project, using correct contact names to maximise success, and regional links to universities or disciplinary affiliations, as well as personal heritage. Flattery has been found to be a useful tool deployed to persuade individuals to participate. Accessing firms is both an art (persuading individuals to participate in the study) and a science (identifying firms and developing robust survey instruments). Many academics learn this art by a process of trial and error.

The internet and, particularly, targeted e-mails have become an important technique for accessing informants (Harvey, 2010). E-mail remains an important tool to arrange interview times. Targeting correspondence, whether that is e-mail or social media, directly to named individuals reduces the influence of gatekeepers and the speed of access. Access by e-mails and social networking through apps on mobile phones allows the researcher to time the contact at relatively quiet work periods, such as during commuting times, early in the morning or late afternoon. Researchers also know when messages have been read through alerts, and can maximise their impact by using other prompts, including viewing profiles which send alerts to respondents.

Researchers face difficult decisions about how forthcoming they should be concerning the demands that a researcher might place on potential respondents. Often a rough estimate of the interview length is provided, but the researcher must not mislead potential respondents. All research projects go through a formal process of ethical review. This process includes the identification of firms, access and ethical consent. The deployment of ethical consent forms before an interview has been found to intimidate some potential interviewees whilst reassuring others. In some of our projects, firms have been approached with a request for a discussion or chat about issues facing their firm and/or sector. This is an attempt to replace the formality of an interview situation with a less intimidating discussion. In our experience, the most effective technique is to e-mail the ethical consent form once an interview has been arranged. This also provides reassurance once the interviewee knows exactly what has been discussed.

The interview and accessing information

While access to the firm may have been achieved with the arrangement of an interview, access to information still needs to be negotiated (Ostrander, 1993; Wrigley et al., 2003). The interview setting is a social interaction and requires considerable communication skills as well as interviewing techniques, to ensure the interviewee feels comfortable with the process, and for the researcher to navigate the potential blocks on information the interviewee may establish. Developing a typology of interview questions and improvised interventions appropriate to the research (Dillon, 1990), as well as spending time before and at the beginning of the interview to develop a rapport (Elwood and Martin, 2000), are tools to enable the researcher to be flexible to the situation. The interview process itself, however, enhances these positionalities and generates a microclimate of politics and social identities that actively impacts on the information generated. The researcher's ability to navigate this climate is central to their ability to access relevant topics and data.

Gender, ethnicity and status are aspects of identity that are difficult to avoid in the research arena, and the manufacturing sector has a distinct profile: it is heavily dominated by males and includes a diverse range of organisational forms. In the corporate interview setting the researcher may have less power than the interviewee (McDowell, 1992). As a junior researcher within this setting, the power dynamic is intensified, and the junior researcher's lack of experience and status often leads to loss of control during the interview (Harvey, 2010). However, status as a university researcher in a manufacturing setting can also change these power dynamics. University academics are themselves perceived as relative elites in some communities. Engagement with universities for some manufacturing firms is an unknown process and may induce caution, perceptions of inferiority, but also excitement to showcase the firm's achievements. The diverse nature of management teams in the sector makes it extremely difficult to anticipate the nature of the 'elite', and therefore the position of the researcher before the interview.

Understanding the identity of the respondent and their organisational role and history is important (Oinas, 1999). The researcher needs to be aware of whether they are getting the 'corporate spiel' or the individual's knowledge, expertise and experiences. This can often be tested by cross-checking information with other sources, such as media reports, websites, company articles and industry experts. It is important to remember that a respondent will only be aware of part of an event, and that post-rationalisation, or selective forgetting, combined with face-saving or face-enhancing strategies, will distort the types of information given to a researcher. Triangulating information obtained from interviewees with other sources such as other representatives from the firm, or by accessing industry gossip, is important. Whilst the corporate interview provides a valuable opportunity to obtain insights into company behaviour, it must be stressed that interviews are selective and distorted accounts of events.

Ongoing access and maintaining the relationship

The relationship that is developed by the researcher and the participants through the fieldwork process should not end after a successful interview. The researcher-researched relationship is complex and sometimes tensions emerge between the researcher's need for data and the interviewee's personal circumstances, experiences and opinions. The interview setting can generate a very unusual, and temporary, occasion of intense communication and trust. An interview may explore extremely sensitive or distressing information that is unintentionally shared. In these situations, the researcher has the ethical obligation to discuss how this data is used within the project.

Throughout the study the researcher must maintain a constructive relationship with informants to facilitate future access to firms and any successful university–industry collaboration that might develop. The researcher must recognise from the start of their project the importance of dedicating time to cultivating relationships with participants, as this leads to increased loyalty to the researcher and the university that they represent. Post-interview relationship management may start with a polite message of gratitude to thank the interviewee for their time and help. Maintaining this relationship can be difficult, and the researcher must have techniques in place to solidify the relationship throughout the research (Figure 10.1).

It is the researcher's responsibility to provide the information and feedback that was promised initially, and promptly. Maintaining communication with participants allows for subsequent information-gathering and to provide ongoing feedback about research findings and developing resources for participants. Social media provides a quick, direct and manageable avenue for ongoing communication with multiple participants. Project Twitter feeds, blogs and webpages allow researchers to update project findings and maintain a community of participants. Maintaining up-to-date contact details with individual participants is important. Developing a professional social network group, such as on LinkedIn, can help ensure that contact details are up to date and that notices about the research reach participants, even years after the initial interview. This can also be successfully achieved by sustaining a good relationship with gatekeepers. Organisational structures frequently change through job moves and restructuring, but gatekeepers, whether internal or external to the organisation, can provide an ongoing route into the current organisation.

The impact from research is a core consideration of any research project and should be considered along with access throughout the project. A standard approach is to provide a general summary of the research, such as an industry report, after completion of the research project, as a token of appreciation or as a record of the engagement. It is important that no firm or individual is named in these reports. Such reports should provide an overview of the project's outcomes and their implications. This approach has three limitations. First, it is difficult to determine what industry participants would want from the research project, and this requires a very different style of communication to the standard academic publication. The type of information considered as useful by participants may not have been the object of the research, but might still be specified by participants during discussions over access. Second, timings are very difficult and project summaries inherently come at the end of the project, which may be up to three years after the initial contact, at which point the information may no longer be relevant to the participants. Third, the provision of a written summary does not facilitate a discussion around project outcomes. A better approach would be to consider organizing an interactive briefing event or tailored seminar, and this could take the form of a webinar.

Conclusions

Access and research engagement is a social process that is built upon connections and interactions between two communities. Access is a critical methodological problem that is framed by the social and spatial setting of the individual, organisation or place under study. Impressions of participants and the researcher must be carefully managed.

The researcher requires a repertoire of skills to access organisations and participants. The skills are a combination of learnt practices through experience and mentoring, but can also be developed systematically through guided approaches to managing the access process. The framework explored in this chapter provides a methodological tool to support the design of a process for accessing organisations (see Figure 10.1). This chapter has focused primarily on accessing the manufacturing sector, because this environment generates distinct challenges for researchers. Nevertheless, this framework can be applied to access all types of organisations, as it highlights the processes that need to be managed and negotiated during the corporate interview process.

The fieldwork process is a learning curve. Preparation is vital, but the multitude of settings and encounters will always throw up unexpected situations. This only highlights the need to be reflexive and prepared during the research process. The framework presented and explored in this chapter will assist novice researchers in the field by highlighting critical points in accessing companies. At each stage of the framework, access to different elements of the research process must be negotiated. Understanding these issues should help researchers remain open to opportunities, increase their awareness of potential pitfalls, and provide them with a repertoire of potential methods to overcome them.

Note

1. The FAME database provides financial information on UK and Irish registered companies.

References

Aberbach, J.D. and Rockman, B.A. (2002) Conducting and coding elite interviews. *PS: Political Science and Politics*, 35, 673–676.

Atkinson, R. and Flint, J. (2001) Accessing hidden and hard-to-reach populations: snowball research strategies. *Social Research Update*, 33, 1–4.

Bryson, J.R. (2009) Management control and business and professional services expertise: 'walking' reputational capital, golden handcuffs, client intimacy and zipper relationships. In: Henning, K. and Michulitz, C. (eds), *Management Cybernetics 2020*. Berlin: Duncker & Humblot Verlag, pp. 40–57.

Campbell, L.M., Gray, N.J., Meletis, Z.A., Abbott, J.G. and Silver, J.J. (2006) Gatekeepers and keymasters: dynamic relationships of access in geographical fieldwork. *Geographical Review*, 96, 97–121.

Cochrane, A. (1998) Illusions of power: interviewing local elites. *Environment and Planning A*, 30, 2121–2132.

Cormode, L. and Hughes, A. (1999) The economic geographer as a situated researcher of elites. *Geoforum*, 30, 299–300.

Crang, M. (2005) Qualitative methods: there is nothing outside the text? *Progress in Human Geography*, 29, 225–233.

Desmond, M. (2004) Methodological challenges posed in studying an elite in the field. *Area*, 36, 262–269.

Dillon, J.T. (1990) *The Practice of Questioning*. London: Routledge.

Dodds, S. and Hess, A.C. (2020) Adapting research methodology during COVID-19: lessons for transformative service research. *Journal of Service Management*. DOI: 10.1108/JOSM-05-2020-0153.

Elwood, S.A. and Martin, D.G. (2000) 'Placing' interviews: location and scales of power in qualitative research. *Professional Geographer*, 52, 649–657.

England, K.R.L. (1994) Getting personal: reflexivity, positionality, and feminist research. *Professional Geographer*, 46, 80–89.

Gubrium, J.F. and Holstein, J.A. (2002) *Handbook of Interview Research: Context and Method*. Thousand Oaks, CA: SAGE.

Harvey, W.S. (2010) Methodological approaches for interviewing elites. *Geography Compass*, 4, 193–205.

Healey, M.J. and Rawlinson, M.B. (1993) Interviewing business owners and managers: a review of methods and techniques. *Geoforum*, 24, 339–355.

Herod, A. (1993) Gender issues in the use of interviewing as a research method. *Professional Geographer*, 45, 305–317.

Herod, A. (1999) Reflections on interviewing foreign elites: praxis, positionality, validity, and the cult of the insider. *Geoforum*, 30, 313–327.

Holstein, J.A. and Gubrium, J.F. (1995) The active interview. Sage University Paper.

Hughes, A. (1999) Constructing economic geographies from corporate interviews: insights from a cross-country comparison of retailer-supplier relationships. *Geoforum*, 30, 363–374.

Hughes, A. and Cormode, L.E. (1998) Theme issue: researching elites and elite spaces. *Environment and Planning A*, 30, 2095–2162.

Hughes, A. and Cormode, L.E. (1999) Special Issue. Networks, cultures and elite research: the economic geographer as situated researchers. *Geoforum*, 30, 299–363.

Lobe, B., Morgan, D and Hoffman, K.A. (2020) Qualitative data collection in an era of social distancing. *International Journal of Qualitative Methods*. https://doi.org/10.1177/1609406920937875

McDowell, L. (1992) Valid games? A response to Erica Schoenberger. *Professional Geographer*, 44, 212–215.

McDowell, L. (1998) Elites in the City of London: some methodological considerations. *Environment and Planning A*, 30, 2133–2146.

McGuirk, P.M. and O'Neill, P. (2016) Using questionnaires in qualitative human geography. In: Hay, I. (ed.), *Qualitative Research Methods in Human Geography*. Toronto: Oxford University Press, pp. 246–273.

Newton, J., Franklin, A., Middleton, J. and Marsden, T. (2012) (Re-)negotiating access: the politics of researching skills and knowledge for 'sustainable communities'. *Geoforum*, 43, 585–594.

Oinas, P. (1999) Voices and silences: the problem of access to embeddedness. *Geoforum*, 30, 351–361.

Ostrander, S.A. (1993) Surely you're not in this just to be helpful. Access, rapport, and interviews in three studies of elites. *Journal of Contemporary Ethnography*, 22, 7–27.

Papacharissi, Z. (2009) The virtual geographies of social networks: a comparative analysis of Facebook, LinkedIn and ASmallWorld. *New Media and Society*, 11, 199–220.

Papacharissi, Z. (2013) A networked self: identity performance and sociability on social network sites. In: Lee, F.L.F., Leung, L., Qiu., J.L. and Chu, D.S.C. (eds), *Frontiers in New Media Research*. New York: Routledge, pp. 207–221.

Poon, J.P.H. (2005) Quantitative methods: not positively positivist. *Progress in Human Geography*, 29, 766–772.

Rice, G. (2010) Reflections on interviewing elites. *Area*, 42, 70–75.

Schoenberger, E. (1991) The corporate interview as a research method in economic geography. *Professional Geographer*, 43, 180–189.

Sin, C.H. (2003) Interviewing in 'place': the socio-spatial construction of interview data. *Area*, 35, 305–312.

Smith, K.E. (2006) Problematising power relations in 'elite' interviews. *Geoforum*, 37, 643–653.

Teti, M., Schatz, E. and Liebenberg, L. (2020) Methods in the time of COVID-19: the vital role of qualitative inquiries. *International Journal of Qualitative Methods*. https://doi.org/10.1177/1609406920920962

Turner, S. (2013) Red stamps and green tea: fieldwork negotiations and dilemmas in the Sino-Vietnamese borderlands. *Area*, 45, 396–402.

van Dijck, J. (2013) 'You have one identity': performing the self on Facebook and LinkedIn. *Media, Culture and Society*, 35, 199–215.

Ward, K.G. and Jones, M. (1999) Researching local elites: reflexivity, 'situatedness' and political-temporal contingency. *Geoforum*, 30, 301–312.

Welch, C., Marschan-Piekkari, R., Penttinen, H. and Tahvanainen, M. (2002) Interviewing elites in international organizations: a balancing act for the researcher. *International Business Review*, 11, 611–628.

Woods, M. (1998) Rethinking elites: networks, space, and local politics. *Environment and Planning A*, 30, 2101–2119.

Wrigley, N., Currah, A. and Wood, S. (2003) Commentary. *Environment and Planning A*, 35, 381–387.

11 Reading manufacturing firms and new research agendas: scalar-plasticity, value/risk and the emergence of Jenga Capitalism

John R. Bryson

Manufacturing matters (Bryson et al., 2015). It is important to appreciate that whilst money makes the world go round, all sizes of manufacturing companies play a central role in this whirlwind. Manufacturing companies design and fabricate the products that underpin the activities of financial institutions and markets. The use of the term 'whirlwind' in this context is deliberate, as this highlights that this is a violent and destructive process that is also perhaps impossible to control. Conflating money with manufacturing is intended to emphasise that these two processes can never be separated. Manufacturing is an exercise in financial investment and in the management and manipulation of money.

In 2003, John Allen published an influential book on *Lost Geographies of Power*. In this he argued that geographers have 'lost the sense in which geography makes a difference to the exercise of power' (Allen, 2003: 1). The book highlighted that it is important to stand back and reflect on existing research agendas. This chapter develops an approach to setting out a research agenda for manufacturing research based on identifying topics that have been 'lost', 'overlooked' or which are 'emergent'.

Within the city-region literature there has emerged a recent conceptual interest in the concept of 'seeing like a region' or to 'see like a city' or even to 'see like a state' (Magnusson, 2011; Addie, 2017; Amin and Thrift, 2017). These forms of metaphor are intended to persuade readers or listeners to consider cities and regions from a particular perspective. In this case, the focus is on trying to appreciate complexity. An alternative rhetorical device is to shift from 'seeing' towards 'reading'. Seeing involves the action of being conscious of that which is around you, whilst reading involves engaging with the elements that are included in a text and with the complete text; comprehension is greater than the individual elements or parts. It might be difficult to 'see like a manufacturing firm', but reading firms represents a very different challenge. Applying 'reading' as a method or approach to identifying a research agenda for manufacturing raises the interesting question of how to read manufacturing or production processes. Manufacturing research is already informed by implicit approaches to reading production processes. Much research is centred on comprehension, including learning a vocabulary and then combining the application of this vocabulary to comprehend some business process. In the case of reading manufacturing firms and production processes, the texts are organisations, production processes, interfirm relationships and regulatory frameworks including trade regulations and standards.

An important cross-cutting theme to consider in developing a research agenda on manufacturing is the contribution that social science makes to the wider society. There is a developing debate on responsible business (Claydon, 2011; United Nations, 2019), but this approach also needs to be applied to academia. What are the characteristics of a responsible academic? What role should social science play? Is this around research-informed teaching and/or wider societal impacts on policy development and approaches to managing and organising business? It is important that the manufacturing research agenda resonates with wider societal needs and that social science continues to be considered by funders, and potential and actual students, to be relevant. For at least the next decade, the primary challenges facing manufacturing will revolve around decarbonisation, cybersecurity, skill shortages, enhancing supply chain security and resilience, and in engaging with the developing national debates on economic security and national security. This is the context for this chapter, which develops and applies an approach to reading businesses to identify a research agenda for manufacturing. The chapter proceeds as follows. First, it develops an approach to reading businesses as a method to identify new research agendas. Second, the reading business approach is applied to manufacturing to identify six new research agendas. Third, the chapter concludes by reflecting on this approach.

Reading firms as an approach to identifying research agendas

How does one read a business? This is a question that is rarely asked. The answer is complex. Any reading of a business will suffer from information asymmetry, including information that can never be known. There is a real danger that business is considered to be a rational process with informed entrepreneurs and managers making correct decisions. This is not the case: too often, business decisions must be made rapidly, and there is never sufficient information to make a completely informed decision. All firms are people-centric, highly politicised and culturally inflected. There is a real danger that patterns and regularities regarding firm behaviour are identified, and then it is assumed that these are meaningful patterns which are the outcome of rational decision-making processes. Many of these patterns will be shaped by serendipity, improvisation, and by decisions that were made in the past. The latter may reflect 'obsolescent logic' in which a decision made at some time in the past no longer reflects present-day circumstances (Salder and Bryson, 2019: 809). In this case, a company may work around the constraints imposed by this type of obsolescence to avoid writing off sunk costs.

Reading a business is a process in which a reader, or readers, needs to identify and understand the structures, systems and processes that lie behind the creation of all forms of value. There are multiple ways in which firms create value, including processes that enhance profitability. Reading is a process of continual analysis and must precede and follow any policy or firm-level intervention. In this account, the emphasis is on an evidence-based informed view of production processes based on collecting information, understanding business processes, and in appreciating the interplay between a firm's business model, operational processes, employees, and the co-creation of value with customers. Reading a business may focus on the now, but it can also explore the past as well as the future. There is a danger that the application of this approach to the future is based on extrapolations from the past. It is important to consider potential disruptions including innovation, regulatory change and alterations in consumer behaviour.

The first stage in reading is based on acquiring understanding of a vocabulary. Reading manufacturing requires identifying the elements, processes and vocabulary that are required for comprehension. This vocabulary includes terms and concepts used in practice and in research (Clark, 1998). Some of the practitioner vocabulary will be sector-specific. This vocabulary includes firms, strategic relationships, foreign direct investment, non-tariff barriers, research and development, innovation, power, dynamics, offshoring, reshoring, outsourcing, value, risk, risk-reward ratios, value for money, brands/branding, competitiveness, productivity and EBITA (earnings before interest, taxes and amortisation).

The second stage involves rules that have been developed to enhance understanding. This is the grammar that support comprehension. For manufacturing this 'grammar' includes identifying the relationships between societal needs or consumer demand, and product development and design processes. A product is then created via the configuration of a production process, and this includes design, management and value. This configuration process will reflect some combination of obsolete logic, sunk costs, technology and geography, and will involve various forms of interfirm relationship. The latter may be formal, including strategic partnerships, or informal or price-based. The completed product is monetarised in some way. Eventually the product becomes obsolete and is reclassified as waste; waste may become a resource, as products can be upcycled or recycled (Figure 11.1).

Figure 11.1 is a stylised account of a production process. The following points must be noted. First, some of these linkages are two-way, for example, production design may require alterations to product design (Bryson and Rusten, 2011). Second, some products are designed before a clear societal need is identified, and manufacturers then must create consumer demand (Bryson and Rusten, 2011: 187). This is an important point as it illustrates the interlinkages between production and consumption. Third, the strength and direction of the relationships between these stages in the production process are important research questions in their own right. Fourth, production processes have negative impacts that include creating extra-network effects that enhance risk, and these risks may be difficult to control (Bryson and Vanchan, 2020). These extra-network effects include climate change, but also opioid addiction. In 2017, more people died in the United States from overdoses involving opioids than from HIV- or AIDS-related illnesses at the peak of the AIDS epidemic (DeWeerdt, 2019). There are also more direct supply chain effects, including unsustainable production practices that have major environmental consequences, that raise issues regarding equity and environmental justice (Goldstein and Newell, 2019a, 2019b).

Reading a business raises a series of foundational questions that should inform all attempts at reading a production process or reading supply chains or production networks. These include:

1. What is being produced?
2. How are these manufactured goods produced?
3. Have these products changed over time and what are the implications of any changes for the configuration of the production process?
4. What values are being produced, for whom and where, including the creation of values-in-use? Have these values altered over time?

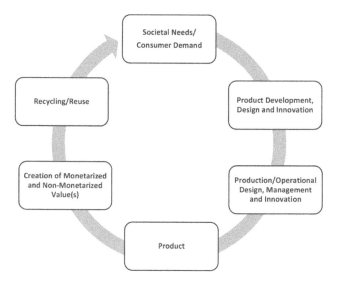

Figure 11.1   Manufacturing from product development, fabrication, monetisation to recycling

5. Where is the primary source of value, and of which value?
6. How are these values produced? What are the trade-offs that have been considered regarding different blends of value that are incorporated into the product/process?
7. What are the operational scales at which these values are produced?
8. What are the most important processes, and which contribute the most value and for whom?
9. What roles do data, data analytics and enterprise resource planning (ERP) systems play in underpinning the value creation process?
10. What are the interrelationships between inputs and outputs or productivity?
11. What alternative production processes exist, and why was this particular production process selected, including the geography of this process?
12. What are the interfirm dynamics of this production process, including the distribution of power and returns?
13. What intra-firm dynamics are involved in this production process?
14. Is this a spatial or an aspatial process, or what are the spatial and aspatial aspects of this process?
15. How has the production process been subdivided into discrete but linked tasks by the application of a division of labour?
16. Is there a spatial division of labour in which tasks are undertaken in particular locations? Has the spatial division of labour altered? How do

regulations, compliance and taxation influence decisions regarding the configuration of production networks?

17. What are the labour implications of this production process?
18. What are the power dynamics of this production process?
19. What are the relationships between these production processes and land? What role does land play in corporate decisions? Existing facilities may be landlocked, forcing a company to enhance land-related productivity or to relocate; forced relocation due to landlocking might result in transferring production to another facility.
20. What are the environmental implications of this production process? Supply chains are constructed on place-based relationships that result in environmental and social impacts.
21. What are the risks, including pollution, and who is accountable for these risks?
22. Who directly and indirectly experiences these risks, including any financial gains and losses?
23. What resources (tangible and intangible) are required, including those owned or coordinated and controlled by the firm?
24. What contradictions exist within this process, including perverse outcomes?
25. What are the relationships between insurance and/or finance, and the configuration of this process including financialisation?
26. What technological solutions have been developed to support this production process?
27. What near-to-market innovations, including regulatory change, might disrupt this production process or displace this product?
28. Is the product recycled? If so, how is the product recycling process configured?

These 28 questions provide a framework for reading all types of businesses including manufacturing-orientated business. It must be noted that there are many other questions that could be added to this list.

These 28 questions are a starting point for exploring the evolving configuration of manufacturing production processes and related risks. The emphasis placed on risk in some of these questions highlights the interrelationships between risks and returns, and suggests that research also needs to focus on existing and emergent risks. There is an important relationship between risk identification and management, and the design of operational processes that support the fabrication of products. Cutting across these issues are skills or capabilities as well as online platforms and data analytics. Enterprise resource planning (ERP) systems are becoming increasingly important as integrated platforms designed to manage all aspects of production-based or distribution businesses. These systems align financial management, human resources, supply chain management, manufacturing and distribution with the core accountancy function within a corporate setting. They track all aspects of production, distribution and finance and are playing an important role in both everyday management and organisational strategy. There is an important research agenda to be developed on the ways in which ERP systems are used to support production, distribution and financial management.

All these 28 questions revolve around the issue of value. The concept of value is critical for understanding all types of production processes. There are many different types of value. There is a tendency to focus too much on profit, monetarised value, surplus value or return on investment (ROI). This is unfortunate. There is a substantial literature on non-price-based sources of competitiveness (Koutsoyiannis, 1982; Bryson and Ronayne, 2014; Bryson and Vanchan, 2020), including the relationship between monetarised values and values-in-use (Bryson et al., 2020). This also includes a focus on the creation of wider societal and environmental values. This highlights the ongoing shift by companies towards the pursuit of purpose over profit. Companies may apply approaches based on responsible business or corporate social responsibility, including balancing cost minimisation and profit maximisation, with alternative values related to sustainability and responsible employment practices.

This approach to reading firms is one way of identifying topics and themes that require further research. It also highlights the holistic nature of business and manufacturing. Thus, a focus on reward must be placed in the context of risk; different risk-reward ratios reflect differences in configuring the technological-production interface and in configuring global production networks (GPNs) (Bryson and Vanchan, 2020). The same product can be produced using very different GPNs, with great differences in the relationship between technology, people, geography and production. These types of issues are reflected in research topics that include understanding new forms of risk, research on different forms of value and skills and capabilities, including a research agenda on risks, rewards and contingency planning. There are cross-cutting themes including exploring new and existing global societal challenges and business and social responsibility. This includes a focus on decarbonising existing products, and production processes combined with designing goods for effective recycling, and the development of new products to support the shift towards the net zero greenhouse gas emissions target (Milne et al., 2019).

A research agenda for manufacturing industries in the global economy

This approach to reading firms is holistic. Initially the focus is on reading the complete firm, and then topics, themes and processes can be identified that require further research; but these should be placed within the context of the complete firm and/or production process. The following six subsections explore topics and themes that require further research and that come from applying a holistic approach to reading manufacturing companies.

A new manufacturing research agenda on risk and the emergence of Jenga Capitalism

The academic debates on manufacturing, and production in general, as well as globalisation, tends to ignore or neglect risk (see Beck, 1992; Bryson and Vanchan, 2020). Risk, and the trade-offs with reward, is an important and much under-researched topic. Different sectors, firms, individuals and countries have different attitudes to risk. The emphasis in the globalisation literature is on the benefits that come from globalisation rather than the risks, additional costs and complexities. This is an account in which companies benefit by stripping out costs via the configuration of GPNs designed to maximise profitability. There is another side to globalisation, or to the ongoing global shift, that has been revealed by COVID-19. This is to acknowledge that globalisation comes with benefits and risks (Bryson and Vanchan, 2020). Economic geographers have begun to consider inter-network and intra-network risks, but with a focus on the configuration of GPNs (Coe and Yeung, 2015) rather than developing a more holistic analysis of risk and globalisation. There are two critical research gaps that need to be explored – system convergence and organisational risk and uncertainty – and these will be discussed in turn.

First, within economics there is a literature on economic convergence and divergence (Daniels et al., 2011). This approach assumes that all economies should converge at some time in the future, and this convergence is defined as per capita income convergence. The critical word here is 'convergence', but used to explore a very different process. Globalisation, and the configuration of all GPNs, are exercises in another form of convergence: this can be best described as system convergence. As systems converge across the world, or are coupled together in complex ways, then this supports enhanced connectivity between different systems, processes and places. These connections between places and systems become denser and more critical. On the one hand, this has many benefits that have been well documented by academics. On the other hand, this process comes with many undocumented risks. System and place convergence means that the complete system, or a GPN, becomes less resilient and is saturated with unknown risks. Any disruption anywhere in this system has the potential to ricochet throughout the system, causing major disruptions. COVID-19 is a perfect example of this. Enhanced connectivity between places now means that disease anywhere may rapidly become disease everywhere. It also means that a GPN can cease to function because of some disruption to the systems that support it. This disruption might be linked to problems in cloud-based services or in the application of an Internet of Things (IoT) approach to the supporting computer architecture that sits behind the real-time coordination of a GPN.

It is important to appreciate how precarious global systems are to disruption. Satellites, even the Global Positioning System (GPS), can be rendered inoperable for a period by a solar flare. A solar flare could disrupt electrical grids, the internet, as well as satellite communications. The internet relies on hundreds of thousands of miles of critical undersea cables that circle the globe. These cables carry more than 90 per cent of global communications, including the data exchanges which underpin trillions of dollars of financial transactions every day. These cables are at risk of sabotage and any disruption would ripple throughout the global economy.

System convergence of any type, including enhanced connectivity, comes with manageable and perhaps unmanaging risks. There is an important research agenda here that needs to explore the types of risks that are quantified on a daily basis by actuaries. These risks can affect both sides of a balance sheet, and their assessment, quantification and management require valuation, liability management and asset management skills. Many of these will be extra-network risks that are created by convergence and by the configuration of effective GPNs (Bryson and Vanchan, 2020). The risks related to this type of system or network convergence, combined with enhanced place-to-place connectivity, can be understood in two ways.

On the one hand are domino effects, or chain reactions, in which disruption in one part of a GPN or converged system has the potential to disrupt production and consumption processes across the globe. For COVID-19, the domino effect disrupted GPNs that were involved in the production of personal protection equipment (PPE). This produced major problems for companies, their employees as well as governments. Nevertheless, the primary point of disruption was at the point of consumption, and the failure of these GPNs contributed to enhanced disease transmission and death.

On the other hand, system convergence across capitalism is perhaps best described as representing a new epoch. This is not the Anthropocene, but the emergence of 'Jenga Capitalism'. Jenga is a board game in which players take turns to remove one block at a time from a tower constructed of 54 wooden blocks. Each block that is removed is placed on the top of the structure and the structure becomes progressively less stable. Globalisation has resulted in system convergence combined with enhanced connectivity. The outcome is similar to a game of Jenga. Eventually in a Jenga game, removing one block and replacing it will result in the complete collapse of the structure. COVID-19 is one moment in Jenga Capitalism. Other pandemics will follow, given the increase in human population, combined with increased density, and place-based convergence. Thus, one element of this new Jenga Capitalism epoch will be that the twenty-first century will become known as the pandemic century. There have been other indications of Jenga Capitalism. These include SARS in 2003, the Japanese earthquake of 2011 that disrupted production across the planet, and the 2010 volcanic eruption of Eyjafjallajökull in Iceland. This eruption disrupted air travel across Western and Northern Europe and across the Atlantic for six days.

The application of the term 'Jenga' to 'capitalism' creates a new metaphor. This is a rhetorical device with a difference, as those applying it can imagine a Jenga tower but can also play the Jenga game. This is an example of an action-based metaphor. To appreciate the value of this new metaphor it is important to explore the interrelationships between the biological and the biographical. The biological includes survival, whilst the biographical is based on survival combined with differential outcomes. Biographies shape biological outcomes. One of the most important points to appreciate is that the system convergence and the enhanced place-to-place connectivity which characterises Jenga Capitalism increases uncertainty, including unmanageable risks, and these impact on individual biographies. These impacts increase inequalities, morbidity and mortality. A key characteristic of Jenga Capitalism is the reach of these impacts rather than their duration. During the Jenga epoch a problem that emerges in one system or place can rapidly be transmitted to many other places. A local problem becomes a global problem. This highlights the importance of scale and in applying a multi-scalar approach to exploring Jenga Capitalism. In this context, it is important to appreciate that each place is connected to other places in very different ways. The implication is that not all places will be impacted in the same way by the same disruption.

Malicious attacks on computer servers, mobile devices, electronic systems and networks are central to Jenga Capitalism. Any disruption to these systems results in domino effects. These attacks include industrial espionage, which is another overlooked research area. A classic example of a cyberattack and its impacts as part of Jenga Capitalism occurred in June 2019. Norsk Hydro, a Norwegian global aluminium producer, experienced a malicious hack on its core services. This is an excellent example of a GPN being disrupted by a cyber-attack. This was a ransomware attack involving 22,000 computers located across 170 sites in 40 countries. The company's Chief Information Officer (CIO) opened the ransom note that appeared on the company's computers, which stated that 'Your files have been encrypted with the strongest military algorithms ... without our special decoder it is impossible to restore the data' (Tidy, 2019). The initial outcome was that the company's 35,000 employees had to return to using paper and pens, and many of the company's production lines ceased to operate. Production lines were switched back to manual functions, and retired colleagues returned to the company to provide training in how to run these production lines without computers. Norsk Hydro did not pay the ransom, and this attack resulted in additional costs for this company of over £45 million. The Norsk Hydro case highlights the importance of effective contingency planning for all companies and GPNs. These plans must include no linkages to existing converged systems. Thus, contingency planning must assume that all digital platforms and converged systems are no longer functional.

System convergence, combined with place-based connectivity, are core drivers behind the uncertainty that is central to Jenga Capitalism. Every month new examples of Jenga Capitalism events occur. In March 2021, the *Evergreen* container ship became wedged across the Suez Canal for six days. Around 12 per cent of global trade is transported via this canal. This blockage meant that over 420 ships had to wait for this container ship to be freed. This blockage impacted upon supply chains for months. The Evergreen was impounded for three months, but the blockage also disrupted the planned geography of freight traffic with container ships unable to meet their agreed schedules. These ships carry completed manufactured goods and components including semiconductors. The canal's blockage added another level of disruption to the global distribution of computer chips. On Friday 19 March 2021, there was a fire at a semiconductor chip fabrication plant owned by Renesas. This facility was located in the city of Naka, Japan. The fire commenced in a plating tank and resulted in an electrical overcurrent. The resulting blaze damaged 11 of this plant's fabrication units and took five hours to extinguish. It was expected to take three months for production to return to pre-fire rates. This factory produced chips for the automotive industry and there is currently a global shortage. In February 2021, chip-making plants were closed in Texas due to weather conditions and a drought in Taiwan was also threatening the manufacture of wafers. The automotive industry is reliant on a limited number of chip manufacturers, with production concentrated in Asia, particularly in Taiwan and Korea.

Governments are becoming increasingly concerned about the impact of supply chain disruptions, including COVID-19 and the US-China trade war, on the supply of computer chips. This issue is behind strategies intended to enhance national resilience through approaches based on economic sovereignty. An excellent example is the European Union's Digital Compass plan that was announced on 9 March 2021 (European Commission, 2021). This plan is intended to double the manufacture of semiconductor chips in Europe, to represent 20 per cent of the global market by 2030. This is a policy based on digital sovereignty intended to safeguard European citizens against supply chain disruptions and overdependency on chip-making plants located in other national jurisdictions.

Second, researching and writing about companies and organisational forms is a very different process from being involved in the management of a business. I have been involved with the establishment of two companies and have been a member of the board of a number of companies. I have also advised large international businesses, including one project which resulted in the sale of a division for over $7 billion. As a company director, I am very aware that this role comes with personal liabilities. There are over 50 activities that a director can engage in that could lead to some form of legal action, and some could result in a custodial sentence. There are two points to explore that come from this experience. First, it is important to appreciate that managing a company involves negotiating trade-offs in every decision-making process. Core strategic decisions are the outcome of a complex evidence-based informed discussion that is complicated by power dynamics that are played out between board members and the executive. Nevertheless, many decisions are made rapidly, and some with little or no evidence to support the decision-making process. Second, all these companies have tried to reduce uncertainty and enhance certainty. This is a complex process, but surprise is to be avoided. Avoiding surprise and enhancing certainty involves risk identification, mitigation and adaptation. This should be an ongoing process for all organisations, and there should be a continual organisational dialogue around risk. Identifying, mitigating and adapting to risks by firms is something that is underplayed in much of the literature on manufacturing. Inappropriate management decisions, including approaches to risk management, combined with serendipity, can destroy a company in a very short period. COVID-19 has highlighted the precarious nature of many companies.

Whilst writing this section, I have before me copies of the current 'combined risk grids' for two companies I am involved with. Every well-managed company will have one of these grids as a rolling document that is continuously updated. For larger firms, there is an intra-firm app that managers consult to obtain a real-time assessment of company performance related to risk. A risk grid is context-dependent, but the approach tends to be common across firms. The grids that are before me include nine columns: key risks, likelihood, impact, numeric score, controls, responsibility, further actions, type, and committee responsible. This grid is colour-coded to identify changes made during the last iteration of the grid. These include additional risks added to the grid, any alterations in risk scores and in control measures. It is difficult to identify any commonalities between these risk grids, as they are constructed to meet each board's appreciation of the risks facing one company. Risks are sector- and company-specific. Nevertheless, there are risks related to dependency (key employees, other firms), recruiting and retaining employees, skill deficiencies including those at the level of the board, complying with statutory regulations, external environment, sales/revenue, health and safety (employees, customers and visitors), cybersecurity, failure of core systems, disruptive innovation, legal action, industrial action, inappropriate use of company resources, quality issues, financial control, emergence of unanticipated and uninsured costs, catastrophic loss of facilities, server failure, competition, government policy, reputational damage, social media and public perception.

All companies are exposed to risks. Some are well known and have been experienced in the past, some may be anticipated, and some are ignored. Risk management is an ongoing corporate process, but it is also one that in the context of some of the social science debates on manufacturing is too often ignored. Risk is related to reward, and companies must balance profitability and cost control against risk. There is an important research agenda here that includes exploring contingency planning, and the role this plays in altering the configuration of GPNs and production processes. This is partly about under-standing the ways in which risk management is reflected in adaptations and alterations in company practices. This research agenda on risk must be aligned with research on values and alternative values.

A new manufacturing research agenda on value and alternative values

There are many different types of business decisions. These involve immediate decisions that reflect the everyday management of some production or busi-ness task. These immediate decisions balance cost, value realisation, capacity and capabilities in real time. These decisions may be about the immediate term, but they may also be about longer-term relationship-building. A product might be provided at cost to facilitate the development of a longer-term relationship with a potential client. Thus, the concept of a cost-capability ratio (Coe and Yeung, 2015) is one that must be extremely fluid as it reflects the moment-by-moment or sales-by-sales process by which a company balances immediate demands on its processes versus longer-term objectives. Companies configuring GPNs may be managing a set of interfirm transactions that are intended to be agile as supply is matched with demand in real time. This is an ongoing adjustment process reflecting different solutions to balancing capacity with demand, but in real time.

Longer-term decisions include fixed capital investments, and related revenue costs, and the configuration of 'value networks' (Bryson et al., 2018), or networks of organisations or actors, involved in coordinating processes that result in the creation of value both for those involved in the value network, and for those utilising the values-in-use provided by the goods and service products produced. A value network plays a critical role at the level of both an individual firm and a supply chain or GPN. These longer-term decisions have very different characteristics to the more immediate real-time decisions required to balance a GPN. Two characteristics are critical. First, there are longer-term decisions that result in sunk costs, or investment that is incurred, cannot be recovered and must be written off if there is some change in the configuration of a value network and linked production process. Sunk costs can be compared to 'prospective costs', which are future costs that could be avoided if appropriate action is taken. Second, sunk costs may reflect decisions that were the outcome of some partially rational decision-making process. This is a partially rational process given the constraints of information asymmetry and other constraints on decision-making. These other constraints may be geographical in that investment planned to be fixed in place may not be fixed in the best location. The best location may already have been acquired by another value network, or the best location may have constraints linked to uneven connectivity or skill shortages. Sunk costs may eventually come to reflect logic that has become obsolete (Salder and Bryson, 2019). A company must balance the tensions between writing off sunk costs with an assessment of the 'value' of investing in any alternative resource, including alternative places. There will come a time when the only option is to write off this investment.

These longer-term investments include relationships with other companies. A process of relationship-building reflects an investment in time; time is a proxy measure of revenue expenditure. Such relationships take many forms and reflect the multitudinous ways in which a company becomes embedded. These may be short-term well-defined relationships and much longer-term relationships. These relationships may be severed by regulatory change; for example, the introduction of mandatory auditor rotation for larger firms across the European Union (Gardner and Bryson, 2020). They may also become sunk costs that reflect another form of obsolete logic. If this is the case, then the relationships may be severed and replaced by some alternative solution.

Reading a business, or a GPN, is an exercise in understanding the interplay between different scales and durations of decision-making. These scales and durations range from micro-decisions that represent the everyday decisions made to address routine problems, to major strategic decisions involving billions of dollars. All these decisions focus on balancing value against risk in the context of a discussion around different alternatives to operational delivery. There is no one way of realising value, but different approaches come with different cost-value-risk profiles. Balancing a company's cost-value-risk profile is an ongoing process, but the focus should ideally be on long-term sustainability.

Economic geographers, and all social scientists, interested in unravelling the complexity of production must develop an approach to conceptualising and measuring all forms of value (Bryson et al., 2018; Bryson and Vanchan, 2020) in relation to risk. Much of the economic geography literature has focused on cost minimisation, or profit maximisation, and ignored other motivations and processes that influence and inform corporate decision-making and the configuration of GPNs. A more holistic approach is required that must engage with the debate on alterity or diversity in economic relationships, but also with new and alternative approaches to production (Bryson and Taylor, 2010; Gibson-Graham, 2020). These alternative approaches include the recent emphasis on 'slow fashion' versus 'fast fashion' (Bryson and Vanchan, 2020), but also alternative forms of production intended to address private and public sector failure (Bryson et al., 2018). A holistic approach must also engage with exploring the role governments play as enablers, creators and regulators of value. Too frequently, the research focus on governments is centred on regulations and fixing market failures rather than on, for example, 'using public-sector procurement policy to stimulate as much innovation as possible – social, organisational and technological' (Mazzucato, 2021: 6). This also includes a discussion regarding the allocation of risks and rewards between business and government. In this context, it is important to appreciate that some of the products, and their GPNs, that have played critical roles in reconfiguring socio-economies emerged from government-funded initiatives. Thus, Mazzucato identifies 20 product areas in which the innovation was undertaken as part of government-funded space programmes. These include laptops, home insulation, memory form mattresses, ear thermometers, LEDs, camera phones and the computer mouse (Mazzucato, 2021: 86-87).

There are many different values to elucidate and explore. On the one hand, there is the dominant approach that focuses on profit or surplus. The danger is that this approach has a tendency to assume rational decision-making processes exist that are able to maximise profit. On the other hand, there are non-price-based forms of value. These include non-monetarised forms that eventually influence or are reflected in monetarised forms of value. It is important to appreciate that non-monetarised and monetarised forms of value may be related. These non-monetarised forms of value include the values related to place, and the power of place in influencing value (Allen, 2003; Rusten et al., 2007). They also include firms that balance profit with wider societal and environmental business impacts. This may be positioned within an approach based on corporate social responsibility or responsible business.

For social scientists it is important to unravel the multiple ways in which companies create value. This debate must explore approaches to responsible versus irresponsible business. A responsible business is one that creates more value for society than it extracts as part of a monetarisation or value capture process. This includes values created for individual consumers and the wider society. The alternative are businesses that extract more value than they contribute, and this may include transferring social and environmental costs to other companies, citizens and governments. These are parasitic companies in which the profit motive is linked to a primary focus on cost control, with no concern for the negative externalities that are created by this approach to running and managing a business. A responsible business focuses on developing solutions to the challenges faced by individuals and societies, creating values-in-use which underpin revenue generation but also enhances corporate sustainability and resilience.

An alternative account of value is found in the financialisation literature (Epstein, 2005; Muellerleile, 2009; French et al., 2011; Bryson et al., 2017b). There is much research to undertake here. This includes understanding the relationships between decisions made by financial institutions and the configuration of production systems (Billing and Bryson, 2019). It also includes companies that have developed multiple business models, and one of these might be a business model focused on financialisation rather than on manufacturing. Financialisation also includes corporate decisions regarding investments that might impact on the value of a company's shares, but not on production processes or profitability. This includes stock buyback schemes and dividend payments that are reflected in share prices. This reflects financial engineering designed to benefit a company's shareholders, including members of the firm's management team. A manufacturing-orientated corporation may also act as if it is a financial institution as it engages in financial engineering to generate revenue through the manipulation of money. In 2013, Apple had $145 billion in cash, but still decided to borrow $17 billion by issuing a bond. Apple had decided that borrowing was more effective and less expensive than using its own cash reserves, for three reasons. First, these cash reserves were scattered across the globe. Returning them to the United States, at that time, would have resulted in Apple having to pay American taxes. Second, Apple could obtain extremely low interest rates given the then demand for high-quality corporate bonds. Third, part of the rationale behind this bond was to contribute to financing a $100 billion payback to Apple's shareholders in the form of increased dividends and stock buybacks. Stock buyback reduces the number of shares and increases the value of remaining shares, but there is no 'real' increase in Apple's value. This was an exercise in value manipulation. For Apple, part of the problem that it faced in 2013 reflected the company's success in tax planning, based on keeping profits offshore. Apple was borrowing to create better returns for shareholders, and much of this borrowing was nothing to do with creating innovative new products or services (Foroohar, 2016).

The relationship between value and power is important. This includes the appropriation of value between participants in a value network. It also includes understanding inequalities, including those who may experience some form of disadvantage in the distribution of returns. Value creation occurs throughout a production process. This includes product development and design, procurement, logistics, financialisation, and operational management or production engineering. Operational management is a critical business process that combines engineering with business and management. In universities, research and teaching in operational management is undertaken in both engineering departments and business schools. It is important to explore the relationships between value creation and operational or production management.

A manufacturing research agenda on operational management and geography

The business and management literature on firms and the economy is siloed. Thus, departments of marketing, management, entrepreneurship, finance and taxation, strategy, international business and operations have emerged, and each comes with a specialist literature. There are very few attempts to develop an integrated approach to understanding business (see Bryson et al., 2020). The strategy debate in business and management includes a focus on understanding the governance and configuration of global commodity chains (GCC) and global value chains (GVC). The current business and management focus is on understanding the configuration of business models and this includes complex multi-sided business models (Bryson et al., 2020). The business model literature has been ignored by geographers (see Bryson et al., 2018). The multi-sided business model literature highlights the ways in which different types of value can be combined within the same company.

The key point to note is that there is a literature on strategy, and one on operations. The operational literature has been largely ignored by geographers (Bryson and Vanchan, 2020; Bryson et al., 2020). There are two important research gaps here. On the one side, much of the geographical literature has focused on the relationship between place and production. This includes the GPN approach, and research that focuses on understanding offshoring, reshoring and outsourcing (Peck, 2019). The focus has been on exploring and discussing strategy, rather than on operations and the role they play in the configuration of GPNs. Thus, understanding cost-capability ratios requires an appreciation of operational issues. A problem with the cost-capability ratio approach (Coe and Yeung, 2015) emerges when this ratio is explored through the lens of the well-developed literature on production planning (Mula et al., 2006). Production planning is about negotiating trade-offs between cost and capacity, and the effectiveness of this negotiation process reflects capability. Capability is partly a reflection of experience and the ability of a firm to measure and regulate production processes in real time. Perhaps the cost-capability ratio is better defined as a cost-capacity-capability ratio. There is already a 'process capability index', or 'process capability ratio', in the operations literature (Montgomery, 2004). This is a statistical measure of the ability of a process to produce outputs within an agreed specification, and this index is applied in real time by companies. There are many complex measurement processes that have been developed in the operations literature that are used to configure and manage production processes within factories. All these approaches have been overlooked in the strategy literature and in the geographical literature (Bryson and Vanchan, 2020).

There is an important research gap here that can best be defined as the opportunity to develop an operations-informed view of production. This would include understanding how firms are increasingly substituting the advantages held by place with technological solutions. The GPN approach, and the economic geography literature, has yet to acknowledge the importance of trade-offs that companies make between locational benefits versus tech-nological substitution. Thus, a production process can be located in a place which has comparatively inexpensive factor inputs: land, labour, resources. Alternatively, a technological solution, for example based on the construction of a smart factory in a high-cost labour location, or a factory designed around Industry 4.0, may outperform a factory based in a location with access to low-cost labour. Another example is that reshoring can only be understood by exploring the relocation of tasks between one place and another, and any alterations in these tasks including changes to product and process design (Vanchan et al., 2018). Offshoring and reshoring involves some alterations in tasks, including technological or labour substitution and/or some alterations in product. These changes reflect alterations in both product design and operational configurations. In any case, it will be increasingly important for social science to move beyond the simple offshoring and reshoring dualism to focus on rightshoring or blended shoring (Bryson, 2007). Binary opposites must be mutually exclusive to have any real conceptual value; seeming opposites are much more complex, and often reflect a continuum or a gradient.

There is well-developed technical literature in engineering on production planning. This is the process by which a company utilises the resources, including employees, materials and production capacity, to provide products to meet the needs of different customers. A production plan is perhaps the corporate equivalent of the cost-capability ratio (Coe and Yeung, 2015). A production plan covers a period known as the planning horizon and is focused on matching existing resources to the required levels of production, focusing on product mix, factory loads, scheduling and logistics. This approach must be based on a detailed understanding of resource availability, materials and estimates of future demand. At the centre of production planning is the product, or service, and the interface between production capacity, capability and consumer demand (Mula et al., 2006). A core gap in the social science literature is based around exploring the interrelationships between production planning and the management of uncertainty and risk.

Operational management places people and their interface with machines at the centre of production processes. Thus, developments in Industry 4.0, or the fourth industrial revolution, involve the application of artificial intelligence (AI), machine learning and developments in robotics to production systems. These applications alter the skill sets required to support production, as well as transforming the relationship between production, place and space. The reconfiguration of a GPN may be in response to technological innovation and/or alterations in government regulations including tariff and non-tariff barriers. Developments in Industry 4.0 reconfigure the relationship between people and production, but people still remain critical. There remains an important research agenda on skills and capabilities and production process innovations, and it is to this that we now turn our attention.

Returning people to the centre of the research agenda

There is an important distinction to make in all research undertaken on firms: firms do not make decisions, as decisions are made by individuals employed by firms. Corporate decisions reflect bounded rationality, urgency, the distractions of the immediate problem, improvisation and irrationality. These decisions will be influenced by corporate culture, but this then reflects differences between national cultures. For firms, place matters in multiple ways, and one of these impacts is centred on the interrelationships between place, culture and decision-making. Understanding the ways in which decisions are made by people, and the influences on these decision-making processes, is too often overlooked. Decision-making always involves power dynamics, information asymmetry, bounded rationality, and is also a culturally inflected process.

There is a well-developed literature on skills focusing on pathways into the labour market, training and hard-to-fill vacancies (Bryson et al., 2017a; Lowe et al., 2018). There is also the older literature on deskilling (Braverman, 1974), and the more recent literature on the impacts AI and other forms of technological innovation will have on labour markets (Bryson, 2018). An important issue to consider is to develop a people-centric account of manufacturing. This would shift the focus away from exploring the relationship between the requirements of firms and labour market supply, to focus on people. Further research is required to explore the experience of work, including a focus on the relationship between working in manufacturing and identity. This also includes exploring the development of career pathways over the life course, and research on hard-to-fill vacancies and labour exploitation.

A region that develops an identity based around a dominant industry may develop a localised culture that forms around highly visible companies and the experiences of the local workforce. The company and the nature of the work becomes imprinted on employees and on a place. This process of place-based imprinting, and the legacy effects, is an important manufacturing research agenda. A factory located in a small-town setting may act to catalyse social connections that cut across, for example, race, gender, age and class. Such a factory may be a setting that encourages social interactions enhancing social cohesion and reducing segregation. Factory closure stops these daily interactions and may lead to an increase in segregation.

A people-informed view of GPNs is required in which research explores the interactions between people working across different locations. There needs to be a focus on two forms of people-based embeddedness: on the one hand, embeddedness within a firm; and on the other hand, embeddedness within wider networks that support the development of a career. Production is a people-centric process, and this implies that it is culturally, politically and socially inflected. It is the people, and the decisions that they make, that are central to manufacturing processes. This includes those involved in creating algorithms that control production processes and logistics systems, those working on the shop floor, and those involved in strategic decision-making.

In 2016, Carr and Gibson argued that the experiences and knowledge of those who make things are absent from the debate on production. This is surprising. They argue that there needs to be more attention given to understanding the social life of making, combined with appreciating industrial cultures, workers and their capacities. A key part of this research must focus on rethinking production and skills as the economy and society transitions towards new forms of clean production and green growth.

There is a tension here, in that across the social sciences there is a tendency to separate production from consumption. Thus, the GPN literature shines a spotlight on production, and underplays consumption. This is unfortunate. Marx was very aware that production and consumption cannot be conceptually or practically separated. To Marx, 'production is also immediately consumption' (Marx, 1973: 90), and the term 'productive consumption' should be used to describe the relationships between these activities. Thus, production is aligned with consumption, and vice versa. Another important research gap is in understanding localised consumer preferences and the ways in which international businesses customise their products to meet the needs of consumers in specific markets. This is about targeting and tailoring the product/service, and has important implications for design, production, marketing and distribution. This suggests that the GPN approach should be reframed to focus on global production consumption networks (GPCNs). The danger in isolating consumption from production is that this ignores the role consumers play in shaping the activities of producers, and vice versa. This has become particularly important with the emergence of social media and the role this can play in forcing companies to alter their strategies and even to reconfigure GPNs. Social media, including bloggers, vloggers and consumer review sites, influences consumer behaviour and directly impacts on company performance and behaviour. This includes consumer pressure to enhance corporate social responsibility in the Anthropocene.

TRACAST and the manufacturing research agenda on care, responsibility and the Anthropocene

A new geological epoch has been proposed: the Anthropocene. The Anthropocene is defined as that period in which there has been significant human impact on the Earth's ecosystems, including anthropogenic climate change. The Anthropocene highlights the complex interrelationships between human activity and environmental processes. Douglas Adams, the novelist, identified a spurious economic phenomenon which he labelled the 'Shoe Event Horizon' (Adams, 1980), in which shoe production and consumption come to define a moment in economic history. The term 'horizon' refers to a bedding surface in geology in which there is some marked change in lithology. The Anthropocene reflects a similar change in lithology. COVID-19 has been described as a disease of the Anthropocene (O'Callaghan-Gordo and Antó, 2020). An alternative reading of COVID-19 is that the pandemic has highlighted the precarious nature of the Anthropocene. A virus has shattered 'the very foundations of our lives, causing not only an immense amount of suffering, but also economic havoc' (Žižek, 2020: 3). There will be a COVID-19 horizon in the Anthropocene.

In 2004, Doreen Massey published a paper under the title 'Geographies of Responsibility' in which she explored the relationships between identity and responsibility. A geography of responsibility has yet to emerge that acts as a cross-cutting theory within the discipline of geography. There are a number of papers that engage with this concept. In 1984, Richard Morrill, proclaimed that geographers have a 'six-fold responsibility: to truth and scientific integrity; to the discipline of geography, a body of knowledge and a corps of people; to the physical environment; to our communities; to our society; and to humanity' (Morrill, 1984: 1). This represents one definition of responsibility. The primary focus, perhaps for geographers, should be on developing a debate on responsibility and place/space relationships. This debate must include a concern with identifying and addressing inequalities, but also reducing the negative impacts of human actions on Planet Earth, but also on outer space, which needs to include a concern with preventing the transmission of biological material and pollutants to other planets but also with reducing orbital debris.

Recently, Gibson-Graham et al. (2019a, 2019b) have engaged with the debate on the Anthropocene by setting out a case for economic geography to identify and encourage ethical economic actions that would be transformational. This is a call for economic geographers to recognise the interrelationships between industrial manufacturing, climate change and growing socio-economic inequalities. This is a call for geographers and other social scientists to position manufacturing for the Anthropocene in a discourse based on care. Part of this involves decarbonising production processes, including GPNs, and part of this involves redesigning products to reduce environmental pollution and increase recyclability.

Much of the social science literature on manufacturing has focused on production and the geographies of production, but has tended to ignore or neglect what is being produced: the product or the service. This is surprising. There needs to be a renewed focus on products and services including a focus on their design, but also the ways in which products are continually redesigned to reduce costs and defects (see Bryson and Rusten, 2011). This process of redesign also includes reducing environmental impacts, including the decarbonisation of production processes, products and logistics.

It is possible to argue that GCC, GVC and GPN research needs to undergo some form of revival or renaissance. One of the problems is that these approaches are partial, in that they focus on supply chains rather than corporations and tend to overlook environmental and other negative impacts. A key omission is the absence of any robust methodological approach that can be applied to track entire supply chains. Recently, there has been a major conceptual and methodological development that has the potential to overcome the impasse being experienced by studies that adopt a chain or network metaphor. In 2019, Goldstein and Newell introduced the 'Tracking Corporations Across Space and Time' (TRACAST) methodological framework (Goldstein and Newell, 2019b). The TRACAST methodological process 'enables us to more deeply understand why and how supply chains take the forms that they do and their corresponding impacts on people and the planet' (Goldstein and Newell, 2019b: 106492). This approach can be applied by academics, non-governmental organisations (NGOs) and corporate actors to enhance supply chain transparency and to shift towards more environmentally and socially responsible sourcing. This approach identifies 'hotspots', or places with severe social and environmental impacts related to a specific product's supply chain. This also includes identifying key nodes and corporate actors involved in a hotspot (Cho et al., 2021).

TRACAST's focus on investigating specific companies was inspired by NGO and activist research on corporate transparency that focused on investigating specific companies. One of the most exciting aspects of the TRACAST approach is the application of methodologies developed in environmental science and physical geography, including geographic information system (GIS) data and environmental sensors, to identify the localised environmental impacts of supply chains. This includes linking Costco's beef supply chain in

California to the environmental burden of air pollution related to the emission of PM2.5 particles in the San Joaquin Valley (Chamanara et al., 2021). The concept of 'teleconnections' provides an additional approach to understanding the complex links between 'geographically separate sites of production and consumption' (Goldstein and Newell, 2019b: 106492). In atmospheric science, teleconnections are climate anomalies that are related to one another over long distances. This concept highlights the importance of exploring the interrelationships between specific companies and land use change.

The GPN literature has perhaps been too centred around understanding the business and corporate dimensions of production networks. This is unfortunate. A GPN contains important teleconnections that create environmental and social hotspots. Applying methodologies developed in physical geography and environmental sciences to identify and track hotspot geographies created by corporations is a major innovation. Geography used to pay especial attention to the complex interrelationships between human activity, space and place. Over time, the research focus has narrowed within economic geography to explore corporate behaviour isolated from wider environmental and socio-economic impacts. The TRACAST approach has the potential to return geography to its disciplinary roots in understanding the interface between human activity and the environment. TRACAST has opened a new research agenda on corporations and the wider impacts of their production or supply networks. For academics, it provides a methodological process that can underpin comparative research whilst providing companies and activists with a new methodological tool.

Products and services are produced to create values-in-use for consumers, and financial and other returns for producers. Both products and services can be differentiated based on their social and environmental dimensions rather than solely on price. Differentiation will increasingly include repairability and recyclability, with companies positioning their products within a discourse based around the circular economy. On 1 January 2021, the French government introduced alterations to labelling regulations for smartphones, fridges and other consumer electronic products based around the provision of a mandated repairability score. This initiative is intended to discourage or limit manufacturers of consumer goods from deploying a strategy based on planned obsolescence. The introduction of planned obsolescence as a management strategy can be traced back to Alfred P. Sloan Jr who transformed General Motors (GM) in the 1920s by introducing products with built-in design obsolescence (Bryson and Rusten, 2011). The shift towards environmentally friendly products, including mono-material products designed to enhance recyclability, will represent another form of non-price-based competitiveness. The application of the circular economy to manufacturing transforms product design and production planning. Production planning must increasingly include approaches to product recycling based on deposit return and reward schemes. For some products, the future lies in mono-material designs. Mono-material, or mono-fibre, products are designed to be remade. This includes products and packaging.

The future research agenda on manufacturing must include exploring new ways of designing and producing products that will reduce the environmental impacts of production processes. It must include a focus on the circular economy and recyclability. The debate on the Anthropocene, responsibility and care highlights the importance of considering the role social science should play in identifying and facilitating alternative pathways that produce better outcomes for all life on Earth. This includes rethinking the economy to enhance social and environmental impacts, and to reduce negative impacts (Gibson-Graham, 2014). This is to argue that the economy, as it currently functions, has no long-term future, and that an alternative approach to economic practice is required (Mazzucato, 2021). Currently, these are niche debates in economic geography, but they must become central. A core research agenda must be to facilitate alternative pathways to economic futures.

Scalar-plasticity, global production networks and the scale question

Identifying the linkages between production processes and societal and environmental impacts highlights the importance of exploring the interrelationships between company activity and scale. The conventional approach is to apply a multi-scalar approach based on exploring the interplay between the local, regional, national, and international or global scales. The emphasis has been on understanding the hierarchical ordering of sociospatial relationships. There are many examples of the application of a multi-scalar approach to exploring sociospatial relationships. Thus, to Smith the world should be considered 'as a "profit surface" produced by capital itself, at three separate scales' (Smith, 2008: 197), and these scales 'are strictly spatially nested' (Jones et al., 2017: 139). In his discussion of the scale question in urban theory, Brenner noted that 'the concept of scale is an essential basis for deciphering the vertical differentiation and stratification of sociospatial relations among (for instance) global, supranational, national, regional, and/or local levels' (Brenner, 2019: 265). He then highlights the dangers of the methodological dead end of 'scale-centrism', or the limits of scale. This echoes the emphasis placed by Massey on the importance of delineating between spatial and aspatial processes (Massey, 1984). In Méndez's important account of climate change and environmental justice a multi-scalar approach is adopted that 'brings into focus the multiple scales (that is, locally, regionally, statewide, nationally, and internationally) in policymaking and environmental justice advocacy' (Méndez, 2020: 2). One of the challenges related to scale is that the academic debate tends to be grounded in discussions of geopolitics, governance or state theory (Brenner, 2019). This is unfortunate, as there are many ways in which scale is constructed through a complex interplay between human activities, place and space (Bryson et al., 2021). On the one hand, scale is a political or administrative construct, with defined boundaries that can be identified on maps. On the other hand, scale is the outcome of a set of processes in real time that work across administrative or governance boundaries.

An alternative approach to scale is required which acknowledges that scale reflects, or is defined as, the geographic or spatial reach of a set of actions. There is a danger in treating scale as something that lies outside an organisation or individual; scale is socially constructed through interactions between people, place and space. Thus, every individual or organisation socially creates their own applied or working definition of a set of locales or regions. This also applies to the international or the global. The key point is that a company's working definition of a specific scale, with one exception, emerges through practice, performance and embeddedness. The one exception is the national: this has a legal definition based on national jurisdictions, and reflects a boundary that determines approaches to taxation, employment, trade and regulations.

The everyday construction or configuration of scale implies that scale is an extremely complex process. The multi-scalar approach obscures this complexity. The alternative is to adopt the concept of 'scalar-plasticity' to highlight the multiple interlayering of geographical relationships that exist between different places and that have different characteristics. In this new and novel approach, scale becomes a much more fluid and dynamic process, based on organisations and individuals configuring their interrelationships with place and space in real time. Linking the term 'plasticity' with 'scale' highlights that the spatial reach of actions involves the creation of multiple connections between an organisation, place and space, and that new connections are continually made, and existing connections broken. Scalar-plasticity emphasises the ability of an organisation, or GPN, to form or reform, or organise and reorganise, its spatial reach. This includes blending material with virtual or online connections. Existing material or virtual connections may be destroyed or removed and replaced as a GPN is reconfigured in real time. These real-time adjustments also include alternative pathways that have been designed into the configuration of GPNs to enhance resilience and reflect contingency planning. Algorithms play an important role in these real-time adjustments (Bryson et al., 2020). These real-time adjustments are constrained by path dependency based on fixed capital investments, and investments in establishing and maintaining interfirm relationships. Such adjustments include network alterations that reflect new forms of learning, the application of new technologies to production processes and the establishment of new relationships. They also reflect alterations in the cost or profit surface that underpins every product's GPN and that emerges from the current configuration of a GPN's approach to scalar-plasticity. In this approach, each organisation enacts its own definitions of multiple locals and regions and, combined, these form an organisation's international and/or global reach. The boundaries and interconnections between these scales are also blurred, fluid and plastic. These are not necessarily strictly spatially nested. For some organisations some of their 'locals' will play a much more important role in defining their international or global reach. Thus, there are more strategic places, or places that play a very specific role in the configuration of an organisation's profit surface. It is important to appreciate that every organisation, and perhaps every product, will have its one profit surface that reflects the enactment of scalar-plasticity in real time.

The spatial reach of a GPN is thus defined by a set of actions that determine the interrelationships between tasks (for example, production inputs, production, design, innovation, distribution, sales, recycling), places and space. A spatial reach is configured to meet the needs of a particular product in the context of a specific organisational setting. A corporation will be involved in configuring many different production networks, and each will be based on the enactment of a set of specific inter-place, or trans-local, based configurations. New methodologies and tools need to be developed to identify and understand the spatial reach of production/consumption processes as they are socially constructed by organisations. The application of the TRACAST methodological framework should enable scholars to explore global flows of components and goods, and this includes delimitating the spatial reach of their actions by identifying environmental and social hotspots (Goldstein and Newell, 2019b). These hotspots are identified not based on existing administrative boundaries, but by identifying their precise geographic configurations.

Understanding scale as the outcome of a process of social construction based on performance, practice and enactment challenges existing approaches to scale in the chain and network literatures: GCCs, GVCs and GPNs. These approaches treat scale as a given, rather than as the outcome of a set of social relationships between people, organisations, place and space. This process involves blending decisions that have been made in the past that reflect obsolete logic (Salder and Bryson, 2019), or sunk costs, with decisions that are made in real time and decisions that alter existing geographical configurations, or the spatial reach of a GPN. At any one time, a GPN is the outcome of trade-offs between sunk costs, obsolete logic and current operations. Sunk costs also include contractual relationships.

There has been a shift in the GPN debate from GPN 1.0' to GPN 2.0 (Coe and Yeung, 2015; Vanchan et al., 2018; Bryson and Vanchan, 2020). This reflects a renewed emphasis on understanding dynamics. Nevertheless, it is time to challenge the ways in which scale is considered within GPN 1.0 and 2.0. By definition, a GPN must be 'global', but the use of the term 'global' in this context ignores the fact that every corporation constructs their own definition of global. Every corporation has configured scale through the ongoing accumulation of a set of decisions, contractual agreements and investments that define its spatial reach.

A GPN is the outcome, at any one point in time, of a process that involves the configuration of a set of spatial and aspatial relationships. The implication is that it is timely for the GPN approach to develop a more nuanced approach to place, space and scale. This would require major revisions to the GPN approach and the development of a GPN 3.0 approach. GPN 3.0 would engage with the TRACAST methodology to identify the geography of hotspots and key nodes. This could include a focus on understanding the configuration of 'scalar-plasticity production networks' (SPNs). It would also need to shift the object of research away from understanding GPNs to positioning GPNs in the context of an organisational or corporate setting. Thus, a corporation will be involved in the real-time simultaneous configuration of many SPNs. An important research agenda exists in understanding this process of simultaneous configuration in the context of inter- and intra-firm negotiated and non-negotiated trade-offs. A more radical change would involve acknowledging that not all production configurations adopt a network form. This then would result in a focus on identifying and understanding 'scalar-plasticity production configurations' (SPCs).

GPN 3.0 must also begin to explore the configuration of the material with virtual spaces of production. The virtual becomes an increasingly important dimension to the ways in which organisations configure their SPNs. New forms of value and risk, as well as contingency planning, are increasingly created by blending the material with the virtual. The scalar-plasticity approach acknowledges the multiple and plastic nature of the material and virtual sociospatial relationships that underpin the configuration of profit surfaces as well as surfaces that reflect alternative forms of value.

Conclusions: constructing a responsible research agenda

All social scientists should reflect on what they are trying to achieve. Part of this should include exploring and reflecting on the role and purpose of universities, including the balance between research, teaching and broader societal contributions. Identifying a research agenda must balance tensions between the institutional structures that have developed to regulate academia, including recruitment and promotional criteria, and societal impacts. All academic disciplines must ensure that they remain relevant, as the alternative is that they become increasingly irrelevant. The eventual outcome would be a decline in student numbers and in government funding targeted to support a discipline. Ultimately, it means the shrinkage of departments, and departmental closures, as universities shift resources to more relevant disciplines.

The approach to reading firms that is outlined in this chapter is intended to develop a more holistic approach to understanding firms, and this then underpins the identification of new research agendas. This approach can operate at different levels of analysis. The initial focus is on identifying research areas that require further attention. Once a topic, theme or problem is selected, then the process of reading can continue, but focused on a particular societal and related research challenge. Nevertheless, the reading firms approach emphasises the importance of placing a focus on any one corporate process or activity within the wider context of the firm. The emphasis is on firms or corporations initially, rather than supply chains. The supply chain literature tends to isolate supply chains from their corporate setting (Goldstein and Newell, 2019a, 2019b). The GPN literature is a good example: a GPN is not a firm or a corporation but reflects one part of a much more complex organisation's activities. Thus, a corporation will be involved in configuring many different GPNs as well as engaging in financialisation. A firm engages in a continual process of decision-making that involves trade-offs between different investment opportunities. The outcome of this process might be removing capital that could be invested in production and innovation, and allocating this to support some form of financialisation. Investment may be removed, or written off, as a company decides to alter the balance between existing activities and even invest in new revenue-creating activities. The process of reading businesses is about reading signs, but the focus is on comprehension. Comprehension might be the end point, but some research projects should also inform everyday practice and alter behaviour. This is not to argue that all research should produce societal impacts. Rather, the argument is that, where appropriate, research should try to facilitate better societal outcomes. This include engaging with debates on responsible business.

In the introduction to this chapter, the literature on responsible business was highlighted as an entry route towards developing a debate on what it means to be a responsible academic. This is an important issue and raises the following questions:

- Who are academics responsible to, and what is the nature of this responsibility?
- What are the characteristics of a responsible research agenda, compared to an irresponsible research agenda?

A responsible research agenda must not be defined in terms of publication, but must be based on creating wider societal impacts. This must include identifying corporate practices that exploit people, companies and the environment. It must include encouraging and instigating a much broader public and political debate that is intended to develop solutions. COVID-19, and the emergence of this new epoch of Jenga Capitalism, place these questions centre stage to the debate on 'what kind of geography for what kind of public policy?' (Harvey, 1974). or 'what kind of research agenda for what kind of societal impact?'

References

Adams, D. (1980), *The Restaurant at the End of the Universe*. Pan: London.
Addie, J.-P. (2017), From the urban university to universities in urban society. *Regional Studies*, 51(7): 1089–1099.
Allen, J. (2003), *Lost Geographies of Power*. Oxford: Blackwell.
Amin, A. and Thrift, N. (2017), *Seeing Like a City*. Cambridge: Polity.
Beck, U. (1992), *Risk Society: Towards a New Modernity*. London: SAGE.
Billing, C. and Bryson, J.R. (2019), Heritage and satellite manufacturing: firm-level competitiveness and the management of risk in global production networks. *Economic Geography*, 95(5): 423–441.
Braverman, H. (1974), *Labor and Monopoly Capital*. New York: Monthly Review Press.
Brenner, N. (2019), *New Urban Spaces: Urban Theory and the Scale Question*. Oxford: Oxford University Press.
Bryson, J.R. (2007), The 'second' global shift: the offshoring or global sourcing of corporate services and the rise of distanciated emotional labour. *Geografiska Annaler, Series B, Human Geography*, 89: 31–43.
Bryson, J.R. (2018), Divisions of labour, technology and the transformation of work: worker to robot or self-employment and the gig economy. In: Paasi, A., Harrison, J. and Jones, M. (eds), *Handbook on the Geographies of Regions and Territories*. Cheltenham, UK and Northampton, MA, USA: Edward Elgar Publishing, 141–152.
Bryson, J.R., Clark, J. and Vanchan, V. (2015), *Handbook of Manufacturing Industries in the World Economy*. Cheltenham, UK and Northampton, MA, USA: Edward Elgar Publishing.

Bryson, J.R., Kalafsky, R. and Vanchan, V. (2021), Ordinary cities, extraordinary geographies: parallax dimensions, interpolations and the scale question. In: Bryson, J.R., Kalafsky, R. and Vanchan, V. (eds), *Ordinary Cities, Extraordinary Geographies: People, Place and Space*. Cheltenham, UK and Northampton, MA, USA: Edward Elgar Publishing, 1–22.

Bryson J.R., Mulhall, R.A., Lowe, N. and Stern, J. (2017a), Engineering and the skills crisis in the UK and US. In: Zhang, Y. and Gregory, M. (eds), *Value Creation through Engineering Excellence: Building Global Network Capabilities*. London: Palgrave, 327–349.

Bryson, J.R., Mulhall, R.A. and Song, M. (2017b), Urban assets and the financialisation fix: land tenure, renewal and path dependency in the city of Birmingham. *Cambridge Journal of Regions, Economy and Society*, 10(3): 455–469.

Bryson, J.R, Mulhall, R., Song, M., Loo, B., Dawson, R. and Rogers, C. (2018), Alternative-substitute business models and the provision of local infrastructure: alterity as a solution to financialization and public-sector failure. *Geoforum*, 95: 25–34.

Bryson, J.R. and Ronayne, M. (2014), Manufacturing carpets and technical textiles: routines, resources, capabilities, adaptation, innovation and the evolution of the British textile industry. *Cambridge Journal of Regions, Economy and Society*, 7: 471–488.

Bryson, J.R. and Rusten, G. (2011), *Design Economies and the Changing World Economy: Innovation, Production and Competitiveness*. London: Routledge.

Bryson, J.R., Sundbo, J., Fuglsang, L. and Daniels, P. (2020), *Service Management: Theory and Practice*. London: Palgrave.

Bryson, J.R. and Taylor, M. (2010), Mutual dependency, diversity and alterity in production: cooperatives, group contracting and factories. In: Fuller, D., Jonas, A.E. and Lee, R. (eds), *Interrogating Alterity*. Farnham: Ashgate, 75–94.

Bryson, J.R. and Vanchan, V. (2020), Covid-19 and alternative conceptualisations of value and risk in GPN research. *Tijdschrift voor Economische en Sociale Geografie*. https://doi.org/10.1111/tesg.12425.

Carr, C. and Gibson, C. (2016), Geographies of making: rethinking materials and skills for volatile futures. *Progress in Human Geography*, 40(3): 297–315.

Chamanara, S., Goldstein, B. and Newell, J.P. (2021), Where's the beef? Costco's meat supply chain and environmental justice in California. *Journal of Cleaner Production*, 278: 123744. https://doi.org/10.1016/j.jclepro.2020.123744.

Cho, K., Goldstein B., Gounaridis, D. and Newell, J.P. (2021), Where does your guacamole come from? Detecting deforestation associated with the export of avocados from Mexico to the United States. *Journal of Environmental Management*, 278(Pt 1): 111482. doi: 10.1016/j.jenvman.2020.111482.

Clark, G.L. (1998), Stylised facts and close dialogue: methodology in economic geography. *Annals, Association of American Geographers*, 88: 73–87.

Claydon, J. (2011), A new direction for CSR: the shortcomings of previous CSR models and the rationale for a new model. *Social Responsibility Journal*, 7(3): 405–420.

Coe, N. and H.W. Yeung (2015), *Global Production Networks: Theorizing Economic Development in an Interconnected World*. Oxford: Oxford University Press.

Daniels, P.W., Rubalcaba, L., Stare, M. and Bryson J.R. (2011), How many Europes? Varieties of capitalism, divergence and convergence and the transformation of the European services landscape. *Tijdschrift voor economische en sociale geografie*, 102: 146–161.

DeWeerdt, S. (2019), Tracing the US opioid crisis to its roots. *Nature*, 773, S10–S12. doi: https://doi.org/10.1038/d41586-019-02686-2.

Epstein, G.A. (2005), Financialization and the world economy. In: Epstein, G.A. (ed.), *Financialization of the World Economy*. Cheltenham, UK and Northampton, MA, USA: Edward Elgar Publishing, 3–16.

European Commission (2021), *2030 Digital Compass: the European way for the Digital Decade*. European Commission COM(2021) 118 final, accessed 1 April 2021 at https://eur-lex.europa.eu/legalcontent/en/TXT/?uri=CELEX:52021DC0118.

Foroohar, R. (2016), *Makers and Takers: The Rise of Finance and the Fall of American Business*. New York: Crown Business.

French, S., Leyshon, A. and Wainwright, T. (2011), Financializing space, spacing financialization. *Progress in Human Geography*, 35(6): 798–819.

Gardner, E. and Bryson, J.R. (2020), The dark side of the industrialisation of accountancy: innovation, commoditization, colonization and competitiveness. *Industry and Innovation*. DOI: 10.1080/13662716.2020.1738915.

Gibson-Graham, J.K. (2014), Rethinking the economy with thick description and weak theory. *Current Anthropology*, 55(9): 147–153.

Gibson-Graham, J.K. (ed.) (2020), *The Handbook of Diverse Economies*. Cheltenham, UK and Northampton, MA, USA: Edward Elgar Publishing.

Gibson-Graham, J.K., Cameron, J., Healy, S. and McNeill, J. (2019a), Economic geography and ethical action in the Anthropocene: a rejoinder. *Economic Geography*, 95(1): 27–29.

Gibson-Graham, J.K., Cameron, J., Healy, S. and McNeill, J. (2019b), Roepke lecture in economic geography – economic geography, manufacturing, and ethical action in the Anthropocene. *Economic Geography*, 95(1): 1–21.

Goldstein, B. and Newell, J.P. (2019a), Why academics should study the supply chains of individual corporations. *Journal of Industrial Ecology*, 23(6): 1316–1327. 10.1111/jiec.12932.

Goldstein, B. and Newell, J.P. (2019b), How to track corporation across space and time. *Ecological Economics*, 169: 106492. 10.1016/j.ecolecon.2019.106492.

Harvey, D. (1974), What kind of geography for what kind of public policy? *Transactions of the Institute of British Geographers*, 63: 18–24.

Jones, J.P., Leitner, H., Marston, S.A. and Sheppard, E. (2017), Neil Smith's Scale. *Antipode*, 49: 138–152.

Koutsoyainnis, A (1982), *Non-Price Decisions: The Firm in a Modern Context*. London: Macmillan.

Lowe, N., Stern, J., Bryson J.R. and Mulhall, R. (2018), Youth job creation and employer engagement in 285 U.S. manufacturing. In: Andreason, S., Van Horn C., Prince, H. and Greene T. (eds), *Investing in America's Workforce: Improving Outcomes for Workers and Employers*. Kalamazoo, MI: Upjohn Institute, 285–308.

Magnusson, W. (2011), *Politics of Urbanism: Seeing Like a City*. New York: Routledge.

Marx, K. (1973), *Grundrisse*. Harmondsworth: Penguin.

Massey, D. (1984), *Spatial Division of Labour: Social Structures and the Geography of Production*. London: Palgrave.

Massey, D. (2004), Geographies of responsibility. *Geografiska Annaler*, 86(1): 5–18.

Mazzucato, M. (2021), *Mission Economy: A Moonshot Guide to Changing Capitalism*. London: Allen Lane.

Méndez, M. (2020), *Climate Change from the Streets*. New Haven, CT: Yale University Press.

Milne S., Chambers, K., Elks, S., Hussain, B. and McKinnon S. (2019), *Living Carbon Free: Exploring What a Net-Zero Target Means for Households*. Birmingham: Energy Systems Catapult.

Montgomery, D. (2004), *Introduction to Statistical Quality Control*. New York: John Wiley & Sons.

Morrill, R.L. (1984), The responsibility of geography. *Annals of the Association of American Geographers*, 74(1): 1–8.

Muellerleile, C. (2009), Financialization takes off at Boeing. *Journal of Economic Geography*, 9(5): 663–677.

Mula, J., Poler, R., García-Sabater, J.P. and Lario, F.C. (2006), Models for production planning under uncertainty: a review. *International Journal of Production Economics*, 103(1): 271–285.

O'Callaghan-Gordo, C. and Antó, J.M. (2020), COVID-19: the disease of the Anthropocene. *Environmental Research*, 187. doi: 10.1016/j.envres.2020.109683.

Peck. J. (2019), *Offshore: Exploring the Worlds of Global Outsourcing*. Oxford: Oxford University Press.

Rusten, G., Bryson, J.R. and Aarflot, U. (2007), Places through products and products through places: industrial design and spatial symbols as sources of competitiveness. *Norwegian Journal of Geography*, 61(3): 133–144.

Salder, J. and Bryson, J.R. (2019), Placing entrepreneurship and firming small town economies: manufacturing firms, adaptive embeddedness, survival and linked enterprise structures. *Entrepreneurship and Regional Development*, 31(9): 806–825.

Smith, N. (2008), *Uneven Development: Nature, Capital, and the Production of Space* (3rd edn). Athens, GA: University of Georgia Press.

Tidy, J. (2019), How a ransomware attach cost on firm £45m. *BBC News*. Accessed 29 October 2020 at: https://www.bbc.co.uk/news/business-48661152.

United Nations (UN) (2019), *The Ten Principles of the UN Global Compact*. Accessed 1 April 2021 at: https://www.unglobalcompact.org/what-is-gc/mission/principles.

Vanchan, V., Mulhall, R. and Bryson, J. (2018), Repatriation or reshoring of manufacturing to the U.S. and UK: dynamics and global production networks or from here to there and back again. *Growth and Change*, 49: 97–121.

Žižek, S. (2020), *Pandemic: COVID-19 Shakes the World*. New York: Polity.

Index